KB158979

지금,
멋진 영어 한 줄의
타이밍

Ernest Hemingway 3

열두 달
멋진 영어
시리즈 ❸

꼬박꼬박
하루 하나씩
어니스트
헤밍웨이
영어 읽기

지금,
멋진 영어 한 줄의
타이밍

Ernest Hemingway 3

이충호 지음

bs
브레인스토어

Prologue

헤밍웨이는 시작부터 끝까지 명성의 울짱을 벗어난 적이 없었다. 간단명료한 그의 문장처럼 그는 삶도 자기만의 방식으로 간단명료하게 마침표를 찍으며 전설의 담벼락을 높였다. 이런 그의 명성과 전설은 주거니 받거니 끊임없이 회자(膾炙)되고 그 열기는 지금도 식을 줄을 모른다. 그가 들려주는 이야기가 우리 마음에 좀처럼 지워지지 않는 무늬를 만들기 때문일 것이다. 나 역시 성긴 울타리 틈새로 거인의 정원을 엿보다가 그가 던진 미끼 하나를 덥석 물었던 적이 있다. The first draft of anything is shit(모든 초고는 쓰레기다). 작가로 입문하기 전 초벌로 원고를 쓰는 내내 의심과 두려움, 캄캄한 공포와 마주할 때 의지했던 헤밍웨이의 말이다. 그렇다, 글도 우리의 삶도, 모든 일은 수십, 수백 번 고쳐 쓰는 일이다.

사랑과 야망의 생로병사를 좇아가는 게 인생이다. 거울 속에 비치는 주름과 흰머리를 홀로 들여다보게 될 때 나오는 회한의 눈물이나 관조(觀照)의 힘이 아마 자신의 진가(眞價)일 것이다. 부디 헤밍웨이에서 뽑아낸 열정과 눈물, 지혜와 미학이 당신의 가슴으로 건너가 당신의 무늬를 만들고 당신의 영어를 적셔주는 청춘의 샘이 되었으면 한다. 그의 작품 속에 들어 있는 '인문 영어' 문장들을 뽑아 '멋진 영어' 시리즈를 이어가려고 한다. 그의 문체로 풀어낸 젊은 날의 사랑과 노년의 성찰은 마치 계절을 따라 익어간 과일처럼 고상한 뒷맛을 남긴다. 헤밍웨이 과일바구니에는 다섯 개를 담았다. 그의 명성이 시작된 『태양은 다시 떠오른다 The Sun Also Rises(1926)』부터 『무기여 잘 있어라 A Farewell to Arms(1929)』, 『킬리만자로의 눈 The Snows of Kilimanjaro(1936)』, 『누구를 위하여 종은 울리나 For Whom the Bell Tolls(1940)』 그리고 그의 노벨 문학상 수상에 기여한 『노인과 바다 The Old Man and the Sea(1952)』까지.

『태양은 다시 떠오른다』는 스물일곱 살의 헤밍웨이가 발표한 첫 장편소설이다. 인류 역사상 그 유례를 찾아볼 수 없는 세계대전을 치르고 난 후 정신적 불모지에서 무기력할 수밖에 없었던 '길 잃은 세대(Lost Generation)'가 겪는 시대적 불안과 상실감을 그렸다. 이전의 도덕과 윤리가 무너진 자리에 뿌리 내린 환멸과 상실감으로 인해 새로운 가치를 찾아 헤매야 했던 젊은 세대의 혼돈과 방황, 로맨스를 간결하고 깔끔하면서도 생생하고 풍부한 스타일로 담아낸 걸작이다.

헤밍웨이가 자신의 경험을 바탕으로 쓴 자전적 소설 『무기여 잘 있어라』는 그 스스로 『로미오와 줄리엣』에 비교했을 만큼 불운한 청춘들의 사랑이야기를 담은 비극 소설이다. 스스로 "사랑을 하지 않는다"고 말할 정도로 삶을 방치했던 남자가 진정한 사랑을 만나면서 삶과 사랑의 소중함을 깨닫는 과정을 그렸고, 이데올로기가 주는 공허함과 세상에 내던져져 죽음으로 향할 수밖에 없는 인간의 숙명을 그린 전쟁소설이다.

『킬리만자로의 눈』은 그가 쓴 70여 편에 달하는 단편 중에서 최고의 작품이자 가장 많은 사랑을 받는 작품이다. 돈 많은 여자들을 유혹하며 일탈적인 삶을 살다가 평생 꿈이었던 글쓰기를 시작하며 아프리카에 갔다가 사소한 사고로 죽음 앞에 서게 된 남자의 마음을 따라가는 이야기다. 아프리카의 뜨거운 태양 아래서 대면하게 된 고독과 공허, 그리고 삶의 마지막 순간에 찾아온 절대 자유가 소설 첫머리에 올린 '무엇을 찾아 그 높은 곳까지 왔는지 아무도 그 이유를 알지 못하는 킬리만자로의 표범' 제사(題詞)와 어우러지며 신비를 더한다.

『누구를 위하여 종은 울리나』는 1936년 발발한 스페인 내전에 참전해 철교 폭파 비밀 지령을 받은 미국인 로버트 조던이 1937년 5월 말의 토요일 오후부터 그다음 주 화요일 오전까지 벌어진 투쟁을 그린 연대기 소설이자 전장 속에서 나즈막히 울려 퍼지는 희망의 종소리 같은 러브 스토리다. '당신 안에 내가 있다(The me in thee)' 라는 조던의 말을 빌려 죽음을 삶으로 연결하는 동시에 존 던(John Donne)의 시에서 따온 소설의 제목을 통해 연대의 가치를 역설하고 있다.

『노인과 바다』는 헤밍웨이가 가시나무새가 되어 부른 마지막 노래였다. 켈트 신화에 나오는 가시나무새는 평생 뾰족하고 긴 가시가 박힌 가시나무를 찾아다니다가 마침내 찾은 그 가시나무로 돌진해 가시에 박혀 죽으면서 가장 아름다운 노래를 불렀다고 한다. 84일째 고기를 잡지 못했던 멕시코 만류의 늙은 어부 산티아고가 혼자 먼 바다로 나가 크고 힘센 청새치와 사투를 벌이는 이틀의 시간을 통해 '파멸할지언정 패배하지 않겠다'는 한 인간의 실존적 투쟁과 불굴의 의지를 그려내고 있다.

제자에게 소중한 시간을 만들어 주었던 화요일의 모리 교수처럼(『Tuesdays With Morrie』) 토요일마다 내 영혼과 육체에 건강함을 불어넣어 주시는 이원상 선생님과, 집필에 필요한 헤밍웨이를 챙겨주며 응원해 준 친구 류재량에게 이 자리를 빌어 감사의 인사를 전하고 싶다.

2020년 6월

이충호

Contents

07 July

08 August

09 September

10 October

11 November

12 December

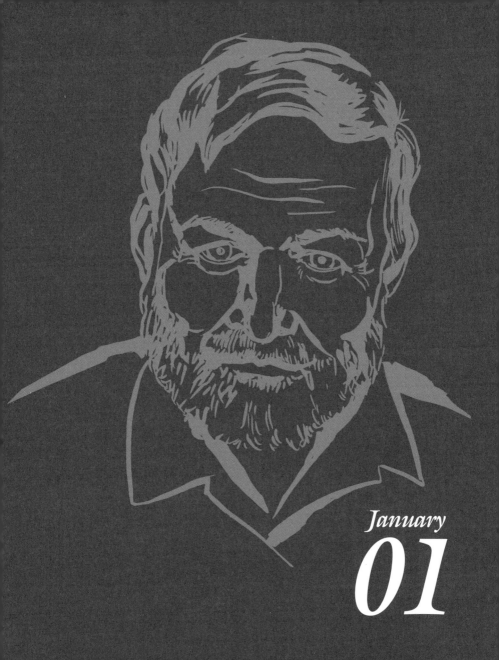

January
01

Everybody gets everything wrong.

우리 모두는 모든 것에 대해 오해하며 살고 있다.

MON

All countries look just like the moving pictures

어떤 나라든 꼭 영화같이 보이는 법이야

"All my life I've wanted to go on a trip like that," Cohn said. He sat down. "I'll be too old before I can ever do it."
"Don't be a fool," I said. "You can go anywhere you want. You've got plenty of money."
"I know. But I can't get started."
"Cheer up," I said. "All countries look just like the moving pictures."

"난 평생 그런 여행을 하고 싶었어. 하지만 그런 여행 한 번 못 해 보고 아주 늙어버릴 것 같아." 콘이 말했다.
"바보 같은 소리 마. 넌 원하는 곳이라면 어디라도 갈 수 있잖아. 돈이 많으니."
"그야 그렇지. 하지만 선뜻 출발할 수가 없단 말이야."
"기운을 내. 어떤 나라든 꼭 영화같이 보이는 법이야."

문장분석

"All my life/ I've wanted to go on a trip like that," Cohn said. He sat down. "I'll be
~같은
too old/ before I can ever do it."

"Don't be a fool," I said. "You can go anywhere you want. You've got plenty of
많은, 충분한
money."

"I know. But I can't get started."
시작하다
"Cheer up," I said. "All countries look (just) like the moving pictures."

plenty [plénti] 많음, 가득, 풍부, 많은
cheer [tʃíər]
  환호, 갈채, 격려, 응원하다, 기운을 북돋우다
Cheers! 건배

juvenile [dʒúːvənəl] 젊은, 어린, 소년소녀
rejuvenation [ridʒùːvənéiʃən]
  회춘, 젊어지기, 다시 젊어짐

Nobody ever lives their life all the way up except bull-fighters

투우사 외에 자신의 삶을 철저하게 사는 사람은 없다

"I can't stand it to think my life is going so fast and I'm not really living it."

"Nobody ever lives their life all the way up except bull-fighters."

"I'm not interested in bull-fighters. That's an abnormal life. I want to go back in the country in South America. We could have a great trip."

"삶이 이렇게 빠르게 달아나고 있는데 정말 진정한 삶을 살고 있지 않다는 생각을 하면 견딜 수가 없어."

"투우사 외에 자신의 삶을 철저하게 사는 사람은 없어."

"난 투우사에겐 흥미가 없어. 그건 비정상적인 삶이야. 난 남아메리카 시골에 들어가고 싶어. 우리가 함께 가면 멋진 여행이 될 텐데."

문장분석

"I can't stand it to think my life is going so fast and I'm not really living it."
  endure

"Nobody ever lives their life all the way up except bull-fighters."
                    철저히

"I am not interested in bull-fighters. That's an abnormal life. I want to go back in
  ~에 관심이 없다
the country in South America. We could have a great trip."
                                현재 사실의 반대

endure [endjúər] 견디다, 참다
bull [bul] 황소(ox)
abnormal [æbnɔ́:rməl] 보통과 다른, 정상이 아닌

except [iksépt] …을 제외하고, …외에는(but)
expect [ikspékt] 기대하다, 기다리다

Do you realize you've lived nearly half the time you have to live already?

네가 살아갈 인생의 절반 가까이를 이미 살았다는 사실을 깨닫고 있는 거니?

"Listen, Jake," he leaned forward on the bar. "Don't you ever get the feeling that all your life is going by and you're not taking advantage of it? Do you realize you've lived nearly half the time you have to live already?"
"Yes, every once in a while."

"이봐, 제이크," 그가 카운터 위로 몸을 내밀었다. "네 인생이 저만치 달아나 버리고 있는데 그걸 조금도 이용하고 있지 않다고 생각해 본 적 없어? 네가 살아갈 인생의 절반 가까이를 이미 살았다는 사실을 깨닫고 있는 거야?"
"그럼, 가끔 그런 생각이 들긴 하지."

문장분석

"Listen, Jake," he leaned forward on the bar. "Don't you ever get the feeling that
　　　　　　　　　　　앞으로　　　　　　　　　　　　　　　　　　　　　　　　　　　

all your life is going by and you're not taking advantage of it? Do you realize (that)
　　　　　　　　　　　　　　　　　　　　　　이용하다

you have lived nearly half the time you have to live already?"
　　　　　　　　almost　　　　　　　　　　　must

"Yes, (every) once in a while."
　　　　　이따금, 때때로

lean [liːn] 기대다, 의지하다, 기울다
advantage [ædvǽntidʒ] 유리, 이익
disadvantage [disədvǽntidʒ] 불리, 불이익

profit [prɑ́fit] 이익, 수익, 이윤, 소득
realize [ríːəlàiz] 실현하다, 현실화하다, 깨닫다

You can't get away from yourself by moving from one place to another

이 나라에서 저 나라로 옮겨 다닌다고 해서 너 자신한테서 달아날 수 있는 건 아냐

"Listen, Robert, going to another country doesn't make any difference. I've tried all that. You can't get away from yourself by moving from one place to another. There's nothing to that."
"But you've never been to South America."

"이봐, 로버트, 다른 나라에 간다고 해서 달라지는 건 없어. 나도 벌써 그런 건 전부 해봤어. 이 나라에서 저 나라로 옮겨 다닌다고 해서 너 자신한테서 달아날 수 있는 건 아냐. 그래봤자 아무것도 없어."
"하지만 넌 남미에 가 본 적이 없잖아."

문장분석

"Listen, Robert, (going to another country) doesn't make any difference. I have
　　　　　　　　　　주어
tried all that. You can't get away from yourself by moving from one place to
　　　　　　　　　~에서 도망치다　　　　　　~함으로써
another (place). There's nothing to that."

"But you've never been to South America."

difference [dífərəns] 다름, 차이
differentiate [dìfərénʃièit] 구별짓다, 식별하다
abroad [əbrɔ́ːd] 외국에, 해외로

aboard [əbɔ́ːrd] 배에, 배를 타고, (탈 것을) 타고
abort [əbɔ́ːrt] 유산(낙태)하다

I was sorry for him, but it was not a thing you could do anything about

그가 딱하게 느껴졌지만, 나로서는 어떻게 손을 쓸 수가 없었다

I was sorry for him, but it was not a thing you could do anything about, because right away you ran up against the two stubbornnesses: South America could fix it and he did not like Paris. He got the first idea out of a book, and I suppose the second came out of a book too.

그가 딱하게 느껴졌지만, 나로서는 어떻게 손을 쓸 수가 없었다. 남아메리카에 가면 해결될지도 모른다는 것이고 또 파리가 싫다는 이 두 가지 고집에 정면으로 부딪혔기 때문이다. 첫 번째 생각은 책에서 얻은 것이고, 또 아마 두 번째 생각 역시 책에서 얻은 듯했다.

문장분석

I was sorry for him, but it was not a thing you could do anything about, because

right away you ran up against the two stubbornnesses: South America could fix
　　곧바로　　　　~와 충돌하다

it and he did not like Paris. He got the first idea out of a book, and I suppose the

second came out of a book too.

stubborn [stʌ́bərn] 완고한, 고집 센
fix [fíks] 고치다, 정돈하다
suppose [səpóuz] 가정하다, 상상하다, 추측하다

oppose [əpóuz] …에 반대하다, …에 대항하다
appose [əpóuz] 나란히 놓다, 덧붙이다

014

Vocabulary Of The Week

MON

plenty [plénti] 많음, 가득, 풍부, 많은
cheer [tʃiər]
 환호, 갈채, 격려, 응원하다,
 기운을 북돋우다
Cheers! 건배

juvenile [dʒúːvənəl]
 젊은, 어린, 소년소녀
rejuvenation [ridʒùːvənéiʃən]
 회춘, 젊어지기, 다시 젊어짐

TUE

endure [endjúər] 견디다, 참다
bull [bul] 황소(ox)
abnormal [æbnɔ́ːrməl]
 보통과 다른, 정상이 아닌
except [iksépt]
 …을 제외하고, …외에는(but)

expect [ikspékt] 기대하다, 기다리다

WED

lean [liːn] 기대다, 의지하다, 기울다
advantage [ædvǽntidʒ] 유리, 이익
disadvantage [disədvǽntidʒ]
 불리, 불이익
profit [práfit] 이익, 수익, 이윤, 소득

realize [ríːəlàiz]
 실현하다, 현실화하다, 깨닫다

THU

difference [dífərəns] 다름, 차이
differentiate [difərénʃièit]
 구별짓다, 식별하다
abroad [əbrɔ́ːd] 외국에, 해외로
aboard [əbɔ́ːrd]
 배에, 배를 타고, (탈 것을) 타고

abort [əbɔ́ːrt] 유산(낙태)하다

FRI

stubborn [stʌ́bərn] 완고한, 고집 센
fix [fiks] 고치다, 정돈하다
suppose [səpóuz]
 가정하다, 상상하다, 추측하다
oppose [əpóuz]
 …에 반대하다, …에 대항하다

appose [əpóuz]
 나란히 놓다, 덧붙이다

You never know in this town

이 도시에서는 뭐가 어떻게 돌아가는지 전혀 알 수가 없어요

"I don't know. You never know in this town."
"Don't you like Paris?"
"No."
"Why don't you go somewhere else?"
"Isn't anywhere else."
"You're happy, all right."
"Happy, hell!"

"글쎄, 난 모르겠어요. 이 도시에서는 뭐가 어떻게 돌아가는지 전혀 알 수가 없어요."
"파리를 좋아하지 않아?"
"싫어해요."
"그럼 왜 다른 곳으로 가지 않지?"
"갈 곳이 아무 데도 없어요."
"아가씨는 틀림없이 행복해서 그러는 거야."
"행복은 무슨 빌어먹을 행복!"

문장분석

"I don't know. You never know (anything) in this town."

"Don't you like Paris?"

"No."

"Why don't you go somewhere else?"
그 외에

"(There) Isn't anywhere else."

"You're happy, all right."
확실히

"Happy, hell!"
제기랄

hell [hel] 지옥, 저승
inferno [infɔ́:rnou] 지옥, 지옥 같은 장소
kingdom [kíŋdəm] 왕국, 왕토, 영역

heavenly [hévənli] 하늘의, 천상의
wandering [wɑ́ndəriŋ]
헤매는, 종잡을 수 없는, 방랑

016

She was looking into my eyes

그녀는 내 눈을 빤히 들여다보고 있었다

She was looking into my eyes. Her eyes would look on and on after every one else's eyes in the world would have stopped looking. She looked as though there were nothing on earth she would not look at like that, and really she was afraid of so many things.

그녀는 내 눈을 빤히 들여다보고 있었다. 온 세상 사람의 모든 눈이 보는 것을 멈춘 다음에도 그 눈만은 그렇게 계속 뚫어지게 바라보고 있으리라. 그런 눈으로 바라보지 않을 것은 이 세상에 아무것도 없다는 듯 그녀는 바라보고 있었다. 실제로 그녀는 두려운 것이 너무나 많았다.

문장분석

She was looking into my eyes. Her eyes would look on and on / after every one
<u>계속해서</u>

else's eyes in the world would have stopped looking. She looked as though there
<u>마치~처럼</u>

were nothing (on earth) she would not look at like that, and really she was afraid
<u>그런 식으로</u> <u>~을 두려워하다</u>

of so many things.

afraid [əfréid] 두려워하는, 무서워하는
dread [dred] 두려워하다, 무서워하다
fright [frait] 공포, 놀람

freight [freit] 화물, 운송
flight [flait] 날기, 비행

We'd better keep away from each other

우리 서로 멀리하는 게 좋겠어

"And there's not a damn thing we could do," I said.
"I don't know," she said. "I don't want to go through that hell again."
"We'd better keep away from each other."
"But, darling, I have to see you. It isn't all that you know."
"No, but it always gets to be."
"That's my fault. Don't we pay for all the things we do, though?"

"빌어먹을, 우리가 할 수 있는 일이 한 가지도 없어." 내가 말했다.
"모르겠어. 또다시 그런 끔찍한 걸 겪고 싶지 않아." 그녀가 말했다.
"우리 서로 멀리하는 게 좋겠어."
"하지만, 자기. 당신을 만나지 않곤 견딜 수 없어. 그게 당신이 알고 있는 전부
는 아니잖아."
"그렇지. 하지만 늘 이런 식이 되고 말지."
"그건 내 잘못이야. 그래도 우리가 하는 일에 대한 대가는 충분히 치르고 있지
않아?"

문장분석

"And there's not a (damn) thing we could do," I said.

"I don't know," she said. "I don't want to go through that hell again."
겪다

"We'd better keep away from each other."
멀리하다

"But, darling, I have to see you. It isn't all that you know."
must

"No, but it always gets to be."
becomes

"That's my fault. Don't we pay for all the things we do, though?"
대가를 지불하다

damn [dæm] 비난하다, 혹평하다, 제기랄
fault [fɔ:lt] 과실, 잘못(mistake)
though [ðou] …이긴 하지만, 그래도

through [θru:] …을 통하여, …동안 (줄곧)
thorough [θə́:rou] 철저한, 충분한, 완벽한

He was putting himself in my place, I guess

그는 내 입장에 서서 생각하고 있었던 것 같았다

That was where the liaison colonel came to visit me. That was funny. That was about the first funny thing. I was all bandaged up. "You, a foreigner, an Englishman, have given more than your life." He never laughed. He was putting himself in my place, I guess. "Che mala fortuna! Che mala fortuna!"

연락장교 대령이 나를 방문한 게 그곳이었다. 참으로 우스꽝스러운 일이었다. 처음으로 우스꽝스러운 일이었다. 나는 온몸에 붕대를 칭칭 감고 있었다. "귀관은 외국인, 영국인으로서 목숨보다도 더 소중한 것을 바쳤다." 그 장교는 조금도 웃지 않았다. 그는 내 입장에 서서 생각하고 있었던 것 같았다. "체 말라 포르투나! 체 말라 포르투나!"

문장분석

That was (where) the liaison colonel came to visit me. That was funny. That was about the first funny thing. I was all bandaged up. "You, a foreigner, an Englishman, have given more than your life." He never laughed. He was putting
성기에 부상을 입은 것을 의미
himself in my place, I guess. "Che mala fortuna! Che mala fortuna!"
위치, 입장

liaison [liːéizɔːŋ] (F.) 연락, 접촉
colonel [kə́ːrnəl] 대령
bandage [bǽndidʒ] 붕대, 안대

foreigner [fɔ́(ː)rinər] 외국인
laugh [læf] 소리내어 웃다
Che mala fortuna! (I.) 재수가 없었다!

I suppose she only wanted what she couldn't have

그녀는 얻을 수 없는 것만을 몹시 갖고 싶어 하는 것 같았다

I never used to realize it, I guess. I try and play it along and just not make trouble for people. Probably I never would have had any trouble if I hadn't run into Brett when they shipped me to England. I suppose she only wanted what she couldn't have. Well, people were that way. To hell with people.

나는 그런 사실을 한 번도 깨닫지 못했던 것 같다. 나는 그걸 농담으로 삼을 뿐 다른 사람들에게 폐를 끼치지 않으려고 한다. 그들이 나를 영국으로 후송했을 때 브렛을 우연히 만나지만 않았더라면 아마 아무런 문제가 없었을지 모른다. 그녀는 얻을 수 없는 것만을 몹시 갖고 싶어 하는 것 같았다. 어쩌면 인간이란 그런 식인가. 빌어먹을 인간들!

문장분석

I never used to realize it, I guess. I try and play it along and just not make trouble
과거의 습관/ 상태   괴롭히다, 애먹이다
for people. Probably I never would have had any trouble/ if I hadn't run into Brett
                                                                    우연히 만나다
when they shipped me to England. I suppose (that) she only wanted (what)she

couldn't have. Well, people were that way. To hell with people.
                                                ~는 될 대로 되라지

realize [ríːəlàiz] 실현하다, 현실화하다   suppose [səpóuz] 가정하다(assume), 상상하다
probably [prábəbli] 아마, 대개는   encounter [enkáuntər] 조우, 우연히 만나다
ship [ʃip] 배, 배로 보내다, 수송하다

Vocabulary Of The Week

MON

hell [hel] 지옥, 저승
inferno [infə́:rnou]
지옥, 지옥 같은 장소
kingdom [kíŋdəm] 왕국, 왕토, 영역
heavenly [hévənli] 하늘의, 천상의

wandering [wɑ́ndəriŋ]
헤매는, 종잡을 수 없는, 방랑

TUE

afraid [əfréid]
두려워하는, 무서워하는
dread [dred] 두려워하다, 무서워하다
fright [frait] 공포, 놀람
freight [freit] 화물, 운송
flight [flait] 날기, 비행

WED

damn [dæm]
비난하다, 혹평하다, 제기랄
fault [fɔːlt] 과실, 잘못(mistake)
though [ðou] …이긴 하지만, 그래도
through [θruː]
…을 통하여, …동안 (줄곧)

thorough [θə́:rou]
철저한, 충분한, 완벽한

THU

liaison [liːéizɔːŋ] (F.) 연락, 접촉
colonel [kə́:rnəl] 대령
bandage [bǽndidʒ] 붕대, 안대
foreigner [fɔ́(ː)rinər] 외국인
laugh [læf] 소리내어 웃다

Che mala fortuna!
(I.) 재수가 없었다!

FRI

realize [ríːəlàiz]
실현하다, 현실화하다
probably [prɑ́bəbli] 아마, 대개는
ship [ʃip] 배, 배로 보내다, 수송하다
suppose [səpóuz]
가정하다(assume), 상상하다

encounter [enkáuntər]
조우, 우연히 만나다

Then all of a sudden I started to cry

그러고 나서 나는 갑자기 울음을 터뜨렸다

I lay awake thinking and my mind jumping around. Then I couldn't keep away from it, and I started to think about Brett and all the rest of it went away. I was thinking about Brett and my mind stopped jumping around and started to go in sort of smooth waves. Then all of a sudden I started to cry.

나는 잠을 이루지 못한 채 이 생각 저 생각 더듬으며 누워 있었다. 마음에서 그 생각을 떨쳐 버릴 수 없이 브렛에 대해 생각하기 시작하자 다른 상념은 모두 사라져 버렸다. 브렛을 생각하자 마음이 함부로 널뛰는 것이 멈추고 잔잔한 물결 같은 것이 되어 움직이기 시작했다. 그러고 나서 나는 갑자기 울음을 터뜨렸다.

문장분석

I lay awake thinking and my mind jumping around. Then I couldn't keep away
　　　　　　　　　　　　　　　　　　팔짝팔짝 뛰다　　　　　　　　　멀리하다
from it, and I started to think about Brett and all the rest of it went away. I was
　　　　　　　　　　　　　　　　　　　　　　　　　　　　　사라지다
thinking about Brett and my mind stopped jumping around and started to go in

sort of smooth waves. Then all of a sudden I started to cry.
일종의 ~(~ 같은 것)　　　　　　　　　　갑자기

lie [lai] (lay-lain) 눕다, ~이 놓여 있다　　　rest [rest] 나머지, 휴식, 안정
lay [lei] (laid-laid) 눕히다, ~을 놓다　　　smooth [smu:ð] 매끄러운, 부드러운
lie [lai] (lied-lied) 거짓말하다

This was Brett, that I had felt like crying about

브렛은 그런 여자였다. 내가 떠올리면서 울고 싶었던 바로 그런 여자였다

This was Brett, that I had felt like crying about. Then I thought of her walking up the street and stepping into the car, as I had last seen her, and of course in a little while I felt like hell again. It is awfully easy to be hard-boiled about everything in the daytime, but at night it is another thing.

브렛은 그런 여자였다. 내가 떠올리면서 울고 싶었던 바로 그런 여자였다. 그러고 나서 내가 마지막으로 본 그 여자의 모습, 길거리 위쪽으로 걸어가 자동차에 올라타는 모습을 생각했다. 아닌 게 아니라 잠시 후 나는 지옥을 헤매는 것 같은 느낌이 들었다. 대낮이라면 어떤 일이 닥치더라도 감정을 억누르기가 아주 쉬운 법인데 밤에는 정말 어떻게 해 볼 도리가 없는 것이다.

문장분석

This was Brett, that I had felt like crying about. Then I thought of her walking up the street and stepping into the car, as I had last seen her, and of course / in a
~한 때의
little while / I felt like hell again. It is awfully easy to be hard-boiled about every-
잠시 후, 곧   very
thing in the daytime, but at night / it is another thing.

awfully [ɔ́ːfəli] 매우, 무섭게
awesome [ɔ́ːsəm]
　두려운, 경외케 하는, 인상적인, 멋진
terrific [tərífik] 빼어난, 대단한, 아주 좋은, 멋진

hard-boiled
　단단하게 삶은, 무정한, 냉철한, 현실적인
daytime [déitàim] 낮, 주간(의)

We like quiet, like you like noise, my dear

우린 조용한 걸 좋아해요, 당신이 시끄러운 걸 좋아하는 것처럼 말이죠

"Have another brandy," the count said.
"Get it on the hill."
"No. Have it here where it is quiet."
"You and your quiet," said Brett. "What is it men feel about quiet?"
"We like it," said the count. "Like you like noise, my dear."

"브랜디를 한 잔 더 하지요." 백작이 권했다.
"언덕에 가서 해요."
"아니에요. 조용한 이곳에서 해요."
"당신은 또 그 '조용' 타령이군요. 도대체 남자들은 그 '조용'에서 뭘 느끼는 거죠?" 브렛이 물었다.
"우린 조용한 걸 좋아합니다. 당신이 시끄러운 것을 좋아하는 것처럼 말이죠." 백작이 대답했다.

문장분석

"Have another brandy," the count said.
먹다, 마시다
"Get it on the hill."

"No. Have it here where it is quiet."

"You and your quiet," said Brett. "What is it men feel about quiet?"
또 늘 하는~이야기
"We like it," said the count. "Like you like noise, my dear."
~처럼

count [kaunt] 백작
crown [kraun] 왕관, 왕권
clown [klaun] 어릿광대

royal [rɔ́iəl] 왕의, 왕족의
loyal [lɔ́iəl] 충성스러운, 성실한

Injustice everywhere

세상이 온통 부정부패로 가득하더군

"Not so good, Jake. Injustice everywhere. Promoter claimed nigger promised let local boy stay. Claimed nigger violated contract. Can't knock out Vienna boy in Vienna. 'My God, Mister Gorton,' said nigger, 'I didn't do nothing in there for forty minutes but try and let him stay. That white boy musta ruptured himself swinging at me. I never did hit him.'"

"별로 좋지 않았어. 세상이 온통 부정부패로 가득하더군. 프로모터는 검둥이가 지방 청년을 마지막까지 때려눕히지 않기로 약속했다고 우겨대는 거야. 검둥이가 계약을 위반했다는 거야. 빈에서는 빈 선수를 케이오시킬 수 없다는 거지. 검둥이가 말하더군. '정말 기가 막혀요, 고턴 씨. 난 40분 동안 그 녀석을 넘어뜨리지 않으려고 노력했다고요. 그 백인 선수가 나를 때리려다가 제풀에 쓰러진 게 틀림없어요. 난 그를 한 번 때려 보지도 못했거든요.'"

문장분석

"Not so good, Jake. Injustice everywhere. Promoter claimed (that) nigger promised let local boy stay. (Promoter) Claimed (that) nigger violated contract. (Nigger) Can't knock out Vienna boy in Vienna. 'My God, Mister Gorton,' said nigger, 'I didn't do anything in there for forty minutes but try and (let) him (stay.)'
except

That white boy musta ruptured himself swinging at me. I never did hit him.'"
must have

injustice [indʒʌ́stis] 부정, 불법, 불의, 불공평
claim [kleim] 요구하다, 주장하다, 청구하다
nigger [nígər] 흑인, 검둥이

violate [váiəlèit] 어기다, 침해하다
rupture [rʌ́ptʃər] 파열, 파괴, 찢다

Road to hell paved with unbought stuffed dogs

지옥 가는 길이 네가 사지 않은 박제 개로 포장되어 있을 거야

"Mean everything in the world to you after you bought it. Simple exchange of values. You give them money. They give you a stuffed dog."
"We'll get one on the way back."
"All right. Have it your own way. Road to hell paved with unbought stuffed dogs. Not my fault."

"그걸 사고 나면 이 세상 모든 것을 얻은 기분이 들 거야. 단순한 가치의 교환이지. 너는 그들에게 돈을 지불하는 거야. 그러면 그들은 너에게 박제한 개 한 마리를 주는 거고."
"돌아오는 길에 한 마리 사도록 해."
"좋아. 마음대로 해. 지옥 가는 길이 네가 사지 않은 박제 개로 포장되어 있을 거야. 하지만 그건 내 잘못이 아냐."

문장분석

"Mean everything in the world to you / after you bought it. Simple exchange of values. You give them money. They give you a stuffed dog."

"We'll get one on the way back."
　　　　　　　　　　돌아오는 길에
"All right. Have it (all) your own way. Road to hell (is) paved with unbought stuffed
　　　　　　　네 멋대로 해라
dogs. (That's) Not my fault."

value [vǽljuː] 가치, 유용성, 진가
valueless 가치가 없는, 하찮은
invaluable [invǽljuəbəl]
　값을 헤아릴 수 없는, 매우 귀중한(priceless)

stuff [stʌf] …에 채우다(채워 넣다)
pave [peiv] (도로를) 포장하다

Vocabulary Of The Week

MON

lie [lai] (lay-lain) 눕다, ~이 놓여 있다
lay [lei] (laid-laid) 눕히다, ~을 놓다
lie [lai] (lied-lied) 거짓말하다
rest [rest] 나머지, 휴식, 안정
smooth [smuːð] 매끄러운, 부드러운

TUE

awfully [ɔ́ːfəli] 매우, 무섭게
awesome [ɔ́ːsəm]
　두려운, 경외케 하는, 인상적인, 멋진
terrific [tərífik]
　빼어난, 대단한, 아주 좋은, 멋진

hard-boiled
　단단하게 삶은, 무정한, 냉철한,
　현실적인
daytime [déitàim] 낮, 주간(의)

WED

count [kaunt] 백작
crown [kraun] 왕관, 왕권
clown [klaun] 어릿광대
royal [rɔ́iəl] 왕의, 왕족의
loyal [lɔ́iəl] 충성스러운, 성실한

THU

injustice [indʒʌ́stis]
　부정, 불법, 불의, 불공평
claim [kleim]
　요구하다, 주장하다, 청구하다
nigger [nígər] 흑인, 검둥이
violate [váiəlèit] 어기다, 침해하다

rupture [rʌ́ptʃər] 파열, 파괴, 찢다

FRI

value [vǽljuː] 가치, 유용성, 진가
valueless 가치가 없는, 하찮은
invaluable [invǽljuəbəl]
　값을 헤아릴 수 없는,
　매우 귀중한(priceless)
stuff [stʌf] …에 채우다(채워 넣다)

pave [peiv] (도로를) 포장하다

MON

Ought not to daunt you and never be daunted

사람들을 주눅 들게 하지 말라, 또 남한테 주눅 들지도 말라

"Certainly like to drink," Bill said. "You ought to try it some times, Jake."
"You're about a hundred and forty-four ahead of me."
"Ought not to daunt you. Never be daunted. Secret of my success. Never been daunted. Never been daunted in public."

"술을 마시는 건 과연 좋은 거야. 제이크, 너도 가끔 시험해 봐야 해." 빌이 말했다.
"넌 나보다 144년이나 앞서 있군그래."
"사람들을 주눅 들게 하지 말라. 또 남한테 주눅 들지도 말라. 내 성공의 비결이야. 절대로 주눅 들지 않았지. 사람들이 있는 앞에서는 절대로 그런 적이 없어."

문장분석

"Certainly like to drink," Bill said. "You <u>ought to</u> try it some times, Jake."
　　　　　　　　　　　　　　　　　　　　should

"You're <u>about</u> a hundred and forty-four <u>ahead of</u> me."
　　　　　대략　　　　　　　　　　　　　앞서는

"<u>Ought not to</u> daunt you. Never be daunted. (That is the) Secret of my success. (I
　should not

have) Never been daunted. (I have) Never been daunted in public."
　　　　　　　　　　　　　　　　　　　　　　공개적으로, 대중 앞에서

certainly [sə́:rtənli] 확실히, 꼭, 반드시, 정말
daunt [dɔːnt]
　으르다, 움찔하게 하다, …의 기세를 꺾다

public [pʌ́blik] 공중의, 일반 국민의, 공공의
publicity [pʌblísəti] 널리 알려짐. 명성, 평판, 공개
publicize [pʌ́bləsàiz] 선전(공표, 광고)하다

TUE

It's a wonder they ever find any one to marry them

남자들이 결혼할 상대를 찾아내는 건 참 놀라운 일이에요

"You know how the ladies are. If there's a jug goes along, or a case of beer, they think it's hell and damnation."
"That's the way men are. I voted against prohibition to please him, and because I like a little beer in the house, and then he talks that way. It's a wonder they ever find any one to marry them."

"여자들이 그렇죠. 술병이나 맥주 상자가 돌면 지옥이다, 파멸이다 하고 생각해 버리니까요."
"남자들이 그렇더군요. 난 저 사람 기분을 맞춰 주려고, 또 집에서 맥주를 조금 마시는 걸 좋아하기 때문에 금주법에 반대표를 던졌어요. 그런데도 저 사람이 저런 소리를 한다니까요. 남자들이 결혼할 상대를 찾아내는 건 참 놀라운 일이에요."

문장분석

"You know how the ladies are. If there's a jug goes along, or a case of beer,/ they
계속하다
think (that) it's hell and damnation."

"That's the way men are. I voted against prohibition to please him, and because I
~에 반대하여
like a little beer in the house, and then/ he talks that way. It's a wonder (that) they

ever find any one to marry them."
어쨌든

jug [dʒʌg] 주전자, 항아리, 위스키 병
damnation [dæmnéiʃən] 비난, 악평, 파멸
prohibition [pròuhəbíʃən] 금지

please [pliːz] 기쁘게 하다, 만족시키다
wonder [wʌ́ndər] 불가사의, 경이, 놀라움, 기적

Fake European standards have ruined you

사이비 유럽 기준이 널 망치고 만 거야

"You're an expatriate. You've lost touch with the soil. You get precious. Fake European standards have ruined you. You drink yourself to death. You become obsessed by sex. You spend all your time talking, not working. You are an expatriate, see? You hang around cafés."

"넌 국적상실자야. 조국의 땅과 접촉을 잃어버렸단 말이야. 귀하신 몸이 된 거지. 사이비 유럽 기준이 널 망치고 만 거야. 죽도록 술만 퍼마시고. 섹스에 사로잡혀 있고. 넌 모든 시간을 일하는 데 쓰는 것이 아니라 지껄이는 데 허비하거든. 넌 국적상실자야, 알겠어? 카페나 헤매고 다니고 말이야."

문장분석

"You're an expatriate. You've lost touch with the soil. You get precious. Fake
European standards have ruined you. You drink yourself to death. You become
<small>become</small>
obsessed by sex. You spend all your time (in) talking, not working. You are an
<small>죽을 때까지</small>
expatriate, see? You hang around cafés."
<small>understand   어슬렁거리다, 방황하다</small>

expatriate [ekspéitrièit]
  국외로 추방하다, 국외로 이주한 사람
soil [sɔil] 흙, 토양, 국토, 나라
precious [préʃəs] 비싼, 귀중한

ruin [rúːin] 파멸, 파괴하다
obsess [əbsés] 사로잡히다

I'm fonder of you than anybody on earth

난 이 세상의 어느 누구보다도 널 좋아해

"Listen. You're a hell of a good guy, and I'm fonder of you than anybody on earth. I couldn't tell you that in New York. It'd mean I was a faggot. That was what the Civil War was about. Abraham Lincoln was a faggot. He was in love with General Grant."

"이봐, 넌 무척 좋은 놈이야. 그리고 난 이 세상의 어느 누구보다도 널 좋아해. 뉴욕에서는 너한테 이런 말을 못했지. 그런 말을 하면 나를 동성애자라고 할 테니 말야. 남북전쟁이 그것 때문에 일어난 거야. 에이브러햄 링컨은 동성애자였거든. 그랜트 장군한테 반해 버린 거야."

문장분석

"Listen. You're a hell of a good guy, and I am fonder of you than anybody on
　　　　　　　　대단한, 엄청난(강조)　　　　　　　　～을 더 좋아하다
earth. I couldn't tell you that in New York. It would mean (that) I was a faggot.

That was what the Civil War was about. Abraham Lincoln was a faggot. He was in
　　　정체, 본질, 내용
love with General Grant."
～와 사랑에 빠지다

fond [fɑnd] 좋아서, 애정 있는　　　　　　　　general [dʒénərəl] 육군 대장, 일반의
faggot [fǽgət] 남성 동성애자　　　　　　　　civil [sívəl] 시민의, 국내의
heterosexual 이성애자

It must have been pleasant for him to see her looking so lovely

그렇게 아름다운 그녀의 모습을 바라보는 것이 그에겐 기분 좋은 일임에 틀림없었다

He could not stop looking at Brett. It seemed to make him happy. It must have been pleasant for him to see her looking so lovely, and know he had been away with her and that every one knew it. They could not take that away from him.

그는 브렛을 바라보지 않고서는 견딜 수가 없었다. 그게 그를 행복하게 해주는 모양이었다. 그렇게 아름다운 그녀의 모습을 바라보고, 그녀와 함께 놀러 갔다 왔고 또 그 사실을 다들 알고 있다는 것이 그에게는 기분이 좋은 일임에 틀림없었다. 아무도 그에게서 그런 즐거움을 뺏을 수 없었다.

문장분석

He could not stop looking at Brett. It seemed to make him happy. It must have
　　　　　　　　　　　　　　　　 ~한 모양이다
been pleasant for him to see her looking so lovely, and know he had been away
　　　　　　　　　　　　　　 ~처럼 보이다
with her and that every one knew it. They could not take that away from him.

must have pp ~했음에 틀림 없다　　　　may have pp ~했을지도 모른다
cannot have pp ~했을리 없다　　　　　　pleasant [pléznt] 즐거운, 기분좋은, 유쾌한
should have pp
　~했어야 했다(하지만 ~하지 않았다)

Vocabulary Of The Week

MON

certainly [sə́:rtənli]
확실히, 꼭, 반드시, 정말
daunt [dɔ:nt]
으르다, 움찔하게 하다,
…의 기세를 꺾다

public [pʌ́blik]
공중의, 일반 국민의, 공공의
publicity [pʌblísəti]
널리 알려짐. 명성, 평판, 공개
publicize [pʌ́bləsàiz]
전(공표, 광고)하다

TUE

jug [dʒʌg] 주전자, 항아리, 위스키 병
damnation [dæmnéiʃən]
비난, 악평, 파멸
prohibition [pròuhəbíʃən] 금지
please [pli:z]
기쁘게 하다, 만족시키다

wonder [wʌ́ndər]
불가사의, 경이, 놀라움, 기적

WED

expatriate [ekspéitrièit]
국외로 추방하다, 국외로 이주한 사람
soil [sɔil] 흙, 토양, 국토, 나라
precious [préʃəs] 비싼, 귀중한
ruin [rú:in] 파멸, 파괴하다
obsess [əbsés] 사로잡히다

THU

fond [fɑnd] 좋아서, 애정 있는
faggot [fǽgət] 남성 동성애자
heterosexual 이성애자
general [dʒénərəl] 육군 대장, 일반의
civil [sívəl] 시민의, 국내의

FRI

must have pp ~했음에 틀림 없다
cannot have pp ~했을리 없다
should have pp
~했어야 했다(하지만 ~하지 않았다)
may have pp ~했을지도 모른다

pleasant [pléznt]
즐거운, 기분좋은, 유쾌한

February
02

**There is nothing noble in being superior
to your fellow man; true nobility is
being superior to your former self.**

타인보다 우수하다고 해서 고귀해지지 않는다.
진정으로 고귀한 것은 과거의 자신보다 더 나아지는 것이다.

MON

Under the wine I lost the disgusted feeling and was happy

포도주 덕택에 나는 불쾌한 기분을 잊고 행복했다

It was like certain dinners I remember from the war. There was much wine, an ignored tension, and a feeling of things coming that you could not prevent happening. Under the wine I lost the disgusted feeling and was happy. It seemed they were all such nice people.

그날 저녁 식사는 내가 기억하고 있는 전쟁터의 어느 저녁 식사와 같았다. 포도주는 많았고, 긴장은 무시해 버리고, 도저히 막을 수 없는 어떤 일이 다가오고 있다는 느낌이 들었다. 포도주 덕분에 나는 불쾌한 기분을 잊고 행복했다. 하나같이 좋은 사람들이라는 생각이 들었다.

문장분석

It was like certain ⟨dinners⟩ I remember from the war. There was much wine,

an ignored tension, and a feeling of ⟨things coming⟩ that you could not prevent

happening. Under the wine/ I lost the disgusted feeling and was happy. It

seemed (that) they were all such nice people.
　　　　　　　　　　　　　　　　　　very

certain [sə́ːrtən] 확신하는, 어떤
ignore [ignɔ́ːr] 무시하다
prevent [privént] 막다, 방해하다

disgust [disgʌ́st]
　혐오, 구역질, 정떨어지게 하다, 메스껍게 하다
seemingly [síːmiŋli] 보기엔, 외관상, 겉으로는

There is no reason why because it is dark you should look at things differently

어둡다고 해서 사물을 다르게 바라봐야 할 이유는 없다

I turned off the light and tried to go to sleep. It was not necessary to read any more. I could shut my eyes without getting the wheeling sensation. But I could not sleep. There is no reason why because it is dark you should look at things differently from when it is light. The hell there isn't! I figured that all out once, and for six months I never slept with the electric light off.

나는 불을 끄고 잠을 자려고 했다. 이제는 책을 더 읽을 필요가 없었다. 눈을 감아도 방이 빙빙 돌아가는 듯한 느낌이 들지 않았다. 그런데도 잠이 오지 않았다. 어둡다고 해서 밝을 때와 다르게 사물을 바라봐야 할 이유는 없다. 그럴 이유가 있을 턱이 없지 않은가! 언젠가 한 번은 이런저런 생각을 한 끝에 꼬박 반년 동안 전깃불을 켜 둔 채로 잠자리에 들었다.

문장분석

I turned off the light and tried to go to sleep. It was not necessary to read any
　　　　끄다
more. I could shut my eyes without getting the wheeling sensation. But I could

not sleep. There is no reason why because it is dark you should look at things

differently from when it is light. The hell there isn't (any reason)! I figured that all
　　　　　　　　　　　　　　　　　　　　도대체, 대관절
out once, and for six months/ I never slept with the electric light off.
전력을 다하여

necessary [nésəsèri] 필요한, 없어서는 안 될   reason [ríːzən] 이유, 이성
wheel [hwiːl] 바퀴, 회전시키다   figure [fígjər] 계산하다, 이해하다, 해결하다
sensation [senséiʃən] 감각, 기분, 평판

You had to be in love with a woman to have a basis of friendship

우정의 토대를 쌓으려면 먼저 여자와 사랑을 해 봐야 한다

Women made such swell friends. Awfully swell. In the first place, you had to be in love with a woman to have a basis of friendship. I had been having Brett for a friend. I had not been thinking about her side of it. I had been getting something for nothing. That only delayed the presentation of the bill. The bill always came. That was one of the swell things you could count on.

여자들은 굉장한 친구가 될 수 있다. 굉장히 좋은 친구 말이다. 우정의 토대를 쌓으려면 먼저 여자와 사랑을 해 봐야 한다. 나는 브렛과 오래전부터 친구로 지내 왔다. 그녀 입장이 되어서 생각해 본 적은 한 번도 없다. 아무런 대가도 치르지 않고 뭔가를 얻고 있었던 것이다. 다만 계산서가 나오는 일이 늦어졌을 뿐이다. 그러나 계산서는 언제나 날아들었다. 이것만은 예측할 수 있는 멋진 일이었다.

문장분석

Women made such swell friends. <u>Awfully</u> swell. In the first place, you had to <u>be</u>
                                         very

<u>in love with</u> a woman to have a basis of friendship. I had been having Brett for a
~와 사랑에 빠지다

friend. I had not been thinking about her side of it. I had been getting something

<u>for nothing</u>. That only delayed the presentation of the bill. The bill always came.
무료로, 거저

That was one of the swell (things) you could <u>count on</u>.
                                               기대하다, 믿다

swell [swel] 부풀다, 굉장한, 훌륭한　　　　presentation [prèzəntéiʃən] 증여, 제출, 제시
basis [béisis] 기초, 토대　　　　　　　　　bill [bil] 청구서, 지폐, 법안
delay [diléi] 미루다, 연기하다

THU

I paid my way into enough things that I liked

내가 좋아하는 것을 충분히 얻기 위해 나는 나름대로 값을 치렀다

You paid some way for everything that was any good. I paid my way into enough things that I liked, so that I had a good time. Either you paid by learning about them, or by experience, or by taking chances, or by money.

조금이라도 도움이 될 만한 모든 것을 위해 어떤 방법으로든 그 대가를 치렀다. 내가 좋아하는 것을 충분히 얻기 위해 나는 나름대로 값을 치렀고, 그래서 즐거운 시간을 보냈다. 그것들에 관해서 배운다든지, 경험을 한다든지, 위험을 무릅쓴다든지, 아니면 돈을 지불함으로써 값을 치렀다.

문장분석

You **paid** some way for (everything) that was any good. I **paid** my way into enough
방식으로
(things) that I liked, so that I had a good time. **Either** you paid by learning about
them, **or** by experience, **or** by taking chances, **or** by money.
모험하다

pay for 대가를 지불하다, 계산하다
pay into ~에 돈을 붓다, 불입하다
pay for performance 성과급 프로그램

performance [pərfɔ́rməns] 수행, 이행, 성과
experience [ikspíəriəns] 경험, 체험

The world was a good place to buy in

이 세상은 무언가를 구입하기에 좋은 곳이다

Enjoying living was learning to get your money's worth and knowing when you had it. You could get your money's worth. The world was a good place to buy in. It seemed like a fine philosophy. In five years, I thought, it will seem just as silly as all the other fine philosophies I've had.

삶을 즐긴다는 것은 지불한 값어치만큼 얻어 내는 것을 배우는 것이고 그렇게 얻었다는 것을 아는 것이다. 누구나 돈을 지불한 값어치만큼 손에 넣을 수 있을 것이다. 이 세상은 무언가를 구입하기에 좋은 곳이다. 이건 아주 멋진 철학처럼 보인다. 그러나 앞으로 5년 후에는 내가 일찍이 알고 있던 모든 훌륭한 철학이 그랬던 것처럼 이것 역시 그저 어리석게 보일 것이다.

문장분석

Enjoying living was learning to get your money's worth and knowing when you had it. You could get your money's worth. The world was a good place to buy in. It seemed like a fine philosophy. In five years, I thought, it will seem just as silly as silly as all the other fine philosophies (that) I've had.

worth [wəːrθ] …의 가치가 있는, 값어치
philosophy [filάsəfi] 철학
silly [síli] 어리석은(stupid)

in five years 5년 후
within five years 5년 이내

Vocabulary Of The Week

MON

certain [sə́:rtən] 확신하는, 어떤
ignore [ignɔ́:r] 무시하다
prevent [privént] 막다, 방해하다
disgust [disgʌ́st]
혐오, 구역질, 정떨어지게 하다,
메스껍게 하다

seemingly [sí:miŋli]
보기엔, 외관상. 겉으로는

TUE

necessary [nésəsèri]
필요한, 없어서는 안 될
wheel [hwi:l] 바퀴, 회전시키다
sensation [senséiʃən]
감각, 기분, 평판
reason [rí:zən] 이유, 이성

figure [figjər]
계산하다, 이해하다, 해결하다

WED

swell [swel] 부풀다, 굉장한, 훌륭한
basis [béisis] 기초, 토대
delay [diléi] 미루다, 연기하다
presentation [prèzəntéiʃən]
증여, 제출, 제시
bill [bil] 청구서, 지폐, 법안

THU

pay for 대가를 지불하다, 계산하다
pay into ~에 돈을 붓다, 불입하다
pay for performance
성과급 프로그램
performance [pərfɔ́:rməns]
수행, 이행, 성과

experience [ikspíəriəns] 경험, 체험

FRI

worth [wə:rθ]
…의 가치가 있는, 값어치
philosophy [filɑ́səfi] 철학
silly [síli] 어리석은(stupid)
in five years 5년 후
within five years 5년 이내

All I wanted to know was how to live in it

내가 알고 싶은 것은, 이 세상에서 어떻게 살아가느냐 하는 것이다

Perhaps that wasn't true, though. Perhaps as you went along you did learn something. I did not care what it was all about. All I wanted to know was how to live in it. Maybe if you found out how to live in it you learned from that what it was all about.

그러나 어쩌면 그것도 진실은 아닐지 모른다. 아마 살아가면서 무언가를 배우는 것일 것이다. 나는 그것이 무엇이든 아랑곳하지 않았다. 내가 알고 싶은 것은, 이 세상에서 어떻게 살아가느냐 하는 것이다. 만약 이 세상에서 어떻게 살아나갈 것인가를 알아낸다면 그것이 무엇인지는 저절로 알게 되리라.

문장분석

Perhaps that wasn't true, though. Perhaps as you went along / you did learn
something. I did not care what it was all about. All I wanted to know was how to
live in it. Maybe if you found out how to live in it/ you learned (from that) what it
was all about.

perhaps [pərhǽps]
  아마, 형편에 따라서는, 혹시, 어쩌면
though [ðou] …이긴 하지만, 어쩌면

through [θru:] …을 통하여, 처음부터 끝까지
thorough [θə́:rou]
  철저한, 충분한, 완벽한, 완전한

What a lot of bilge I could think up at night

밤이 되면 얼마나 쓸데없는 생각을 많이 하는가

I liked to see him hurt Cohn. I wished he would not do it, though, because afterward it made me disgusted at myself. That was morality; things that made you disgusted afterward. No, that must be immorality. That was a large statement. What a lot of bilge I could think up at night. What rot, I could hear Brett say it.

나는 그가 콘의 감정을 상하게 하는 것을 보고 싶었다. 하지만 나중에 스스로에 대해서 불쾌해지기 때문에 그가 그런 짓을 하지 않았으면 하고 바랐다. 그게 바로 도덕이라는 것이다. 나중에 불쾌하게 느끼게 해 주는 것 말이다. 아니, 부도덕이라고 해야 할까. 이건 엄청난 진술이지. 밤이 되면 얼마나 쓸데없는 생각을 많이 하는가! 시시한 소리! 이렇게 말하는 브렛의 목소리가 들리는 것 같다.

문장분석

I liked to <u>see</u> him <u>hurt</u> Cohn. I wished (that) he would not do it, though, because afterward it made me disgusted at myself. That was morality; (things) that <u>made you disgusted</u> afterward. No, that must be immorality. That was a large
~임에 틀림없다
statement. What a lot of bilge/ I could think up/ at night. What rot, I could hear

Brett say it.

disgusted [disgʌ́stid] 정떨어진, 싫증난, 화나는
disgusting [disgʌ́stiŋ] 구역질나는, 정말 싫은
morality [mɔ(:)rǽləti] 도덕(성)
immorality [imərǽləti] 부도덕, 패덕

bilge [bildʒ]
데데한 이야기, 허튼소리(nonsense), 웃음거리
rot [rɑt] 썩음, 부패, 허튼소리

As long as a bull-fighter stays in his own terrain he is comparatively safe

투우사가 자신의 영역에 머물고 있는 한 비교적 안전하다

Belmonte's great attraction is working close to the bull. In bull-fighting they speak of the terrain of the bull and the terrain of the bull-fighter. As long as a bull-fighter stays in his own terrain he is comparatively safe. Each time he enters into the terrain of the bull he is in great danger.

벨몬테의 가장 큰 매력은 황소에 바싹 붙어서 싸운다는 점이었다. 투우에는 흔히 황소의 영역과 투우사의 영역이 있다고들 한다. 투우사가 자신의 영역에 머물고 있는 한 비교적 안전하다. 소의 영역으로 들어갈 때마다 그는 큰 위험에 빠진다.

문장분석

Belmonte's great attraction is working close to the bull. In bull-fighting/ they
일반인
speak of the terrain of the bull and the terrain of the bull-fighter. As long as a
~하는 한
bull-fighter stays in his own terrain/ he is comparatively safe. Each time he enters
Whenever
into the terrain of the bull/ he is in great danger.

attraction [ətrǽkʃən]
(사람을) 끄는 힘, 매력, 유혹
terrain [təréin] 지대, 지역, 영역, 환경
territory [térətɔ̀ːri] 영토, 영지, 지역, 지방

comparative [kəmpǽrətiv] 비교적인, 상당한
comparable [kámpərəbəl]
비교되는, 필적하는, 상당하는, 동등한

This way he gave the sensation of coming tragedy

이런 방식으로 그는 관중들에게 비극이 닥쳐오리라는 느낌을 주었다

Belmonte, in his best days, worked always in the terrain of the bull. This way he gave the sensation of coming tragedy. People went to the corrida to see Belmonte, to be given tragic sensations, and perhaps to see the death of Belmonte.

전성기 시절 벨몬테는 언제나 소의 영역에서 싸웠다. 이런 방식으로 그는 관중들에게 비극이 닥쳐오리라는 느낌을 주었다. 사람들은 벨몬테를 보려고, 비극적 감정을 맛보려고, 어쩌면 벨몬테가 죽는 것을 목격하려고 투우장으로 몰려들었던 것이다.

Belmonte, in his best days, worked always in the terrain of the bull. This way/
전성기
he gave the sensation of coming tragedy. People went to the corrida/ to see

Belmonte, to be given tragic sensations, and perhaps to see the death of

Belmonte.

terrain [təréin] 지대, 지역, 영역, 환경
corrida [kɔːríːdə] (Sp.) 투우
tragedy [trǽdʒədi] 비극

tragic [trǽdʒik] 비극의, 비극적인
sensation [senséiʃən] 감각, 지각, 기분, 흥분

It is the simplest country to live in

이 나라처럼 살기 편한 곳이 없다

The waiter seemed a little offended about the flowers of the Pyrenees, so I overtipped him. That made him happy. It felt comfortable to be in a country where it is so simple to make people happy. You can never tell whether a Spanish waiter will thank you. Everything is on such a clear financial basis in France. It is the simplest country to live in.

웨이터는 피레네 산맥 야생화로 만든 술 때문에 조금 화가 난 것 같기에 팁을 듬뿍 주었다. 그러자 그는 행복한 표정을 지었다. 사람들을 흐뭇하게 하는 게 이렇게 간단한 나라에 머물고 있어 마음 편했다. 스페인 웨이터라면 고마워할지 어떨지 도무지 분간할 수 없다. 프랑스에서는 모든 것이 이처럼 뚜렷하게 돈에 바탕을 두고 있다. 이 나라처럼 살기 편한 곳이 없다.

문장분석

The waiter seemed a little offended about the flowers of the Pyrenees, so I
~처럼 보이다   약간
overtipped him. That made him happy. It felt comfortable to be in a country
where it is so simple to make people happy. You can never tell whether a Spanish
분간하다
waiter will thank you. Everything is on such a clear financial basis in France. It is
the simplest country to live in.

offend [əfénd]
　성나게 하다, 기분을 상하게 하다, 위반하다
defend [difénd] 막다, 지키다, 방어하다
comfortable [kΛ́mfərtəbəl]
　기분 좋은, 편한, 위안의

financial [finǽnʃəl]
　재정상의, 재무의, 재계의, 금융상의
basis [béisis] 기초, 기저, 토대

Vocabulary Of The Week

MON

perhaps [pərhǽps] 아마, 형편에
따라서는, 혹시, 어쩌면
though [ðou] …이긴 하지만, 어쩌면
through [θruː]
…을 통하여, 처음부터 끝까지

thorough [θə́ːrou]
철저한, 충분한, 완벽한, 완전한

TUE

disgusted [disgʌ́stid]
정떨어진, 싫증난, 화나는
disgusting [disgʌ́stiŋ]
구역질나는, 정말 싫은
morality [mɔ(ː)rǽləti] 도덕(성)
immorality [ìmərǽləti] 부도덕, 패덕

bilge [bildʒ]
데데한 이야기, 허튼소리(nonsense),
웃음거리
rot [rɑt] 썩음, 부패, 허튼소리

WED

attraction [ətrǽkʃən]
(사람을) 끄는 힘, 매력, 유혹
terrain [təréin] 지대, 지역, 영역, 환경
territory [térətɔ̀ːri]
영토, 영지, 지역, 지방
comparative [kəmpǽrətiv]

비교적인, 상당한
comparable [kʌ́mpərəbəl]
비교되는, 필적하는, 상당하는, 동등한

THU

terrain [təréin] 지대, 지역, 영역, 환경
corrida [kɔːríːdə] (Sp.) 투우
tragedy [trǽdʒədi] 비극
tragic [trǽdʒik] 비극의, 비극적인
sensation [senséiʃən]
감각, 지각, 기분, 흥분

FRI

offend [əfénd]
성나게 하다, 기분을 상하게 하다,
위반하다
defend [difénd]
막다, 지키다, 방어하다

comfortable [kʌ́mfərtəbəl]
기분 좋은, 편한, 위안의
financial [finǽnʃəl]
재정상의, 재무의, 재계의, 금융상의
basis [béisis] 기초, 기저, 토대

MON

If you want people to like you you have only to spend a little money

사람들에게 호감을 사려면 돈을 좀 쓰기만 하면 된다

If you want people to like you you have only to spend a little money. I spent a little money and the waiter liked me. He appreciated my valuable qualities. He would be glad to see me back. I would dine there again some time and he would be glad to see me, and would want me at his table. It would be a sincere liking because it would have a sound basis. I was back in France.

사람들에게 호감을 사려면 돈을 좀 쓰기만 하면 된다. 내가 돈을 조금 썼더니 웨이터는 금방 나를 좋아했다. 그는 나를 가치 있는 사람이라고 인정해 주었다. 내가 또 찾아오면 반가워할 것이다. 언제고 또 이곳에서 식사하게 되면 그는 나를 보고 반가워하며 자기 테이블에 앉기를 바랄 것이다. 확실한 근거가 있기 때문에 진심으로 나를 좋아하는 것이리라. 이제 나는 프랑스에 돌아온 것이다.

문장분석

If you (want) people (to) like you/ you have only to spend a little money. I spent a
　　　 ~하기만 하면 된다　　　　　　　약간

little money and the waiter liked me. He appreciated my valuable qualities. He

would be glad to see me back. I would dine there again some time and he would

be glad to see me, and would want me at his table. It would be a sincere liking

because it would have a sound basis. I was back in France.
　　　　　　　　　　　확실한, 건전한

spend [spend] 쓰다, 소비하다(expend)
appreciate [əprí:ʃièit]
　…의 진가를 인정하다, 감상하다, 감사하다

valuable [vǽljuːəbəl] 귀중한, 귀한, 소중한
dine [dain] 저녁 식사를 하다, 식사하다
sincere [sinsíər] 성실한, 진실한, 성심 성의의

That seemed to handle it. That was it

그것으로 일이 해결된 모양이었다. 그랬다

LADY ASHLEY HOTEL MONTANA MADRID
ARRIVING SUD EXPRESS TOMORROW
LOVE JAKE.

That seemed to handle it. That was it. Send a girl off with one man. Introduce her to another to go off with him. Now go and bring her back. And sign the wire with love. That was it all right.

마드리드 호텔 몬타나의 레이디 애슐리
내일 급행으로 도착
사랑하는 제이크.

그것으로 일이 해결된 모양이었다. 그랬다. 여자를 한 남자와 떠나보낸다. 그녀를 또 다른 남자에게 소개하니 또 그 남자하고 도망친다. 이제는 그 여자를 데리러 간다. 그리고 전보에 '사랑하는'이라고 쓴다. 바로 그랬다.

문장분석

LADY ASHLEY HOTEL MONTANA MADRID

ARRIVING SUD EXPRESS TOMORROW LOVE JAKE.

That seemed to handle it. That was it. Send a girl off with one man. Introduce her
　　　～한 모양이다　　　　　바로 그것이다
to another to go off with him. Now go and bring her back. And sign the wire with
　가 버리다
love. That was it all right.
　　　　　　틀림없이

arrival [əráivəl] 도착, 도달　　　　　introduce [intrədjúːs] 소개하다, 도입하다
Sud Express 야간 급행열차의 이름　　wire [waiər] 전신, 전보, 철사
handle [hǽndl] 다루다, 처리하다

I've had such a hell of a time

나 아주 정말 힘들었어

I went over to the bed and put my arms around her. She kissed me, and while she kissed me I could feel she was thinking of something else. She was trembling in my arms. She felt very small.

"Darling! I've had such a hell of a time."

나는 침대로 다가가 두 팔로 그녀를 끌어안았다. 그 여자는 내게 키스를 했다. 내게 키스하는 동안 딴생각을 하고 있다는 걸 느낄 수 있었다. 그녀는 내 팔에 안겨 떨고 있었다. 몸이 아주 작게 느껴졌다.

"자기! 나 아주 정말 힘들었어."

I went (over) to the bed and put my arms around her. She kissed me, and while
　　　　공간의 이동
she kissed me/ I could feel (that) she was thinking of something else. She was
　　　　　　　　　　　　　　　　　　　　　　　　　　　　　그 외에, 다른
trembling in my arms. She felt very small.

"Darling! I've had such a hell of a time."
　　　　　　　　　　　지독한 시간

everyone 모든 사람　　　　　　　　　　a little(few) 약간 있는(긍정)
everyone else 그 사람(들)을 제외한 모든 사람　　little(few) 거의 없는(부정)
tremble [trémbəl] 떨다, 전율하다

God never worked very well with me

하느님은 내게는 별로 효험이 없었어

"You know it makes one feel rather good deciding not to be a bitch."
"Yes."
"It's sort of what we have instead of God."
"Some people have God," I said. "Quite a lot."
"He never worked very well with me."

"화냥년이 되지 않기로 결심하니 기분이 아주 좋아."
"아무렴."
"말하자면 그게 우리가 하느님 대신 믿는 것이기도 하지."
"하느님을 믿는 사람들도 있지. 그런 사람도 꽤 많아." 내가 말했다.
"하느님은 내게는 별로 효험이 없었어."

문장분석

"You know/(it)makes one feel rather good(deciding)not to be a bitch."
　　　　　　　　일반인

"Yes."

"It's sort of what we have instead of God."
　　　　　　　~하는 것　　~대신에
"Some people have God," I said. "Quite a lot."

"He never worked very well with me."
　　　　　유효하게 작용하다

bitch [bitʃ] 암컷　　　　　　　　quiet [kwáiət] 조용한, 말수가 없는
beach [biːtʃ] 해변　　　　　　　　quit [kwit] 그만두다, 끊다
quite [kwait] 상당히, 확실히

We could have had such a damned good time together

우리 둘이 얼마든지 재미있게 시간을 보낼 수도 있었는데

Brett moved close to me. We sat close against each other. I put my arm around her and she rested against me comfortably. It was very hot and bright, and the houses looked sharply white.

"Oh, Jake," Brett said, "we could have had such a damned good time together."

"Yes," I said. "Isn't it pretty to think so?"

브렛이 내 쪽으로 바짝 다가앉았다. 우리는 서로 꼭 붙어 앉아 있었다. 내가 팔을 돌려 브렛을 끌어안자 그녀는 편안한 듯 내게 기댔다. 날씨는 몹시 무덥고 햇살은 쨍쨍 비치고 집들이 희고 뚜렷하게 보였다.

"아, 제이크, 우리 둘이 얼마든지 재미있게 시간을 보낼 수도 있었는데." 브렛이 말했다.

"그래 맞아. 그렇게 생각하기만 해도 기분이 좋지 않아?" 내가 말했다.

문장분석

Brett moved close to me. We sat close <u>against</u> each other. I <u>put</u> my arm <u>around</u>
~대해서
her and she rested against me comfortably. It was very hot and bright, and the

houses <u>looked</u> sharply white.
~처럼 보이다
"Oh, Jake," Brett said, "we could have had such a damned good time together."

"Yes," I said. "Isn't ⓘt pretty ⓣo think so?"

close [klous] 가까운(near), 접근한, 닫은
close [klouz] 감다, 닫다
sharply [ʃáːrpli] 날카롭게. 세게, 격렬하게, 몹시
comfortably [kʌ́mfərtəbəli]

기분좋게, 마음놓고, 안락하게
could have pp
~할 수도 있었는데(과거의 가능성)

Vocabulary Of The Week

**February
WEEK 3**

MON

spend [spend]
쓰다, 소비하다(expend)
appreciate [əprí:ʃièit]
…의 진가를 인정하다,
감상하다, 감사하다

valuable [vǽljuːəbəl]
귀중한, 귀한, 소중한
dine [dain]
저녁 식사를 하다, 식사하다
sincere [sinsíər]
성실한, 진실한, 성심 성의의

TUE

arrival [əráivəl] 도착. 도달
Sud Express 야간 급행열차의 이름
handle [hǽndl] 다루다, 처리하다
introduce [ìntrədjúːs]
소개하다, 도입하다
wire [waiər] 전신, 전보, 철사

WED

everyone 모든 사람
everyone else
그 사람(들)을 제외한 모든 사람
tremble [trémbəl] 떨다, 전율하다
a little(few) 약간 있는(긍정)
little(few) 거의 없는(부정)

THU

bitch [bitʃ] 암컷
beach [biːtʃ] 해변
quite [kwait] 상당히, 확실히
quiet [kwáiət] 조용한, 말수가 없는
quit [kwit] 그만두다, 끊다

FRI

close [klous]
가까운(near), 접근한, 닫은
close [klouz] 감다, 닫다
sharply [ʃáːrpli]
날카롭게. 세게, 격렬하게, 몹시

comfortably [kʌ́mfərtəbəli]
기분좋게, 마음놓고, 안락하게
could have pp
~할 수도 있었는데(과거의 가능성)

MON

I did not know that then, although I learned it later

나는 나중에 그것을 깨달았지만 그때는 그것을 알지 못했다

We were still friends, with many tastes alike, but with the difference between us. He[Priest] had always known what I did not know and what, when I learned it, I was always able to forget. But I did not know that then, although I learned it later.

우리는 역시 다른 점이 많지만 많은 취향이 닮은 친구였다. 그[신부]는 내가 모르는 것, 일단 배워도 늘 잊어버리는 것을 언제나 알고 있었다. 나는 나중에 그것을 깨달았지만 그때는 그것을 알지 못했다.

문장분석

We were still friends, with many tastes alike, but with the difference between us.

그럼에도
He[Priest] had always known what I did not know and what, (when I learned it),

I was always able to forget. But I did not know that then, although I learned it

그때, 당시
later.

alike [əláik]
　(서술적) 서로 같은, 마찬가지의 A and B are alike.
like [laik]
　(…와) 닮은(resembling), …와 같은 A is like B.
difference [dífərəns] 다름, 차이

priest [pri:st] 성직자, 사제
although [ɔːlðóu]
　비록 …일지라도, …이긴 하지만, …이라 하더라도

There isn't always an explanation for everything

세상일이라는 게 언제나 설명할 수 있는 건 아니잖아요

"What an odd thing — to be in the Italian army."

"It's not really the army. It's only the ambulance."

"It's very odd though. Why did you do it?"

"I don't know," I said. "There isn't always an explanation for everything."

"Oh, isn't there? I was brought up to think there was."

"That's awfully nice."

"참, 이상한 일이네요……. 이탈리아 군대에 소속되어 계시다니요."
"군대라고 할 수도 없죠. 앰뷸런스 부대일 뿐인걸요."
"그래도 이상해요. 왜 그러셨어요?"
"나도 모르겠습니다. 세상일이라는 게 언제나 설명할 수 있는 건 아니잖아요."
내가 대답했다.
"오, 그런가요? 나는 언제나 설명할 수 있다고 배웠는데요."
"그것참 훌륭하군요."

문장분석

"What an odd thing—to be in the Italian army."

"It's not really the army. It's only the ambulance."

"It's very odd though. Why did you do it?"
　　　　　　　　그래도

"I don't know," I said. "There isn't always an explanation for everything."

"Oh, isn't there? I was brought up to think (that) there was (always an explanation
　　　　　　　　　　　　기르다, 양육하다
for everything)."

"That's awfully nice."
　　　　　very

odd [ɑd] 이상한, 기묘한, 홀수의
add [æd] 더하다, 가산하다, 추가하다
explanation [èksplənéiʃən] 설명, 해설

awful [ɔ́:fəl] 두려운, 무시무시한, 대단한
awesome [ɔ́:səm]
　경외케 하는, 인상적인, 멋진, 근사한

You will be good to me, won't you?

내게 잘해 줄 거죠, 그렇죠?

I held her close against me and could feel her heart beating and her lips opened and her head went back against my hand and then she was crying on my shoulder.

"Oh, darling," she said. "You will be good to me, won't you?"

What the hell, I thought. I stroked her hair and patted her shoulder. She was crying.

"You will, won't you?" She looked up at me. "Because we're going to have a strange life."

더욱 바짝 끌어안자 심장의 고동이 느껴졌다. 그녀가 입술을 열면서 내 팔에 기댄 채 머리를 뒤로 젖혔다. 그러고 나서 내 어깨에 기대어 울었다. "아, 당신, 내게 잘해 줄 거죠, 그렇죠?" 그녀가 말했다.

도대체 뭐지? 나는 속으로 그렇게 생각했다. 나는 그녀의 머리카락을 쓰다듬으며 가볍게 어깨를 두드려 주었다. 그녀는 여전히 울고 있었다.

"그렇게 해줄 거죠?" 그녀는 내 얼굴을 올려다보았다. "이제부터 우리는 이상한 삶을 살게 될 테니까."

문장분석

I held her close against me and could feel her heart beating and her lips opened
        …을 향하여
and her head went back against my hand and then she was crying on my

shoulder.

"Oh, darling," she said. "You will be good to me, won't you?"

What the hell, I thought. I stroked her hair and patted her shoulder. She was
    도대체 뭐지
crying.

"You will (be good to me), won't you?" She looked up at me. "Because we are

going to have a strange life."
  will

close [klous]
　가까운(near), 접근한, 친밀한, 꼭, 죄어
beat [biːt] 치다, 때리다

shoulder [ʃóuldər] 어깨, 갓길(길 양옆 가장자리)
stroke [strouk] 쓰다듬다, 어루만지다, 주름을 펴다
pat [pæt] 가볍게 두드리다

THU

I knew I did not love Catherine Barkley nor had any idea of loving her

나는 캐서린 바클리를 사랑하지 않았으며 또 앞으로도 사랑하지 않으리라는 사실을 알고 있었다

I knew I did not love Catherine Barkley nor had any idea of loving her. This was a game, like bridge, in which you said things instead of playing cards. Like bridge you had to pretend you were playing for money or playing for some stakes. Nobody had mentioned what the stakes were. It was all right with me.

나는 캐서린 바클리를 사랑하지 않았으며 또 앞으로도 사랑하지 않으리라는 사실을 잘 알았다. 이것은 마치 카드 대신 말로 하는 브리지 게임 같은 것이었다. 브리지처럼 돈을 따기 위해 게임을 하는 척하면 되는 것이다. 무엇을 건 게임인지는 아무도 말하지 않았다. 나야 아무래도 좋았다.

문장분석

I knew (that) I did (not) love Catherine Barkley (nor) had any idea of loving her. This was a game, like bridge, in which you said things instead of playing cards. Like
~대신
bridge/ you had to pretend (that) you were playing for money or playing for
should
some stakes. Nobody had mentioned what the stakes were. It was all right with me.

instead [instéd] 그 대신에, 그보다도
pretend [priténd]
　…인 체하다, …같이 꾸미다, 가장하다
stake [steik] 내기, 내기에 건 돈, 상금

addict [ədíkt] 빠지게 하다, 몰두(탐닉)시키다
addict [ǽdikt]
　어떤 습성에 탐닉하는 사람, 《특히》 (마약) 중독자

FRI

It seemed no more dangerous to me myself than war in the movies

나에게 이 전쟁은 영화 속의 전쟁만큼이나 위험해 보이지 않았다

Well, I knew I would not be killed. Not in this war. It did not have anything to do with me. It seemed no more dangerous to me myself than war in the movies. I wished to God it was over though. Maybe it would finish this summer. Maybe the Austrians would crack. They had always cracked in other wars.

어쨌든 나는 내가 전사하지 않으리라는 것을 알았다. 적어도 이 전쟁에서는 말이다. 이 전쟁은 나와 아무런 상관이 없다. 나에게 이 전쟁은 영화 속의 전쟁만큼이나 위험해 보이지 않았다. 그래도 나는 이 전쟁이 어서 끝나기를 하느님께 간절히 기도했다. 어쩌면 이번 여름에는 끝날지도 모른다. 오스트리아 군대가 항복할지도 모른다. 다른 전쟁에서도 언제나 항복했으니.

문장분석

Well, I knew I would not be killed. Not in this war. It did not have anything to do
~와 상관이 있다

with me. It seemed no more dangerous to me myself than war in the movies. I
~처럼 보이다

wished to God it was over though. Maybe it would finish this summer. Maybe

the Austrians would crack. They had always cracked in other wars.

thou [ðau]
　(인칭대명사 2인칭·단수·주격) 너(는), 그대(는),
　당신(은)
though [ðou] …(이기는) 하지만
thought [θɔːt] 생각하기, 사색, 사고

crack [kræk]
　(채찍 따위로) 찰싹 소리 내다, 금가다, 쪼개지다,
　항복하다
surrender [səréndər] 내어 주다, 항복하다

058

MON

alike [əláik] (서술적) 서로 같은,
마찬가지의 A and B are alike.
like [laik]
(…와) 닮은(resembling),
…와 같은 A is like B.
difference [dífərəns] 다름, 차이

priest [pri:st] 성직자, 사제
although [ɔːlðóu]
비록 …일지라도, …이긴 하지만,
…이라 하더라도

TUE

odd [ɑd] 이상한, 기묘한, 홀수의
add [æd] 더하다, 가산하다, 추가하다
explanation [èksplənéiʃən]
설명, 해설
awful [ɔ́ːfəl]
두려운, 무시무시한, 대단한

awesome [ɔ́ːsəm]
경외케 하는, 인상적인, 멋진, 근사한

WED

close [klous]
가까운(near), 접근한, 친밀한, 꼭, 죄어
beat [bi:t] 치다, 때리다
shoulder [ʃóuldər]
어깨, 갓길(길 양옆 가장자리)
stroke [strouk]

쓰다듬다, 어루만지다, 주름을 펴다
pat [pæt] 가볍게 두드리다

THU

instead [instéd] 그 대신에, 그보다도
pretend [priténd]
…인 체하다, …같이 꾸미다, 가장하다
stake [steik] 내기, 내기에 건 돈, 상금
addict [ədíkt]
빠지게 하다, 몰두(탐닉)시키다

addict [ǽdikt]
어떤 습성에 탐닉하는 사람,
《특히》 (마약) 중독자

FRI

thou [ðau]
(인칭대명사 2인칭·단수·주격) 너(는),
그대(는), 당신(은)
though [ðou] …(이기는) 하지만
thought [θɔ:t] 생각하기, 사색, 사고

crack [kræk]
(채찍 따위로) 찰싹 소리 내다, 금가다,
쪼개지다, 항복하다
surrender [səréndər]
내어 주다, 항복하다

*When spring came, even the false spring,
there were no problems except where to be happiest.
The only thing that could spoil a day was people and
if you could keep from making engagements,
each day had no limits. People were always
the limiters of happiness except for the very few
that were as good as spring itself.*

비록 덧없는 봄일지라도 일단 봄이 오면 어디서 가장 행복할 수 있을까 하는 것 외에는
아무런 문제가 없었다. 하루를 망치는 것은 오로지 사람들 때문이기에 누구와도
만날 약속을 하지 않고 지낼 수 있다면 하루하루가 순조로웠다. 봄이란 계절 그 자체처럼
좋은 몇몇 사람들을 제외하면 나머지 사람들은 대체로 내 행복에 걸림돌이 되었다.

When I could not see her there I was feeling lonely and hollow

그녀를 만나지 못하게 되자 기분이 여간 쓸쓸하고 공허한 게 아니었다

"Catherine asked me to tell you she was sorry she couldn't see you this evening."
I went out the door and suddenly I felt lonely and empty. I had treated seeing Catherine very lightly, I had gotten somewhat drunk and had nearly forgotten to come but when I could not see her there I was feeling lonely and hollow.

"캐서린이 미안하지만 오늘 밤은 만날 수 없다고 전해 달라는군요."
문밖으로 나오니 갑자기 외롭고 공허한 기분이 들었다. 지금껏 나는 캐서린을 만나는 것을 너무도 가볍게 생각해 왔다. 술에 조금 취했다고 그녀를 만나러 오는 것조차 잊을 뻔하지 않았던가. 그러나 막상 그녀를 만나지 못하게 되자 기분이 여간 쓸쓸하고 공허한 게 아니었다.

문장분석

"Catherine asked me to tell you she was sorry she couldn't see you this evening."

I went out the door and suddenly I felt lonely and empty. I had treated seeing

Catherine very lightly, I had gotten somewhat drunk and had <u>nearly</u> forgotten to
almost

come/ but/ when I could not see her there/ I was feeling lonely and hollow.
~할 때

empty [émpti] 빈, 공허한, 비어 있는
treat [triːt] 다루다, 대우하다, 간주하다
somewhat [sʌ́mhwʌt]
　얼마간, 얼마쯤, 어느 정도, 약간(slightly)

lightly [láitli] 조금(a lillte), 가볍게, 살짝, 가만히
hollow [hálou] 속이 빈, 공동(空洞)의

What is defeat? You go home

패전이란 게 뭡니까? 고향으로 돌아가는 겁니다

"I believe we should get the war over," I said. "It would not finish it if one side stopped fighting. It would only be worse if we stopped fighting."

"It could not be worse," Passini said respectfully. "There is nothing worse than war."

"Defeat is worse."

"I do not believe it," Passini said still respectfully. "What is defeat? You go home."

"나도 전쟁이 끝나야 한다고 생각해. 한쪽이 전투를 그만둔다고 해서 끝나진 않아. 우리가 싸우는 걸 그만둔다면 사정은 더욱 나빠질 뿐이지." 내가 말했다.

"이보다 어떻게 더 나빠지겠어요. 전쟁보다 나쁜 게 없죠." 파시니가 공손한 말투로 대꾸했다.

"패배가 더 나빠."

"전 그렇게 생각하지 않습니다. 패전이란 게 뭡니까? 고향으로 돌아가는 겁니다." 파시니가 여전히 공손한 말투로 말했다.

문장분석

"I believe we should get the war over," I said. "It would not finish it if one side stopped fighting. It would only be worse/ if we stopped fighting."
다만, 단지

"It could not be worse," Passini said respectfully. "There is nothing worse than war."

"Defeat is worse."

"I do not believe it," Passini said still respectfully. "What is defeat? You go home."

worse [wəːrs]
(bad, ill의 비교급) 보다 나쁜, (병이) 악화된
respectful [rispéktfəl] 경의를 표하는, 공손한

respective [rispéktiv] 각각의, 각기의, 각자의
defeat [difíːt] 쳐부수다, 좌절시키다
triumph [tráiəmf] 승리

There is no finish to a war

전쟁에는 끝이 없다

"There is nothing as bad as war. We in the auto-ambulance cannot even realize at all how bad it is. When people realize how bad it is they cannot do anything to stop it because they go crazy. There are some people who never realize. There are people who are afraid of their officers. It is with them that war is made."
"I know it is bad but we must finish it."
"It doesn't finish. There is no finish to a war."

"이 세상에 전쟁만큼 나쁜 건 없습니다. 앰뷸런스 부대에나 근무하는 우리는 전쟁이 얼마나 나쁜지 전혀 모르죠. 사람들이 얼마나 나쁜지 알게 되더라도 멈추도록 수를 쓸 수도 없고요. 그렇게 되면 모두 미쳐 버리고 말 테니까요. 그중에는 아무것도 모르는 병사들도 있어요. 장교들을 무서워하는 사람들도 있고요. 전쟁이 일어나는 건 그런 사람들 때문이죠." 파시니가 말했다.
"전쟁이 나쁘단 건 나도 알아. 하지만 어쨌든 끝나야 해."
"끝날 수가 없죠. 전쟁엔 끝이 없으니까요."

문장분석

"There is nothing as bad as war. We (who are) in the auto-ambulance cannot even realize at all how bad it is. When people realize how bad it is/ they cannot do anything to stop it because they go crazy. There are some people who never realize. There are people who are afraid of their officers. It is with them that war is made."
전혀
becmome
강조구문

"I know (that) it is bad/ but we must finish it."

"It doesn't finish. There is no finish to a war."

realize [ríːəlàiz] 실현하다, 현실화하다
afraid [əfréid] 두려워하는, 무서워하는
officer [ɔ́(ː)fisər] 장교, 사관

conflict [kánflikt] 싸움, 다툼, 투쟁, 전투
truce [truːs] 정전, 휴전(협정), 쉼, 일시적 중지

War is not won by victory

전쟁은 승리한다고 해서 이기는 건 아니다

"War is not won by victory. What if we take San Gabriele? What if we take the Carso and Monfalcone and Trieste? Where are we then? Did you see all the far mountains to-day? Do you think we could take all them too? Only if the Austrians stop fighting. One side must stop fighting."

"전쟁에서 승리한다고 해서 반드시 이기는 건 아닙니다. 아군이 산가브리엘레를 점령한다고 한들 그게 무슨 소용입니까? 카로소랑, 몬팔코네랑, 트리에스테를 빼앗은들 무슨 대수냐고요? 그런들 우리가 어디에 머물 수 있나요? 오늘 저쪽 멀리 있는 산들을 모두 보셨죠? 그 산들을 전부 점령할 수 있다고 생각하세요? 오스트리아군이 전투를 중단할 경우에만 가능하죠. 어느 한쪽이라도 그만 둬야 하는 것 아닙니까?"

문장분석

"War is not won by victory. What if we take San Gabriele? What if we take the
··· 하면 어떻게 될까?
Carso and Monfalcone and Trieste? Where are we then? Did you see all the far

mountains to-day? Do you think (that) we could take all them too? Only if the

Austrians stop fighting. One side must stop fighting."

victor [víktər] 승리자, 전승자, 정복자
Austria [ɔ́ːstriə] 오스트리아
Australia [ɔːstréiljə] 오스트레일리아, 호주

demilitarize [diːmílətəràiz]
비군사(비무장)화하다
DMZ demilitarized zone 비무장지대

Even the peasants know better than to believe in a war

시골 농부들도 전쟁을 믿을 만큼 무지하진 않다

"We think. We read. We are not peasants. We are mechanics. But even the peasants know better than to believe in a war. Everybody hates this war."

"There is a class that controls a country that is stupid and does not realize anything and never can. That is why we have this war."

"우리도 생각할 줄 압니다. 책도 읽고요. 우리는 시골 농부가 아닙니다. 기술공이죠. 하지만 시골 농부들도 전쟁을 믿을 만큼 어리석진 않아요. 누구나 전쟁은 끔찍이 싫어한다고요."

"아무것도 깨닫지 못하고 또 깨달을 능력도 없는 우둔한 계급이 있어요. 그자들이 지금 한 나라를 지배하는 거죠. 그런 부류 때문에 지금 이런 전쟁이 벌어지고 있는 겁니다."

문장분석

"We think. We read. We are not peasants. We are mechanics. But even the

peasants know better than to believe in a war. Everybody hates this war."
　　　　　(~할 정도로) 어리석지는 않다

"There is a class that controls a country that is stupid and does not realize

anything and never can. That is why we have this war."

peasant [pézənt] 농부, 소작농, 농군
pigeon [pídʒən] 비둘기
mechanic [məkǽnik] 기계공, 수리공, 정비사

stupid [stjúːpid] 어리석은, 우둔한, 바보 같은
silly [síli] 어리석은(stupid)

Vocabulary Of The Week

MON

empty [émpti] 빈, 공허한, 비어 있는
treat [tri:t]
　다루다, 대우하다, 간주하다
somewhat [sʌ́mhwʌ̀t]
　얼마간, 얼마쯤, 어느 정도,
　약간(slightly)

lightly [láitli]
　조금(a lillte), 가볍게, 살짝, 가만히
hollow [hάlou] 속이 빈, 공동(空洞)의

TUE

worse [wə:rs]
　(bad, ill의 비교급) 보다 나쁜,
　(병이) 악화된
respectful [rispéktfəl]
　경의를 표하는, 공손한

respective [rispéktiv]
　각각의, 각기의, 각자의
defeat [difí:t] 쳐부수다, 좌절시키다
triumph [tráiəmf] 승리

WED

realize [rí:əlàiz]
　실현하다, 현실화하다
afraid [əfréid]
　두려워하는, 무서워하는
officer [ɔ́(:)fisər] 장교, 사관

conflict [kάnflikt]
　싸움, 다툼, 투쟁, 전투
truce [tru:s]
　정전, 휴전(협정), 쉼, 일시적 중지

THU

victor [víktər] 승리자, 전승자, 정복자
Austria [ɔ́:striə] 오스트리아
Australia [ɔːstréiljə]
　오스트레일리아, 호주
demilitarize [diːmílətəràiz]
　비군사(비무장)화하다

DMZ demilitarized zone
　비무장지대

FRI

peasant [pézənt] 농부, 소작농, 농군
pigeon [pídʒən] 비둘기
mechanic [məkǽnik]
　기계공, 수리공, 정비사
stupid [stjú:pid]
　어리석은, 우둔한, 바보 같은

silly [síli] 어리석은(stupid)

MON

What would a man do with a woman like that except worship her?

그런 여자는 남자가 숭배하는 것 말고 뭘 할 수 있을까?

"You are really an Italian. All fire and smoke and nothing inside. You only pretend to be American. I will send Miss Barkley. You are better with her without me. You are purer and sweeter. I will send her. Your lovely cool goddess. English goddess. My God what would a man do with a woman like that except worship her? What else is an English-woman good for?"

"너는 진짜 이탈리아인이야. 온통 불과 연기뿐, 속은 텅 비었어. 너는 미국인인 척하고 있을 뿐이야. 미스 바클리를 보내주지. 나 없이 그녀와 함께 있는 게 훨씬 좋겠지. 넌 나보다 순결하고 착하니까. 그녀를 보내줄게. 자네의 아름답고 냉정한 여신을. 영국의 여신을 말이야. 도대체 그런 여자는 남자가 숭배하는 것 말고 뭘 할 수 있을까? 영국 여자를 어디다 쓰겠냐고?"

"You are really an Italian. All fire and smoke and nothing inside. You only pretend

to be American. I will send Miss Barkley. You are better with her without me. You

are purer and sweeter. I will send her. Your lovely cool goddess. English goddess.

My God/ what would a man do with a woman like that/ except worship her?
예구(머니)
What else is an Englishwoman good for?"

pretend [priténd]
　…인 체하다, …같이 꾸미다, 가장하다
pure [pjuər] 순수한, 순전한, 단순한

goddess [gádis] (절세) 미인, 숭배하는 여성
except [iksépt] …을 제외하고, …외에는(but)
worship [wə́:rʃip] 예배, 참배, 숭배

There are other people who would not make war

전쟁을 싫어하는 사람도 있어요

"There are people who would make war. In this country there are many like that. There are other people who would not make war."
"But the first ones make them do it."
"Yes."
"And I help them."
"You are a foreigner. You are a patriot."

"전쟁을 일으키고 싶어 하는 사람들이 있는 겁니다. 이 나라에는 그런 사람들이 많지요. 전쟁을 싫어하는 사람도 있고요."
"전쟁을 원하는 사람들이 다른 사람들에게 전쟁을 시키는 거군요."
"맞습니다."
"전 그런 사람들을 돕고 있어요."
"외국인인 당신이 애국자입니다."

문장분석

"There are people who would make war. In this country/ there are many like that. There are other people who would not make war."

"But the first ones make them do it."

"Yes."

"And I help them."

"You are a foreigner. You are a patriot."

foreigner [fɔ́(ː)rinər] 외국인, 외인
patriot [péitriət] 애국자
betray [bitréi] 배반(배신)하다

espionage [éspiənὰːʒ]
간첩(탐정) 행위, 정찰, 스파이에 의한 첩보 활동
treaty [tríːti] 조약, 협정

When you love you wish to do things for

사랑을 하면 그 대상을 위해 뭔가 하고 싶어진다

"You should love Him."
"I don't love much."
"Yes," he said. "You do. What you tell me about in the nights. That is not love. That is only passion and lust. When you love you wish to do things for. You wish to sacrifice for. You wish to serve."

"하느님을 사랑해야 합니다."
"저는 누구든 별로 사랑하지 않거든요."
"아니에요. 당신은 사랑하십니다. 밤에 가끔 내게 얘기했잖아요. 그건 사랑이 아닙니다. 한낱 정열과 욕망에 지나지 않아요. 사랑을 하면 그 대상을 위해 뭔가 하고 싶어지죠. 희생하고 싶고 봉사하고 싶어지고요."

문장분석

"You should love Him."
             ‾‾‾
             God

"I don't love much."

"Yes," he said. "You do. What you tell me about in the nights. That is not love.
              ‾‾
              love

That is only passion and lust. When you love/ you wish to do things for. You wish

to sacrifice for. You wish to serve."

passionate [pǽʃənit]
    열렬한, 정열을 품은, 열의에 찬
lust [lʌst] 욕망, 갈망

sacrifice [sǽkrəfàis] 희생, 산 제물, 제물
serve [səːrv] 섬기다, …에 봉사하다
starve [stɑːrv] 굶주리다, 배고프다, 굶어 죽다

You cannot know about it unless you have it

직접 느껴 보지 않고서는 그것에 대해 알 수 없는 법이다

"I don't love."

"You will. I know you will. Then you will be happy."

"I'm happy. I've always been happy."

"It is another thing. You cannot know about it unless you have it."

"Well," I said. "If I ever get it I will tell you."

"저는 사랑을 하지 않습니다."

"중위님은 사랑을 하게 될 거예요. 제가 잘 압니다. 그렇게 되면 당신도 행복해질 겁니다."

"저는 지금도 행복합니다. 지금까지도 늘 행복했고요."

"그것과는 다른 행복이지요. 직접 느껴 보지 않고서는 알 수 없는 행복입니다."

"글쎄요. 만약 제가 그런 사랑을 하게 되면 신부님께도 알려 드리죠." 내가 대답했다.

문장분석

"I don't love."

"You will (love). I know you will (love). Then you will be happy."

"I'm happy. I've always been happy."

"It is another thing. You cannot know about it/ <u>unless</u> you have it."
　　　　　　　　　　　　　　　　　　　　　　　if~not

"Well," I said. "If I ever get it/ I will tell you."
　　　　　　　　　　　　　　　love

unless [ənlés] …하지 않으면, …하지 않는 한
lessen [lésn] 작게(적게) 하다, 줄이다, 줄다
lesson [lésn] 학과, 과업, 수업, 연습

bliss [blis] (더없는) 행복, 희열
bless [bles] …에게 은총을 내리다, …에게 베풀다

God knows I had not wanted to fall in love with her

내가 그녀와 사랑에 빠지리라고는 정말 꿈에도 생각하지 못했다

"Good-by, sweet."
She went out. God knows I had not wanted
to fall in love with her. I had not wanted to
fall in love with any one. But God knows I
had and I lay on the bed in the room of the
hospital in Milan and all sorts of things went
through my head but I felt wonderful.

"잘 있어요. 자기."
그녀가 병실에서 나갔다. 내가 그녀와 사랑에 빠지리라고는 정말 꿈에도 생각
하지 못했다. 나는 어느 누구와도 사랑에 빠지고 싶은 생각이 없었다. 그런데 하
느님께 맹세코 분명히 나는 사랑에 빠졌고, 이렇게 밀라노 병원의 어느 병실에
누워 있는 게 아닌가. 온갖 일이 주마등처럼 머리에 스쳐 갔지만 기분은 하늘을
나는 것처럼 신바람이 났다.

문장분석

"Good-by, sweet."

She went out. <u>God knows</u> I had not wanted to fall in love with her. I had not
        Nobody knows

wanted to fall in love with any one. But God knows I had (fallen in love) and I

lay on the bed in the room of the hospital in Milan and all <u>sorts</u> of things went
                                                    kinds

through my head but I felt wonderful.

lie [lai] (lay [lei]- lain [lein])
눕다, (물건이) 놓여 있다

lay [lei] (p., pp. laid [leid])
눕히다, (물건을) ~에 놓다

through [θru:] ···을 통하여(지나서), ···을 꿰뚫어

thorough [θɔ́:rou]
   철저한, 충분한, 완벽한, 완전한

throw [θrou] (내)던지다

Vocabulary Of The Week

MON

pretend [priténd]
···인 체하다, ···같이 꾸미다, 가장하다
pure [pjuər] 순수한, 순전한, 단순한
goddess [gάdis]
(절세) 미인, 숭배하는 여성

except [iksépt]
···을 제외하고, ···외에는(but)
worship [wə́:rʃip] 예배, 참배, 숭배

TUE

foreigner [fɔ́(:)rinər] 외국인, 외인
patriot [péitriət] 애국자
betray [bitréi] 배반(배신)하다
espionage [éspiənὰ:ʒ]
간첩(탐정) 행위, 정찰,
스파이에 의한 첩보 활동

treaty [trí:ti] 조약, 협정

WED

passionate [pǽʃənit]
열렬한, 정열을 품은, 열의에 찬
lust [lʌst] 욕망, 갈망
sacrifice [sǽkrəfàis]
희생, 산 제물, 제물
serve [sə:rv] 섬기다, ···에 봉사하다

starve [stɑ:rv]
굶주리다, 배고프다, 굶어 죽다

THU

unless [ənlés]
···하지 않으면, ···하지 않는 한
lessen [lésn]
작게(적게) 하다, 줄이다, 줄다
lesson [lésn] 학과, 과업, 수업, 연습
bliss [blis] (더없는) 행복, 희열

bless [bles]
···에게 은총을 내리다, ···에게 베풀다

FRI

lie [lai]
(lay [lei]- lain [lein]) 눕다,
(물건이) 놓여 있다
lay [lei]
(p., pp. laid [leid]) 눕히다,
(물건을) ~에 놓다

through [θru:]
···을 통하여(지나서), ···을 꿰뚫어
thorough [θə́:rou]
철저한, 충분한, 완벽한, 완전한
throw [θrou] (내)던지다

MON

We smelled the dew on the roofs and then the coffee

지붕 위에 내린 이슬과 커피 냄새가 풍겨왔다

I went to sleep again in the morning when it was light and when I was awake I found she was gone again. She came in looking fresh and lovely and sat on the bed and the sun rose while I had the thermometer in my mouth and we smelled the dew on the roofs and then the coffee of the men at the gun on the next roof.

날이 밝을 무렵이 되어 나는 다시 잠이 들었고, 잠에서 깼을 때 그녀는 또 보이지 않았다. 얼마 뒤 그녀가 상큼하고 아름다운 얼굴로 들어와서 침대에 걸터앉았다. 입에 체온계를 물고 있는 동안 해가 떠올랐다. 지붕 위에 내린 이슬 냄새가 났고, 이어 이웃집 옥상의 고사포 사수들이 끓이는 커피 냄새가 풍겨왔다.

문장분석

I went to sleep again in (the morning) when it was light and when I was awake/

I found (that) she was gone again. She came in looking fresh and lovely and sat
~으로 보이는

on the bed and the sun rose/ while I had the thermometer in my mouth and we
~하는 동안

smelled the dew on the roofs and then the coffee of (the men) at the gun on the

next roof.

rise [raiz] (rose-risen) 일어서다, 일어나다
raise [reiz] 일으키다, (위로) 올리다, 끌어올리다
thermometer [θərmɑ́mitər] 온도계, 체온계

thermo [θə́ːrmə]
'열'의 뜻을 갖는 결합사(모음 앞에서는 therm-)
roof [ruːf] 지붕, 지붕 모양의 것

How many people have you ever loved?

이제까지 몇 명이랑 사랑을 나눴죠?

"Tell me. How many people have you ever loved?"
"Nobody."
"Not me even?"
"Yes, you."
"How many others really?"
"None."
"How many have you—how do you say it?—stayed with?"
"None."

"말해 봐요. 이제까지 몇 명이랑 사랑을 나눴지?"
"한 명도 없어."
"나까지도?"
"아니, 당신은 말고."
"정말로 여자를 몇 명이나 사랑했어?"
"한 명도 없어."
"이제까지 여자 몇 명하고…… 그걸 뭐라고 하지? …… 같이 자 봤어?"
"한 명도 없다니까."

문장분석

"Tell me. How many people have you ever loved?"

"Nobody."

"Not me <u>even</u>?"
   심지어, 조차
"Yes, you."

"How many others really?"

"<u>None</u>."
   No one
"How many have you—how do you say it?—<u>stayed with</u>?"
                                      ~의 집에서 머물다
"None."

homosexual 동성애의 (사람), 동성의
heterosexual 이성애(異性愛)의. 다른 성(性)의
bisexual [baisékʃuəl] 양성(兩性)의, 양성애(愛)자

endogamy [endάgəmi] 동족 결혼, 족내혼(族內婚)
exogamy [eksάgəmi] 외혼(제도), 족외혼(族外婚)

You've never belonged to any one else

당신은 이제껏 한 번도 다른 사람의 것이 되어 본 적이 없다

"It's all right. Keep right on lying to me. That's what I want you to do. Were they pretty?"
"I never stayed with any one."
"That's right. Were they very attractive?"
"I don't know anything about it."
"You're just mine. That's true and you've never belonged to any one else. But I don't care if you have. I'm not afraid of them. But don't tell me about them."

"좋아요, 계속 거짓말을 해요. 나도 그랬으면 하니까. 그자들은 예뻤나요?"
"누구하고도 잔 적이 없다니까."
"괜찮아요. 아주 매력적이었나요?"
"난 그런 것에 대해 아무것도 몰라."
"당신은 틀림없이 내 거야. 정말이야. 당신은 이제껏 한 번도 다른 여자의 것이 되어 본 적이 없어. 하지만 설령 그런 일이 있었다 해도 신경 쓰지 않을래. 그들이 겁나지 않으니까. 하지만 그 여자들 얘기는 내게 하지 마."

문장분석

"It's all right. Keep (right) on lying to me. That's what I want you to do. Were they
　　　　　　　　계속해서~하다
pretty?"

"I never stayed with any one."

"That's right. Were they very attractive?"

"I don't know anything about it."

"You're just mine. That's true and you've never belonged to any one else. But I
　　　　　　　　　　　　　　　　　　　　　　　　　　　　　　　다른
don't care if you have (belonged to some one). I'm not afraid of them. But don't

tell me about them."

---

lie [lai] (p., pp. lied [laid]) 거짓말을 하다
lie [lai] (lay [lei] lain [lein]) 눕다, (물건이) 놓여 있다
lay [lei] (p., pp. laid [leid]) 눕히다, (물건을) ~에 놓다

attractive [ətrǽktiv] 사람의 마음을 끄는, 매력적인
belong [bilɔ́(ː)ŋ]
(…에) 속하다, (…의) 것이다, (…의) 소유이다

THU

I loved to take her hair down

나는 그녀의 머리카락을 풀어 주는 것이 좋았다

I loved to take her hair down and she sat on the bed and kept very still, except suddenly she would dip down to kiss me while I was doing it, and I would take out the pins and lay them on the sheet and it would be loose and I would watch her while she kept very still and then take out the last two pins and it would all come down and she would drop her head and we would both be inside of it, and it was the feeling of inside a tent or behind a falls.

나는 그녀의 머리카락을 풀어 주는 것이 좋았다. 머리카락을 풀어 주는 동안 그녀는 침대에 앉아 조금도 움직이지 않았다. 갑자기 허리를 굽혀 내게 키스할 때를 제외하고는. 내가 핀을 뽑아 시트 위에 놓으면 그녀의 머리카락이 풀어졌고, 나는 꼼짝 않고 앉아 있는 그녀를 바라보았다. 그다음 마지막 핀 두 개를 마저 뽑으면 그녀의 머리카락이 모두 흘러내렸다. 그녀가 고개를 숙여 우리 둘 다 머리카락 속에 파묻히면 마치 텐트 안이나 폭포 뒤편에 들어온 것 같은 느낌이 들었다.

문장분석

I loved to take her hair down and she sat on the bed and kept very still, except
(motionless)

suddenly she would dip down to kiss me/ while I was doing it, and I would take

out the pins and lay them on the sheet and it would be loose and I would watch

her/ while she kept very still and then take out the last two pins and it would all
(her hair)

come down and she would drop her head and we would both be inside of it, and

it was the feeling of inside a tent or behind a falls.

still [stil] 정지(靜止)한, 움직이지 않는
dip [dip] 가볍게 머리를 숙이다, 담그다, 적시다
sheet [ʃiːt] 시트, (침구 따위의) 커버, 홑이불

loose [luːs] 매지 않은, 풀린, 흐트러진
lose [luːz] (p., pp. lost) 잃다, 놓쳐버리다

We were thinking the same thing

우리는 같은 생각을 하고 있었다

It was lovely in the nights and if we could only touch each other we were happy. Besides all the big times we had many small ways of making love and we tried putting thoughts in the other one's head while we were in different rooms. It seemed to work sometimes but that was probably because we were thinking the same thing anyway.

밤은 언제나 유쾌했고 서로의 몸이 닿기만 해도 우리는 행복했다. 황홀한 즐거움 말고도 온갖 사소한 방법으로 사랑의 유희를 즐겼다. 우리는 각기 다른 방에 있을 때도 서로의 생각을 상대방에게 알리려고 애썼다. 이따금씩 잘 통할 때도 있었는데, 아마 그것은 두 사람이 같은 생각을 하고 있었기 때문이리라.

문장분석

It was lovely in the nights and if we could only touch each other/ we were happy.

Besides all the big times/ we had many small ways of making love and we tried

putting thoughts in the other one's head/ while we were in different rooms. It

seemed to work sometimes but that was (probably) because we were thinking
~처럼 보이다　　효과가 있다

the same thing anyway.
어쨌든

besides [bisáidz] 그 밖에, 따로, 게다가　　　differ [difər] 다르다
beside [bisáid] …의 곁(옆)에, …와 나란히　　anyway [éniwèi] 어쨌든, 하여튼
thought [θɔːt]
　생각하기, 사색, 사고, think의 과거·과거분사

Vocabulary Of The Week

MON

rise [raiz]
(rose-risen) 일어서다, 일어나다
raise [reiz]
일으키다, (위로) 올리다, 끌어올리다
thermometer [θərmάmitər]
온도계, 체온계

thermo [θə́:rmə]
'열'의 뜻을 갖는 결합사
(모음 앞에서는 therm-)
roof [ru:f] 지붕, 지붕 모양의 것

TUE

homosexual
동성애의 (사람), 동성의
heterosexual
이성애(異性愛)의. 다른 성(性)의
bisexual [baisékʃuəl]
(자웅(雌雄)) 양성(兩性)의,

양성애(愛)자
endogamy [endάgəmi]
동족 결혼, 족내혼(族內婚)
exogamy [eksάgəmi]
외혼(제도), 족외혼(族外婚)

WED

lie [lai]
(p., pp. lied [laid]) 거짓말을 하다
lie [lai]
(lay [lei]- lain [lein]) 눕다,
(물건이) 놓여 있다

lay [lei]
(p., pp. laid [leid]) 눕히다,
(물건을) ~에 놓다
attractive [ətrǽktiv]
사람의 마음을 끄는, 매력적인
belong [bilɔ́(:)ŋ] (…에) 속하다,
(…의) 것이다, (…의) 소유이다

THU

still [stil]
정지(靜止)한, 움직이지 않는
dip [dip]
가볍게 머리를 숙이다, 담그다, 적시다
sheet [ʃi:t]
시트, (침구 따위의) 커버, 홑이불

loose [lu:s] 매지 않은, 풀린, 흐트러진
lose [lu:z]
(p., pp. lost) 잃다, 놓쳐버리다

FRI

besides [bisáidz]
그 밖에, 따로, 게다가
beside [bisáid]
…의 곁(옆)에, …와 나란히
thought [θɔ:t]
생각하기, 사색, 사고,

think의 과거·과거분사
differ [dífər] 다르다
anyway [éniwèi] 어쨌든, 하여튼

MON

I thought girls always wanted to be married

여자들은 언제나 결혼을 하고 싶어 하는 줄 알았다

"There isn't any me. I'm you. Don't make up a separate me."

"I thought girls always wanted to be married."

"They do. But, darling, I am married. I'm married to you. Don't I make you a good wife?"

"You're a lovely wife."

"이미 '나'라는 존재는 없어요. 내가 바로 '당신'이에요. 나를 당신과 떼어놓고 생각하지 말아요."

"여자들은 언제나 결혼을 하고 싶어 하는 줄 알았는데."

"맞아요. 하지만 자기, 난 이미 결혼했어요. 당신과 결혼했다고요. 아내 노릇 잘 하고 있지 않나요?"

"당신은 사랑스러운 아내지."

문장분석

"There isn't any me. I'm you. Don't make up a separate me."
지어내다, 날조하다

"I thought (that) girls always wanted to be married."

"They do. But, darling, I am married. I am married to you. Don't I make you a
want to be married   ~와 결혼한 상태다
good wife?"

"You're a lovely wife."

separate [sépərèit] 잘라서 떼어 놓다, 분리하다   polygamy [pəligəmi] 일부다처(제), 일처다부(제)
separate [sépərit]   monogamy [mənágəmi]
  갈라진, 분리된, 끊어진, 따로따로의   일부 일처제, 일부 일처주의
divorce [divɔ́:rs] 이혼(하다)

You know I don't love any one but you

내가 사랑하는 사람은 당신뿐이라는 거 잘 알잖아요

"You see, darling, I had one experience of waiting to be married."
"I don't want to hear about it."
"You know I don't love any one but you. You shouldn't mind because some one else loved me."
"I do."
"You shouldn't be jealous of some one who's dead when you have everything."
"No, but I don't want to hear about it."
"Poor darling. And I know you've been with all kinds of girls and it doesn't matter to me."

"자기, 나도 한 번 결혼을 기다렸던 적이 있어요."
"그 얘긴 듣고 싶지 않아."
"내가 사랑하는 사람은 당신뿐이라는 거 잘 알잖아요. 예전에 누가 나를 사랑했든 신경 쓰지 말아요."
"어쨌든 기분 나쁜걸."
"모든 걸 가진 사람이 죽은 사람을 질투해서는 안 되죠."
"질투하는 게 아냐. 하지만 그런 얘긴 듣기 싫어."
"답답해요. 난 당신이 온갖 여자를 다 상대했다는 걸 알면서도 조금도 신경 쓰지 않는데."

문장분석

"You see, darling, I had one experience of waiting to be married."

"I don't want to hear about it."

"You know I don't love any one but you. You shouldn't mind because some one
                                            except
else loved me."
다른
"I do."
  mind
"You shouldn't be jealous of some one who's dead / when you have everything."
                              ⌣   though
"No, but I don't want to hear about it."

"Poor darling. And I know you've been with all kinds of girls and it doesn't matter

to me."

experience [ikspíəriəns] 경험, 체험   jealous [dʒéləs] 질투심이 많은
expiration [èkspəréiʃən] 종결, 만료, 만기   matter [mǽtər] 중요하다(count)
mind [maind] 꺼리다, 싫어하다, 신경 쓰다

I'll marry you the day you say

당신이 결혼하자고 하면 바로 그날 결혼하겠어

"You're my religion. You're all I've got."
"All right. But I'll marry you the day you say."
"Don't talk as though you had to make an honest woman of me, darling. I'm a very honest woman. You can't be ashamed of something if you're only happy and proud of it. Aren't you happy?"

"당신이 내 종교예요. 당신은 내가 가진 전부라고요."
"알았어. 하지만 당신이 결혼하자고 하면 바로 그날 결혼하겠어."
"자기, 나를 정식 아내로 맞아들여야 할 것처럼 말하지 마요. 난 이미 정식 아내
라고요. 당신이 행복하고 그걸 자랑스럽게 생각한다면 아무것도 부끄러워할 필
요가 없어요. 지금 행복하지 않아요?"

문장분석

"You're my religion. You're all I've got."

"All right. But I'll marry you/ the day you say."

"Don't talk as though you had to make an honest woman of me, darling. I'm a
　　　　　　　　　마치~처럼(as if)　　　must　　관계한 여자를 정식 아내로 삼다
very honest woman. You can't be ashamed of something/ if you're only happy

and (are) proud of it. Aren't you happy?"
　　　~을 자랑스럽게 여기다

honest [ánist] 정직한, 숨김(이) 없는　　　　shame [ʃeim] 부끄럼, 수치심
honesty [ánisti] 정직, 성실　　　　　　　　proud [praud]
ashamed [əʃéimd] 부끄러이 여기는, 수줍어하는　　거만한(haughty), 잘난 체하는(arrogant), 뽐내는

You'll be sick of me I'll be so faithful

내가 너무 정숙해서 당신이 싫증 낼지 몰라요

"I love you so much and you did love some one else before."
"And what happened to him?"
"He died."
"Yes and if he hadn't I wouldn't have met you. I'm not unfaithful, darling. I've plenty of faults but I'm very faithful. You'll be sick of me I'll be so faithful."

"난 당신을 이렇게 사랑하고 있는데, 당신은 전에 다른 남자를 사랑한 적이 있잖아."
"하지만 그 사람한테 무슨 일이 벌어졌죠?"
"죽었지."
"그래요. 만일 그 사람이 죽지 않았다면 난 당신을 만나지 못했을 거예요. 자기, 난 부정한 여자가 아니라고요. 결점이야 많지만 정숙한 여자라고요. 너무 정숙해서 당신이 싫증 낼지 몰라요."

"I love you so much and you did love some one else before."
　　　　　　　　　　　　　　　　강조
"And what happened to him?"

"He died."

"Yes and if he hadn't (died)/ I wouldn't have met you. I'm not unfaithful, darling. I've

plenty of faults but I'm very faithful. You'll be sick of me I'll be so faithful."
　　　　　　　　　　　　　　　　　　　　　　　　　~에 싫증이 나다

faithful [féiθfəl]
충실한, 성실한, 믿을 수 있는(reliable)
plenty [plénti] 많음, 가득, 풍부, 다량, 충분
fault [fɔːlt] 과실, 잘못(mistake), 허물

be sick of ~에 싫증이 나다
　　　(be tired of, be fed up with)
encounter [enkáuntər] (우연히) 만나다, 조우

Is there anything I do you don't like?

내가 해 준 것 중에서 마음에 들지 않는 게 있었나요?

"You see I'm happy, darling, and we have a lovely time. I haven't been happy for a long time and when I met you perhaps I was nearly crazy. Perhaps I was crazy. But now we're happy and we love each other. Do let's please just be happy. You are happy, aren't you? Is there anything I do you don't like? Can I do anything to please you? Would you like me to take down my hair? Do you want to play?"

"Yes and come to bed."

"봐요, 난 지금 행복해요. 자기, 우리 아주 즐겁게 지내잖아요. 난 오랫동안 행복이란 걸 모르고 살았어요. 그러다가 당신을 처음 만났고 그때 난 정신이 이상했는지도 몰라요. 미쳐 있었을 거예요. 하지만 지금 우린 행복하고 서로 사랑하고 있어요. 그러니 행복한 기분을 마음껏 즐겨요. 당신도 행복하죠? 내가 해 준 것 중에서 마음에 들지 않는 게 있었나요? 어떻게 하면 당신을 즐겁게 해 줄 수 있을까? 내 머리카락을 풀어 내릴까? 나랑 장난치고 싶어요?"

"그래요. 침대로 들어와요."

문장분석

"You see/ I'm happy, darling, and we have a lovely time. I haven't been happy for a long time and when I met you/ perhaps I was <u>nearly</u> crazy. Perhaps I was crazy.
almost
But now we're happy and we love each other. <u>Do</u> let's please just be happy. You
강조
are happy, aren't you? Is there (anything) I do you don't like? Can I do anything to please you? Would you <u>like</u> me <u>to</u> <u>take down</u> my hair? Do you want to play?"
(머리를) 풀다
"Yes and come to bed."

perhaps [pərhǽps]
　아마, 형편에 따라서는, 혹시, 어쩌면

please [pliːz]
　기쁘게 하다, 만족시키다(satisfy), …의 마음에 들다

flirt [fləːrt]
　(남녀가) 새롱(시시덕)거리다, 농탕치다, '불장난'하다

rapture [rǽptʃər] 큰 기쁨, 환희, 황홀, 열중

ecstasy [ékstəsi] 무아경, 황홀, 희열

Vocabulary Of The Week

MON

separate [sépərèit]
잘라서 떼어 놓다, 분리하다
separate [sépərit]
갈라진, 분리된, 끊어진, 따로따로의
divorce [divɔ́:rs] 이혼(하다)

polygamy [pəlígəmi]
일부다처(제), 일처다부(제)
monogamy [mənágəmi]
일부 일처제, 일부 일처주의

TUE

experience [ikspíəriəns] 경험, 체험
expiration [èkspəréiʃən]
종결, 만료, 만기
mind [maind]
꺼리다, 싫어하다, 신경 쓰다
jealous [dʒéləs] 질투심이 많은

matter [mǽtər] 중요하다(count)

WED

honest [ánist] 정직한, 숨김(이) 없는
honesty [ánisti] 정직, 성실
ashamed [əʃéimd]
부끄러이 여기는, 수줍어하는
shame [ʃeim] 부끄럼, 수치심

proud [praud]
거만한(haughty),
잘난체하는(arrogant), 뽐내는

THU

faithful [féiθfəl]
충실한, 성실한, 믿을 수 있는(reliable)
plenty [plénti]
많음, 가득, 풍부, 다량, 충분
fault [fɔːlt] 과실, 잘못(mistake), 허물

be sick of
~에 싫증이 나다
(be tired of, be fed up with)
encounter [enkáuntər]
(우연히) 만나다, 조우

FRI

perhaps [pərhǽps]
아마, 형편에 따라서는, 혹시, 어쩌면
please [pli:z]
기쁘게 하다, 만족시키다(satisfy),
…의 마음에 들다

flirt [flə:rt]
(남녀가) 새롱(시시덕)거리다,
농탕치다, '불장난'하다
rapture [rǽptʃər]
큰 기쁨, 환희, 황홀, 열중
ecstasy [ékstəsi] 무아경, 황홀, 희열

April

04

**The most painful thing is losing yourself
in the process of loving someone too much,
and forgetting that you are special too.**

가장 고통스러운 것은 누군가를 너무나 많이 사랑하는 과정에서 자기 자신을
잃어가는 것과 또한 자기 자신이 특별하다는 것을 잊어버리는 것이다.

It's very restful to have a husband who's not conceited

남편이 잘난 체하지 않는 게 얼마나 마음이 편한지 몰라요

"Wouldn't you like me to have some more exalted rank?"

"No, darling. I only want you to have enough rank so that we're admitted to the better restaurants. You have a splendid rank. I don't want you to have any more rank. It might go to your head. Oh, darling, I'm awfully glad you're not conceited. I'd have married you even if you were conceited but it's very restful to have a husband who's not conceited."

"내가 진급하는 건 안 좋은가 봐?"

"그래요, 자기. 좋은 레스토랑에 들어갈 수 있을 만큼의 계급이면 충분해요. 당신 계급이면 충분해요. 사실은 더 이상 진급하지 않았으면 해요. 그렇게 되면 우쭐해할 테니까요. 아, 자기, 난 당신이 잘난 체하지 않는 게 너무 좋아요. 설령 당신이 잘난 체한대도 결혼하겠지만요. 하지만 남편이 잘난 체하지 않는 게 얼마나 마음이 편한지 몰라요."

문장분석

"Wouldn't you like me to have some more exalted rank?"

"No, darling. I only want you to have enough rank so that we're admitted to the better restaurants. You have a splendid rank. I don't want you to have any more rank. It might go to your head. Oh, darling, I'm awfully glad you're not conceited.
자만하게 만들다   very
I'd have married you/ even if you were conceited but it is very restful to have a
비록~해도
husband who's not conceited."

exalt [igzɔ́:lt] 높이다, 올리다
rank [ræŋk] 계급, 사회층, 신분
admit [ædmit]
…에게 입장을 허가하다, …에게 특권 취득을 인정하다

splendid [spléndid] 빛나는(glorious), 훌륭한
conceit [kənsí:t] 자부심, 자만, 자기 과대 평가

Nobody can help themselves

누구도 자신은 어쩔 수 없어요

"All right. I'm afraid of the rain because sometimes I see me dead in it."
"No."
"And sometimes I see you dead in it."
"That's more likely."
"No it's not, darling. Because I can keep you safe. I know I can. But nobody can help themselves."

"내가 비를 두려워하는 건 가끔씩 빗속에서 내가 죽어 있는 모습을 보기 때문이에요."
"그럴 리가."
"그리고 때론 당신이 죽어 있는 모습도 보여요."
"그건 좀 그럴싸하군."
"아녜요. 그렇지 않아요, 자기. 자기는 내가 안전하게 지켜줄 테니까요. 틀림없이 그럴 수 있을 거예요. 하지만 누구도 자신은 어쩔 수 없잖아요."

문장분석

"All right. I am afraid of the rain because sometimes I see me dead in it."
~이 두렵다

"No."

"And sometimes I see you dead in it."

"That's more likely."

"No it's not, darling. Because I can keep you safe. I know I can (keep you safe).

But nobody can help themselves."

afraid [əfréid] 두려워하는, 무서워하는
fright [frait] 공포, 경악
freight [freit] 화물, 화물 운송

likely [láikli]
있음직한, 가능하다고 생각되는, 정말 같은
protect [prətékt] 보호하다, 막다, 지키다

The last country to realize they were cooked would win the war

궁지에 몰려 있다는 사실을 끝까지 인정하지 않는 나라가 결국은 승리를 거두게 돼 있어

If they killed men as they did this fall the Allies would be cooked in another year. He said we were all cooked but we were all right as long as we did not know it. We were all cooked. The thing was not to recognize it. The last country to realize they were cooked would win the war.

이번 가을처럼 병력을 잃다가는 연합군은 내년에도 궁지에 몰릴 거야. 우리 모두 궁지에 몰려 있다고 그가 말했지만 그 사실을 깨닫지 못하는 한 걱정이 없지. 우린 모두 궁지에 몰려 있어. 한데 문제는 그 사실을 인정하려 하지 않는다는 거야. 궁지에 몰려 있다는 사실을 끝까지 인정하지 않는 나라가 결국은 승리를 거두게 돼 있어.

문장분석

If they killed men as they did this fall/ the Allies would be cooked in another year.
~처럼 killed men

He said we were all cooked but we were all right as long as we did not know it.
~하는 한

We were all cooked. The thing was not to recognize it. The last country to realize
중요한 건 …라는 거야

they were cooked would win the war.

Allies [ǽlaiz]
pl. (a-) 동맹국, (the ~) (제 1·2차 세계 대전 때의) 연합국

cook [kuk] 몹시 지치게 하다, 못쓰게 하다

recognize [rékəgnàiz] 알아보다, 인지하다

last (the ~)
가장 …할 것 같지 않은, 가장 어울리지 않는

realize [rí:əlàiz] 실현하다, 현실화하다

You always feel trapped biologically

인간이라면 언제나 생리적으로 덫에 걸려 있다는 느낌이 들지

"And you don't feel trapped?"
"Maybe a little. But not by you."
"I didn't mean by me. You mustn't be stupid.
I meant trapped at all."
"You always feel trapped biologically."
She went away a long way without stirring
or removing her hand.

"덫에 걸린 듯한 느낌이 들지는 않나요?"
"약간은 그럴지도 모르지. 하지만 당신 때문은 아냐."
"나 때문이라곤 하지 않았어요. 바보같이 굴지 말아요. 어쨌든 덫에 걸린 기분
이 드냐는 거죠."
"인간이라면 언제나 생리적으로 덫에 걸려 있다는 느낌이 들지."
몸을 움직이거나 그녀의 손을 놓은 것도 아닌데 그녀가 마치 멀리 가버린 것 같
은 기분이 들었다.

문장분석

"And you don't feel trapped?"

"Maybe a little. But not by you."

"I didn't mean (trapped) by me. You mustn't be stupid. I meant trapped at all."
조금이라도

"You always feel trapped biologically."
일반인
She went away a long way without stirring or removing her hand.

trap [træp] 올가미, 함정, 덫   biologic [bàiəláɗʒik] 생물학(상)의
little/few 거의 없는(부정)   stir [stəːr] 움직이다, 휘젓다
a little/ a few 조금 있는(긍정)

FRI

If anything comes between us we're gone and then they have us

우리 사이에 무슨 일이 생기면 세상은 우릴 잡아먹을 거예요

"People love each other and they misunderstand on purpose and they fight and then suddenly they aren't the same one."
"We won't fight."
"We mustn't. Because there's only us two and in the world there's all the rest of them. If anything comes between us we're gone and then they have us."
"They won't get us," I said. "Because you're too brave. Nothing ever happens to the brave."

"세상 사람들은 서로 사랑하면서도 일부러 오해를 만들어서 다투고, 그러고 나서 갑자기 다른 사람이 되어 버리죠."
"우리는 싸우지 않을 거야."
"정말로 그러지 마요. 우리 두 사람 외에, 나머지 세상 사람들은 모두 남이니까. 우리 사이에 무슨 일이 생기면 세상은 우릴 먹어 치울 거예요."
"그런 일은 없을 거야. 당신은 무척 용감하니까. 용감한 사람에게는 아무 일도 일어나지 않아." 내가 말했다.

문장분석

"They love each other and they misunderstand <u>on purpose</u> and they fight and
　　　일반인　　　　　　　　　　　　　　　　　　　　　　일부러
then suddenly they aren't the same one."

"We <u>won't</u> fight."
　　　will not
"We mustn't. Because there's only us two and in the world/ there's all the rest of

them. If anything comes between us/ we're gone and then they have us."

"They <u>won't</u> get us," I said. "Because you're too brave. Nothing ever happens to

<u>the brave</u>."
용감한 사람들

misunderstand [misʌndərstǽnd]　　　　　rest [rest] 나머지, 휴식
　오해하다, 잘못 생각하다　　　　　　　　　brave [breiv] 용감한
purpose [pə́ːrpəs] 목적(aim), 의도, 용도　　bravery [bréivəri] 용기, 용감(성), 용맹

Vocabulary Of The Week

MON

exalt [igzɔ́:lt] 높이다, 올리다
rank [ræŋk] 계급, 사회층, 신분
admit [ædmít]
…에게 입장을 허가하다,
…에게 특권 취득을 인정하다

splendid [spléndid]
빛나는(glorious), 훌륭한
conceit [kənsí:t]
자부심, 자만, 자기 과대 평가

TUE

afraid [əfréid]
두려워하는, 무서워하는
fright [frait] 공포, 경악
freight [freit] 화물, 화물 운송

likely [láikli]
있음직한, 가능하다고 생각되는,
정말 같은
protect [prətékt]
보호하다, 막다, 지키다

WED

Allies [ǽlaiz]
pl. (a-) 동맹국, (the ~)
(제 1·2차 세계 대전 때의) 연합국
cook [kuk]
몹시 지치게 하다, 못쓰게 하다

recognize [rékəgnàiz]
알아보다, 인지하다
last
(the ~) 가장 …할 것 같지 않은,
가장 어울리지 않는
realize [rí:əlàiz] 실현하다, 현실화하다

THU

trap [træp] 올가미, 함정, 덫
little/few 거의 없는(부정)
a little/ a few 조금 있는(긍정)
biologic [bàiəláʤik] 생물학(상)의
stir [stə:r] 움직이다, 휘젓다

FRI

misunderstand [mìsʌndərstǽnd]
오해하다, 잘못 생각하다
purpose [pə́:rpəs]
목적(aim), 의도, 용도
rest [rest] 나머지, 휴식
brave [breiv] 용감한

bravery [bréivəri]
용기, 용감(성), 용맹

MON

He knew a great deal about cowards but nothing about the brave

그는 비겁한 사람에 대해선 잘 알지만 용감한 사람에 대해선 아무것도 몰라요

"He was probably a coward," she said. "He knew a great deal about cowards but nothing about the brave. The brave dies perhaps two thousand deaths if he's intelligent. He simply doesn't mention them."
"I don't know. It's hard to see inside the head of the brave."
"Yes. That's how they keep that way."

"그 사람은 아마 비겁한 사람이었을 거예요. 그는 비겁한 사람에 대해선 잘 알지만 용감한 사람에 대해선 아무것도 모르는 사람이에요. 용감한 사람이 영리하다면 아마 이천 번은 죽을 거예요. 그걸 입 밖에 내지 않을 뿐이죠."
"난 모르겠어. 용감한 사람의 머릿속까지 들여다보기는 어려우니까."
"맞아요. 그래서 그들이 용감하게 행동하는 거죠."

문장분석

"He was probably a coward," she said. "He knew a great deal about cowards but
(a lot)
(knew) nothing about the brave. The brave dies perhaps two thousand deaths if
he's intelligent. He simply doesn't mention them."

"I don't know. It is hard to see inside the head of the brave."

"Yes. That's how they keep that way."

probably [prɑ́.bəbli] 아마, 필시, 대개는
coward [káuərd] 겁쟁이, 비겁한
cowardice [káuərdis] 겁, 소심, 비겁

intelligent [intélədʒənt] 지적인, 지성을 갖춘
intelligible [intélədʒəbəl]
　이해할 수 있는, 알기 쉬운, 명료한

Put him in power and see how wise he is

그들에게 권력을 줘 보세요, 얼마나 분별력이 있는지 곧 알게 될 겁니다

"Many of the soldiers have always felt this way. It is not because they were beaten."
"They were beaten to start with. They were beaten when they took them from their farms and put them in the army. That is why the peasant has wisdom, because he is defeated from the start. Put him in power and see how wise he is."

"많은 병사가 늘 이렇게 느껴 왔습니다. 꼭 전쟁에 패배했다고 해서 그런 건 아닙니다."
"그들은 처음부터 패배한 겁니다. 농장에서 군대로 끌려 왔을 때 이미 패배한 거죠. 농부들에게 분별력이 있는 건, 처음부터 패배했기 때문이죠. 그들에게 권력을 줘 보세요. 얼마나 분별력이 있는지 곧 알게 될 겁니다."

문장분석

"Many of the soldiers have always felt this way. It is not because they were beaten."

"They were beaten to start with. They were beaten/ when they took them from
우선, 맨 먼저, 처음에는　　　　　　　　~할 때
their farms and put them in the army. That is why the peasant has wisdom,

because he is defeated from the start. Put him in power and see how wise he is."

soldier [sóuldʒər] 군인
beat [bi:t] 치다, 때려 부수다
peasant [pézənt] 농부, 소작농

wisdom [wízdəm] 현명함, 지혜, 슬기로움
defeat [difí:t] 쳐부수다

Anger was washed away in the river along with any obligation

분노는 모든 의무와 함께 강물 속에서 씻겨 내려갔다

Anger was washed away in the river along with any obligation. Although that ceased when the carabiniere put his hands on my collar. I would like to have had the uniform off although I did not care much about the outward forms. I had taken off the stars, but that was for convenience. It was no point of honor. I was not against them. I was through.

분노는 모든 의무와 함께 강물 속에서 씻겨 내려갔다. 의무는 헌병이 내 멱살을 잡을 때 사라졌다는 말이다. 나는 외적인 형식에 별로 관심을 두지 않는 편이지만 군복을 벗어버리고 싶었다. 소매에서 별을 떼어 버린 것은 그게 편해서였다. 명예를 위해서가 아니었다. 그들을 반대하는 것도 아니었다. 나는 이미 그 일에서 손을 뗐다.

문장분석

Anger was washed away in the river along with any obligation. Although that
　　　　　　　　　　　　　　　　　　　　　　　　　　　　　…이긴 하지만
ceased/ when the carabiniere put his hands on my collar. I would like to have

had the uniform off/ although I did not care much about the outward forms. I

had taken off the stars, but that was for convenience. It was no point of honor. I

was not against them. I was through.
　　　　　　　　　　끝나, 마치어

obligation [àbləgéiʃən] 의무, 책임　　　convenience [kənvíːnjəns] 편리, 편의
cease [siːs] 그만두다, 중지하다　　　　honor [ánər] 명예, 영예, 영광
carabiniere [kæ̀rəbinjɛ́əri]
　(It.) (이탈리아의) 경찰관

I wished I would eat and stop thinking

뭘 좀 먹고 생각하는 것을 그만두고 싶었다

I wished them all the luck. There were the good ones, and the brave ones, and the calm ones and the sensible ones, and they deserved it. But it was not my show any more and I wished this bloody train would get to Mestre and I would eat and stop thinking. I would have to stop.

나는 그들 모두에게 행운을 빌었다. 착한 사람도, 용감한 사람도, 침착한 사람도, 현명한 사람도 있었다. 그들 모두는 행운을 누려 마땅했다. 그러나 이제 더이상 내가 나설 일은 아니었다. 나는 이 빌어먹을 열차가 메스트레에 도착하며 뭘 좀 먹고 생각하는 것을 그만두고 싶을 뿐이다. 어쨌든 생각을 그만해야 했다.

I wished them all the luck. There were the good ones, and the brave ones, and the calm ones and the sensible ones, and they deserved it. But it was not my
luck
show any more and I wished this bloody train would get to Mestre and I would
일, 사업, 기획   어처구니없는(damned)
eat and stop thinking. I would have to stop.

calm [kɑːm] 고요한, 조용한(quiet), 온화한
sensible [sénsəbəl]
  분별 있는, 사리를 아는, 현명한
deserve [dizə́ːrv]
  …할 만하다, 받을 가치가 있다, …할 가치가 있다

bloody [blʌ́di]
  피를 흘리는(bleeding), 유혈의, 피투성이의
bleed [bliːd] 피를 흘리다

I was not made to think but made to eat

나는 생각하기 위해 태어난 게 아니라 먹기 위해 태어났다

I was not made to think. I was made to eat. My God, yes. Eat and drink and sleep with Catherine. To-night maybe. No that was impossible. But to-morrow night, and a good meal and sheets and never going away again except together.

나는 생각하기 위해 태어나지 않았다. 먹기 위해 태어났다. 정말 그렇다. 먹고 마시고 캐서린과 잠을 자도록 만들어졌다. 오늘 밤이라면 가능할지 모른다. 아니, 그렇지 않아. 하지만 내일 밤은 가능할지 모르겠다. 맛 좋은 식사와 시트가 깔린 잠자리 그리고 그녀와 함께할 수 있는 곳이 아니라면 아무 데도 가지 않으리라.

문장분석

I was not made to think. I was made to eat. My God, yes. (I was made to) Eat

and drink and sleep with Catherine. To-night maybe. No, that was impossible.

But to-morrow night, and a good meal and sheets and never going away again

except together.

cogito, ergo sum [kάdʒìtòu-ə́ːrgousʌ́m]
  (L.) (=I think, therefore I exist.) 나는 생각한다,
  그러므로 나는 존재한다
possibility [pὰsəbíləti]
  가능성, 실현성, 있을 수 있음

meal [miːl] 식사, 식사 시간, 한 끼(분)
sheet [ʃiːt] 시트, (침구 따위의) 커버, 홑이불

Vocabulary Of The Week

MON

probably [prάbəbli]
아마, 필시, 대개는
coward [kάuərd] 겁쟁이, 비겁한
cowardice [kάuərdis] 겁, 소심, 비겁
intelligent [intélədʒənt]
지적인, 지성을 갖춘

intelligible [intélədʒəbəl]
이해할 수 있는, 알기 쉬운, 명료한

TUE

soldier [sóuldʒər] 군인
beat [bi:t] 치다, 때려 부수다
peasant [pézənt] 농부, 소작농
wisdom [wízdəm]
현명함, 지혜, 슬기로움
defeat [difi:t] 쳐부수다

WED

obligation [ὰbləgéiʃən] 의무, 책임
cease [si:s] 그만두다, 중지하다
carabiniere [kæ̀rəbinjéəri]
(It.) (이탈리아의) 경찰관
convenience [kənví:njəns]
편리, 편의

honor [άnər] 명예, 영예, 영광

THU

calm [kɑ:m]
고요한, 조용한(quiet), 온화한
sensible [sénsəbəl]
분별 있는, 사리를 아는, 현명한
deserve [dizə́:rv]
…할 만하다, 받을 가치가 있다,

…할 가치가 있다
bloody [blʌ́di]
피를 흘리는(bleeding),
유혈의, 피투성이의
bleed [bli:d] 피를 흘리다

FRI

cogito, ergo sum
[kάdʒitòu-ə́:rgousʌ́m]
(L.) (=I think, therefore I exist.)
나는 생각한다,
그러므로 나는 존재한다

possibility [pὰsəbíləti]
가능성, 실현성, 있을 수 있음
meal [mi:l] 식사, 식사 시간, 한 끼(분)
sheet [ʃi:t]
시트, (침구 따위의) 커버, 홑이불

MON

I had made a separate peace

나는 단독 평화조약을 맺었다

They got off at Gallarate and I was glad to be alone. I had the paper but I did not read it because I did not want to read about the war. I was going to forget the war. I had made a separate peace. I felt damned lonely and was glad when the train got to Stresa.

그들이 갈라라테에서 내리고 나 혼자만 남게 되자 마음이 한결 가벼워졌다. 신문을 갖고 있었지만 전쟁에 관한 소식을 알고 싶지 않아서 읽지 않았다. 전쟁에 대해서는 잊을 작정이었다. 나는 단독 평화조약을 맺은 것이다. 기분이 몹시 쓸쓸했지만 가차가 스트레사에 도착하자 기뻤다.

문장분석

They <u>got off</u> at Gallarate and I was glad to be alone. I had the paper but I did not
  (탈것에서) 내리다

read it because I did not want to read about the war. I was going to forget the

war. I had made a separate peace. I felt <u>damned</u> lonely and was glad when the
                                                      very

train <u>got to</u> Stresa.
    arrive

glad [glæd] 기쁜, 반가운, 유쾌한
alone [əlóun] 다만 홀로, 혼자서, 고독한
separate [sépərèit] 잘라서 떼어 놓다, 분리하다
separate [sépərit]
  갈라진, 분리된, 단독의, 독립된

damned [dæmd, dǽmnid] 저주받은, 지독하게, 굉장히

I did not have the feeling that the war was really over

전쟁이 정말로 끝났다는 느낌이 들지 않았다

The war was a long way away. Maybe there wasn't any war. There was no war here. Then I realized it was over for me. But I did not have the feeling that it was really over. I had the feeling of a boy who thinks of what is happening at a certain hour at the schoolhouse from which he has played truant.

전쟁은 이제 아득하기만 했다. 어쩌면 전쟁이 처음부터 없었는지도 모른다. 이 곳에는 전쟁이 없었다. 그제야 비로소 나에게는 전쟁이 끝났다는 게 실감이 났다. 그러나 전쟁이 정말로 끝났다는 느낌은 들지 않았다. 나는 학교를 땡땡이치고는 지금쯤 학교에서는 무슨 일이 벌어지고 있을까 궁금해하는 학생이 된 기분이었다.

문장분석

The war was a long way away. Maybe there wasn't any war. There was no war here. Then I realized it was over for me. But I did not have the feeling that it was really over. I had the feeling of a boy who thinks of what is happening at a certain hour at the schoolhouse from which he has played truant.

realize [rí:əlàiz] 실현하다, 현실화하다
certain [sə́:rtən] 어떤, 확신하는, 자신하는(sure)
curtain [kə́:rtən] 커튼, 휘장

schoolhouse [skú:lhàus]
(특히 초등학교의) 교사(校舍)
truant [trú:ənt]
게으름쟁이, 꾀부리는 사람, 무단 결석자

We could feel alone when we were together, alone against the others

함께여서 외로운 기분, 즉 세상 사람들에게 맞선 고독을 느낄 뿐이었다

Often a man wishes to be alone and a girl wishes to be alone too and if they love each other they are jealous of that in each other, but I can truly say we never felt that. We could feel alone when we were together, alone against the others. It has only happened to me like that once. I have been alone while I was with many girls and that is the way that you can be most lonely.

남자나 여자나 이따금씩은 혼자 있고 싶을 때가 있다. 사랑하는 사람끼리는 서로의 그런 기분을 질투하는 법이지만 솔직히 우리는 조금도 그런 기분을 느끼지 않았다. 오히려 함께여서 외로운 기분, 다른 세상 사람들에게 맞섰기에 느끼는 고독이었다. 나도 그와 비슷한 기분을 느낀 적이 있다. 많은 여자와 함께 있을 때 오히려 고독을 느꼈는데 그런 경우가 가장 고독했다.

문장분석

Often a man wishes to be alone and a girl wishes to be alone too and if they love each other/ they are jealous of that in each other, but I can truly say (that) I never felt that. We could feel alone when we were together, alone against the
~할 때 ···에 반대하여
others. It has only happened to me like that once. I have been alone while I was
한때 ~하는 동안
with many girls and that is the way that you can be most lonely.

alone [əlóun] (서술적) 혼자서, 고독한
jealous [dʒéləs] 질투심이 많은
jealousy [dʒéləsi] 질투, 투기, 시샘

lonely [lóunli] 외로운, 고독한
loner [lóunər] 혼자 있는(있고 싶어하는) 사람

The night can be a dreadful time for lonely people

고독한 사람에겐 밤이야말로 끔찍한 시간이다

But we were never lonely and never afraid when we were together. I know that the night is not the same as the day: that all things are different, that the things of the night cannot be explained in the day, because they do not then exist, and the night can be a dreadful time for lonely people once their loneliness has started. But with Catherine there was almost no difference in the night except that it was an even better time.

그러나 우리가 함께 있을 때는 결코 고독하지 않았고 두렵지도 않았다. 밤이 낮과 같지 않다는 것, 모든 것이 다르다는 것, 밤에 겪은 것을 낮에 존재하지 않았기에 설명할 수 없다는 것을 나는 잘 안다. 또 고독한 사람에게 일단 고독이 찾아오면 밤이야말로 끔찍한 시간이라는 것도 잘 안다. 그러나 캐서린과 함께 있으면 밤이 더 유쾌하다는 것만 다를 뿐 낮과 거의 다를 게 없었다.

문장분석

But we were never lonely and never afraid/ when we were together. I know that

the night is not the same as the day: that all things are different, that the things

of the night cannot be explained in the day, because they do not then exist, and

the night can be a dreadful time/ for lonely people/ once their loneliness has
일단 …(하면)

started. But with Catherine/ there was almost no difference in the night except

that it was an even better time.
night   훨씬

explain [ikspléin] 설명하다   exist [igzíst] 존재하다, 실재하다
inexplicable [inéksplikəbəl]   existence [igzístəns] 존재, 실재
불가해한, 설명할 수 없는   dreadful [drédfəl] 무서운, 두려운, 무시무시한

The world breaks every one and afterward many are strong at the broken places

이 세상은 모든 사람을 부러뜨리지만 많은 사람은 그 부러진 곳에서 더욱 강해진다

If people bring so much courage to this world the world has to kill them to break them, so of course it kills them. The world breaks every one and afterward many are strong at the broken places. But those that will not break it kills. It kills the very good and the very gentle and the very brave impartially.

사람들이 이 세상에 너무 많은 용기를 갖고 오면 세상은 그런 사람들을 꺾기 위해 죽여야 하고, 그래서 결국에는 죽음에 이르게 한다. 이 세상은 모든 사람을 부러뜨리지만 많은 사람은 그 부러진 곳에서 더욱 강해진다. 그러나 세상은 부러지지 않으려 하는 사람들을 죽이고 만다. 아주 선량한 사람들이든, 아주 부드러운 사람들이든, 아주 용감한 사람들이든 아무런 차별을 두지 않고 공평하게 죽인다.

문장분석

If people bring so much courage to this world/ the world has to kill them to break them, so (of course) it kills them. The world breaks every one and afterward many are strong at the broken places. But those that will not break it kills. It kills
많은 사람들   세상
the very good and the very gentle and the very brave/ impartially.

courage [kə́:ridʒ] 용기, 담력, 배짱
courageous [kəréidʒəs]
  용기 있는, 용감한, 담력 있는
course [kɔːrs] 진로, 행로

coarse [kɔːrs]
  조잡한, 조악(粗惡)한, 거친, 상스러운
impartial [impɑ́ːrʃəl] 공평한, 편견 없는

Vocabulary Of The Week

MON

glad [glæd]
기쁜, 반가운, 유쾌한

alone [əlóun]
다만 홀로, 혼자서, 고독한

separate [sépərèit]
잘라서 떼어 놓다, 분리하다

separate [sépərit]
갈라진, 분리된, 단독의, 독립된

damned [dæmd, dǽmnid]
저주받은, 지독하게, 굉장히

TUE

realize [rí:əlàiz]
실현하다, 현실화하다

certain [sə́:rtən]
어떤, 확신하는, 자신하는(sure)

curtain [kə́:rtən] 커튼, 휘장

schoolhouse [skú:lhàus]
(특히 초등학교의) 교사(校舍)

truant [trú:ənt]
게으름쟁이, 꾀부리는 사람,
무단 결석자

WED

alone [əlóun]
(서술적) 혼자서, 고독한

jealous [dʒéləs] 질투심이 많은

jealousy [dʒéləsi] 질투, 투기, 시샘

lonely [lóunli] 외로운, 고독한

loner [lóunər]
혼자 있는(있고 싶어하는) 사람

THU

explain [ikspléin] 설명하다

inexplicable [inéksplikəbəl]
불가해한, 설명할 수 없는

exist [igzíst] 존재하다, 실재하다

existence [igzístəns] 존재, 실재

dreadful [drédfəl]
무서운, 두려운, 무시무시한

FRI

courage [kə́:ridʒ] 용기, 담력, 배짱

courageous [kəréidʒəs]
용기 있는, 용감한, 담력 있는

course [kɔːrs] 진로, 행로

coarse [kɔːrs]
조잡한, 조악(粗惡)한, 거친, 상스러운

impartial [impá:rʃəl]
공평한, 편견 없는

MON

She was asleep and the sunlight was coming in through the window

그녀는 자고 있었고 창문으로는 햇살이 들어왔다

I remember waking in the morning. Catherine was asleep and the sunlight was coming in through the window. The rain had stopped and I stepped out of bed and across the floor to the window. Down below were the gardens, bare now but beautifully regular, the gravel paths, the trees, the stone wall by the lake and the lake in the sunlight with the mountains beyond. I stood at the window looking out and when I turned away I saw Catherine was awake and watching me.

이튿날 아침잠에서 깨어났을 때의 일이 지금도 생생하다. 캐서린은 자고 있었고 창문으로는 햇살이 들어왔다. 비는 그쳤고 나는 침대에서 일어나 바닥을 가로질러 창가로 다가갔다. 아래쪽에는 지금은 휑하지만 아름답게 잘 정돈된 정원이 있었고 자갈이 깔린 오솔길이며 수목이며 호숫가의 돌담이며 멀리 산을 등지고 햇빛을 받고 있는 호수가 보였다. 창가에 서서 밖을 내다보다가 뒤를 돌아보니 캐서린이 잠에서 깨어 나를 쳐다보고 있었다.

문장분석

I remember waking in the morning. Catherine was asleep and the sunlight was

coming in/ through the window. The rain had stopped and I stepped out of bed

and across the floor/ to the window. Down below/ were the gardens, bare now

but beautifully regular, the gravel paths, the trees, the stone wall by the lake

and the lake in the sunlight with the mountains beyond. I stood at the window

looking out and when I turned away/ I saw Catherine was awake and watching
              ~할 때

me.

irregular [irégjələr] 불규칙한, 변칙의, 비정상의   below [bilóu] …의 아래에(에서, 로)
bare [bɛər] 벌거벗은, 알몸의, 가리지 않은, 드러낸   bellow [bélou] 큰 소리로 울다, 짖다
gravel [grǽvəl] 자갈

Would you like to live after death?

죽은 뒤에도 계속 살고 싶으십니까?

"I had expected to become more devout as I grow older but somehow I haven't," he said. "It is a great pity."

"Would you like to live after death?" I asked and instantly felt a fool to mention death. But he did not mind the word.

"It would depend on the life. This life is very pleasant. I would like to live forever," he smiled. "I very nearly have."

"나이를 먹으면 신앙이 좀 더 두터워질 줄 알았는데 웬일인지 그렇게 되지 않더군. 참으로 딱한 일이지."

"죽은 뒤에도 계속 살고 싶으십니까?" 내가 물었다. 죽음 이야기를 꺼내고 보니 바보 같다는 생각이 들었다. 그러나 그는 신경 쓰지 않았다.

"그야 삶 나름이겠지. 이 세상은 아주 즐거워. 나는 영원히 살고 싶소. 살 만큼 살았는데도 말이야." 그가 미소를 지었다.

문장분석

"I had expected to become more devout as I grow older but somehow I haven't
⎣···하면서, become⎦   ⎣웬일인지⎦
(become more devout)," he said. "It is a great pity."

"Would you like to live after death?" I asked and instantly felt a fool to mention

death. But he did not mind the word.

"It would depend on the life. This life is very pleasant. I would like to live forever,"
⎣~에 달리다⎦
he smiled. "I very nearly have (lived forever)."
⎣almost⎦

devout [diváut] 독실한, 경건한
devote [divóut] 바치다, 헌신하다
pity [píti] 불쌍히 여김, 동정

mind [maind] 싫어하다, 꺼려하다, 신경 쓰다
pleasant [pléznt] 즐거운, 기분 좋은, 유쾌한

The spirit is no older and not much wiser

정신은 더 늙지도 않고 또 그렇다고 해서 훨씬 더 지혜로워지는 것도 아니다

"If you ever live to be as old as I am you will find many things strange."
"You never seem old."
"It is the body that is old. Sometimes I am afraid I will break off a finger as one breaks a stick of chalk. And the spirit is no older and not much wiser."

"자네도 나만큼 나이가 들면 온갖 일이 이상스럽게 생각될 거야."
"지금도 전혀 늙어 보이지 않는데요."
"늙는 건 육체뿐이지. 이따금씩 백묵이 부러지듯 내 손가락이 부러지지나 않을까 겁이 날 때가 있어. 그러면서도 정신은 더 늙지도 않고 또 그렇다고 해서 훨씬 더 지혜로워지는 것도 아냐."

문장분석

"If you ever live to be <u>as</u> old <u>as</u> I am/ you will find many things strange."

"You never <u>seem</u> old."

look

"It is <u>the body</u> that is old. Sometimes I am afraid (that) I will break off a finger <u>as</u>
_{like}
one breaks a stick of chalk. And the spirit is no older and not much wiser."

stick [stik] 막대기, 조각
chalk [tʃɔːk] 분필
choke [tʃouk] 질식시키다, …을 숨 막히게 하다

spirit [spírit] 정신, 마음
zeitgeist [tsáitgàist] (G.) 시대정신(사조)

It is a very unattractive wisdom

그건 아주 탐탁지 않은 지혜야

"You are wise."
"No, that is the great fallacy; the wisdom of old men. They do not grow wise. They grow careful."
"Perhaps that is wisdom."
"It is a very unattractive wisdom."

"당신은 지혜로우십니다."
"아냐. 노인이 지혜로울 거라고 생각하는 건 엄청난 착각이야. 지혜로워지는 게 아니야. 다만 신중해질 뿐이지."
"그게 지혜로워지는 거겠죠."
"그게 지혜라면 아주 탐탁지 않은 지혜야."

"You are wise."

"No, that is the great fallacy; the wisdom of old men. They do not grow wise.
become

They grow careful."

"Perhaps/ that is wisdom."

"It is a very unattractive wisdom."

wise [waiz] 슬기로운, 현명한
wisdom [wízdəm] 현명함, 지혜
likewise [láikwàiz] 똑같이, 마찬가지로

fallacy [fǽləsi] 잘못된 생각, 오류
attractive [ətrǽktiv]
　사람의 마음을 끄는, 매력적인

What do you value most?
Some one I love

자네가 가장 소중하게 생각하는 건 뭔가? 제가 사랑하는 사람입니다

"What do you value most?"
"Some one I love."
"With me it is the same. That is not wisdom. Do you value life?"
"Yes."
"So do I. Because it is all I have. And to give birthday parties," he laughed. "You are probably wiser than I am. You do not give birthday parties."

"자네가 가장 소중하게 생각하는 건 뭔가?"
"제가 사랑하는 사람입니다."
"그건 나도 마찬가지야. 그건 지혜가 아니지. 자넨 삶을 소중하게 생각하나?"
"물론이죠."
"나도 그래. 그게 우리가 갖고 있는 전부니까. 그리고 생일 파티를 하기 위해서도 말이야. 자네가 나보다 현명한지도 모르겠군. 생일 파티 같은 건 열지 않을 테니까."

문장분석

"What do you value most?"

"Some one I love."

"With me/ it is the same. That is not wisdom. Do you value life?"

"Yes."

"So do I. Because it is all I have. And to give birthday parties," he laughed. "You
Me too
are probably wiser than I am. You do not give birthday parties."

value [vǽljuː] 가치, 값을 치다, 소중히 하다   laughter [lǽftər] 웃음, 웃음소리
invaluable [invǽljuəbəl]   so 동사 주어 too
값을 헤아릴 수 없는, 매우 귀중한(priceless)   so 주어 동사 really

110

Vocabulary Of The Week

MON

irregular [irégjələr]
불규칙한, 변칙의, 비정상의
bare [bɛər]
벌거벗은, 알몸의, 가리지 않은, 드러낸
gravel [grǽvəl] 자갈
below [bilóu] …의 아래에(에서, 로)

bellow [bélou] 큰 소리로 울다, 짖다

TUE

devout [diváut] 독실한, 경건한
devote [divóut] 바치다, 헌신하다
pity [píti] 불쌍히 여김, 동정
mind [maind]
싫어하다, 꺼려하다, 신경 쓰다

pleasant [pléznt]
즐거운, 기분 좋은, 유쾌한

WED

stick [stik] 막대기, 조각
chalk [tʃɔːk] 분필
choke [tʃouk]
질식시키다, …을 숨 막히게 하다
spirit [spírit] 정신, 마음

zeitgeist [tsáitgàist]
(G.) 시대정신(사조)

THU

wise [waiz] 슬기로운, 현명한
wisdom [wízdəm] 현명함, 지혜
likewise [láikwàiz]
똑같이, 마찬가지로
fallacy [fǽləsi] 잘못된 생각, 오류

attractive [ətrǽktiv]
사람의 마음을 끄는, 매력적인

FRI

value [vǽljuː]
가치, 값을 치다, 소중히 하다
invaluable [invǽljuəbəl]
값을 헤아릴 수 없는,
매우 귀중한(priceless)
laughter [lǽftər] 웃음, 웃음소리

so 동사 주어 too
so 주어 동사 really

May

05

For Sale: Baby shoes, never worn.

팝니다. 한 번도 신지 않은 아기 신발.

MON

I had expected to become devout myself but it has not come

난 신앙심이 두터워지기를 기대했지만 뜻대로 안 됐어

"I hope you will be very fortunate and very happy and very, very healthy."

"Thank you. And I hope you will live forever."

"Thank you. I have. And if you ever become devout pray for me if I am dead. I am asking several of my friends to do that. I had expected to become devout myself but it has not come."

"I might become very devout," I said. "Anyway, I will pray for you."

"행운을 비네. 자네가 아주 행복하고 또 아주 건강하기를 바라네."

"고맙습니다. 당신도 영원한 삶을 누리시길 빕니다."

"고맙네. 지금도 꽤 오래 살았어. 신앙이 두터워지거든 내가 죽은 후 나를 위해 기도해 주게. 몇몇 친구에게도 그렇게 부탁해 두었어. 난 신앙심이 두터워지기를 기대했지만 뜻대로 안 됐거든."

"어쩌면 제가 아주 경건해질지도 모르죠. 어쨌든 당신을 위해 기도드리겠습니다."

문장분석

"I hope you will be very fortunate and very happy and very, very healthy."

"Thank you. And I hope you will live forever."

"Thank you. I have (lived forever). And if you ever become devout/ pray for me if I am dead. I am asking several of my friends to do that. I had expected to become devout myself but it has not come."

"I might become very devout," I said. "Anyway, I will pray for you."

fortunate [fɔ́:rtʃənit] 운이 좋은, 행운의, 복받은
healthy [hélθi] 건강한, 건장한, 튼튼한
healthful [hélθfəl] 건강에 좋은, 위생적인

devout [diváut] 독실한, 경건한
pray [prei] 기도하다

TUE

Perhaps I have outlived my religious feeling

너무 오래 살아서 종교적인 감정이 없어졌나 봐

"I had always expected to become devout. All my family died very devout. But somehow it does not come."

"It's too early."

"Maybe it is too late. Perhaps I have outlived my religious feeling."

"My own comes only at night."

"Then too you are in love. Do not forget that is a religious feeling."

"나는 늘 경건해지기를 바라 왔어. 내 가족들은 모두 독실한 신앙인으로 죽었지. 하지만 어찌 된 셈인지 나는 그래지지가 않더라고."

"아직 때가 이른가 보죠."

"너무 늦었는지도 모르지. 너무 오래 살아서 종교적인 감정이 없어졌나 봐."

"저한테는 그런 감정이 밤에만 찾아옵니다."

"그렇다면 자네도 사랑을 하고 있군. 잊지 말게나, 그것이 종교적인 감정이라는 걸."

문장분석

"I had always expected to become devout. All my family died very devout. But

somehow/ it does not come."
　　웬일인지

"It's too early."

"Maybe it is too late. Perhaps I have outlived my religious feeling."

"My own comes only at night."
　　···자신의 것

"Then/ too you are in love. Do not forget that is a religious feeling."

expect [ikspékt] 기대하다　　　religious [rilídʒəs] 종교(상)의, 종교적인
outlive [àutlív]　　　　　　　　religion [rilídʒən] 종교
　···보다도 오래 살다, ···보다 오래 계속하다　　devote [divóut] 바치다, 헌신하다

May 115

Are you worried because you haven't anything to do?

할 일이 없는 게 걱정되지 않아요?

"Are you worried because you haven't anything to do?"
"No. I like it. I have a fine life. Don't you?"
"I have a lovely life. But I was afraid because I'm big now that maybe I was a bore to you."
"Oh, Cat. You don't know how crazy I am about you."
"This way?"
"Just the way you are. I have a fine time. Don't we have a good life?"

"할 일이 없는 게 걱정되지 않아요?"
"아니. 난 지금이 좋아. 즐겁게 지내잖아. 당신은 안 그래?"
"나야 행복하죠. 하지만 이렇게 배가 불러오니 당신이 싫증을 느낄까 봐 걱정돼요."
"아, 캣. 당신은 내가 얼마나 당신을 사랑하는지 몰라."
"몸이 이래도?"
"지금의 당신 모습 그대로. 난 행복해. 안 그래?"

문장분석

"Are you worried because you haven't anything to do?"

"No. I like it. I have a fine life. Don't you?"

"I have a lovely life. But I was afraid because I'm big now that maybe I was a bore to you."

"Oh, Cat. You don't know how crazy I am about you."

"This way?"

"Just the way you are. I have a fine time. Don't we have a good life?"

worrier [wə́:riər] 괴롭히는 사람, 걱정 많은 사람
warrior [wɔ́(:)riər] 전사, 투사
bore [bɔːr] 따분한 사람, 싫증나게 하는 사람

boredom [bɔ́:rdəm] 권태, 지루한 것
boresome [bɔ́:rsəm] 지루한, 싫증나는

I'm no good when you're not there

당신이 없으면 나도 아무 쓸모가 없어

"I want us to be all mixed up. I don't want you to go away. I just said that. You go if you want to. But hurry right back. Why, darling, I don't live at all when I'm not with you."

"I won't ever go away," I said. "I'm no good when you're not there. I haven't any life at all any more."

"I want you to have a life. I want you to have a fine life. But we'll have it together, won't we?"

"우리가 아주 하나로 섞여 버렸으면 좋겠어. 당신이 멀리 가는 거 난 싫어요. 방금도 말했지만 가고 싶으면 가도 좋아요. 하지만 서둘러 돌아와 줘요. 아니, 자기, 자기와 함께하는 게 아니면 사는 것 같지 않을 거야."

"절대로 가지 않을 거야. 당신이 없으면 나도 아무 쓸모가 없어. 더 이상 살아가는 게 아니니까." 내가 말했다.

"난 당신이 삶을 누리길 원해요. 멋진 삶을. 하지만 우린 함께 그걸 누릴 거야, 그렇죠?"

문장분석

"I want us to be all mixed up. I don't want you to go away. I just said that. You go if you want to. But hurry right back. Why, darling, I don't live at all when I'm not with you."
곧 바로 / 아니, 저런 / 전혀 if

"I won't ever go away," I said. "I'm no good/ when you're not there. I haven't any life at all/ any more."
will not / 전혀 / 더 이상

"I want you to have a life. I want you to have a fine life. But we'll have it together, won't we?"

mixture [míkstʃər] 혼합, 조합, 섞기
purity [pjúərəti] 청정, 순수
farewell [fɛ̀ərwél] 안녕!(goodbye!)

adieu [ədjú:] 안녕!(goodbye!)
ciao [tʃau] (It.) 차오, 안녕(만남·작별 인사)

Let's go to sleep at exactly the same moment

우리 같은 순간 같이 잠들기로 해요

"Grand."

"Oh, you're sweet. And I'm not crazy now. I'm just very, very, very happy."

"Go on to sleep," I said.

"All right. Let's go to sleep at exactly the same moment."

"All right."

But we did not. I was awake for quite a long time thinking about things and watching Catherine sleeping, the moonlight on her face. Then I went to sleep, too.

"행복해."

"아. 당신은 다정한 사람이야. 그리고 지금 난 정신이 이상하지 않아요. 정말, 정말, 정말로 너무 행복하다고요."

"자. 어서 잠이나 자요."

"좋아요. 우리 같은 순간 같이 잠들기로 해요."

그러나 우리는 그렇게 하지 못했다. 나는 꽤 오랫동안 깨어서 이런저런 일을 생각하며 캐서린이 얼굴에 달빛을 받으며 잠든 모습을 지켜보았다. 그러다가 나도 잠이 들고 말았다.

문장분석

"Grand."

"Oh, you're sweet. And I'm not crazy now. I'm just very, very, very happy."

"Go on to sleep," I said.
···으로 나아가다
"All right. Let's go to sleep at exactly the same moment."

"All right."

But we did not. I was awake for quite a long time thinking about things and
꽤
watching Catherine sleeping, the moonlight on her face. Then I went to sleep,

too.

---

grand [grænd] 굉장한, 멋진(very satisfactory)
momentary [móumantèri]
　순간의, 잠깐의, 덧없는(transitory)
momentous [mouméntas]
　중대한, 중요한, 쉽지 않은

momentum [mouméntam]
　운동량, 여세, 추진력, 계기, 요소
moonlit [mú:nlit] 달빛에 비친, 달빛어린

MON

fortunate [fɔ́ːrtʃənit]
운이 좋은, 행운의, 복받은
healthy [hélθi]
건강한, 건장한, 튼튼한
healthful [hélθfəl]
건강에 좋은, 위생적인

devout [diváut] 독실한, 경건한
pray [prei] 기도하다

TUE

expect [ikspékt] 기대하다
outlive [àutlív]
…보다도 오래 살다,
…보다 오래 계속하다
religious [rilídʒəs]
종교(상)의, 종교적인

religion [rilídʒən] 종교
devote [diváut] 바치다, 헌신하다

WED

worrier [wə́ːriər]
괴롭히는 사람, 걱정 많은 사람
warrior [wɔ́(ː)riər] 전사, 투사
bore [bɔːr]
따분한 사람, 싫증나게 하는 사람
boredom [bɔ́ːrdəm] 권태, 지루한 것

boresome [bɔ́ːrsəm]
지루한, 싫증나는

THU

mixture [míkstʃər] 혼합, 조합, 섞기
purity [pjúərəti] 청정, 순수
farewell [fèərwél] 안녕!(goodbye!)
adieu [ədjúː] 안녕!(goodbye!)
ciao [tʃau]
(It.) 차오, 안녕(만남·작별 인사)

FRI

grand [grænd]
굉장한, 멋진(very satisfactory)
momentary [móuməntèri]
순간의, 잠깐의, 덧없는(transitory)
momentous [mouméntəs]
중대한, 중요한, 쉽지 않은

momentum [mouméntəm]
운동량, 여세, 추진력, 계기, 요소
moonlit [múːnlit]
달빛에 비췬, 달빛어린

You'll fall in love with me all over again

당신은 다시 처음부터 나한테 사랑에 빠지게 될 거예요

"Oh, you're so sweet. And maybe I'd look lovely, darling, and be so thin and exciting to you and you'll fall in love with me all over again."
"Hell," I said, "I love you enough now. What do you want to do? Ruin me?"
"Yes. I want to ruin you."
"Good," I said, "that's what I want too."

"아, 자긴 정말 다정한 사람이야. (머리를 자르면) 더 예뻐 보일 거예요. 자기. 몸이 날씬해져서 당신 마음을 설레게 하면 당신은 다시 처음부터 나한테 사랑에 빠지게 될 거예요."
"이봐! 지금도 당신을 충분히 사랑하고 있어. 당신은 내가 어떻게 해 주기를 바라는 거야? 나를 무너뜨리겠다는 거야?"
"음. 맞아요. 당신을 무너뜨리고 싶어요."
"좋아. 나도 바라는 바야." 내가 대꾸했다.

문장분석

"Oh, you're so sweet. And maybe I'd look lovely, darling, and be so thin and exciting to you and you'll fall in love with me all over again."

"Hell," I said, "I love you enough now. What do you want to do? Ruin me?"

"Yes. I want to ruin you."

"Good," I said, "that's what I want too."

exciting [iksáitiŋ]
　흥분시키는, 자극적인, 몹시 흥취를 자극하는
excited [iksáitid] 흥분한, 활발한
thin [θin] 얇은, 가는, 홀쭉한

fat-free 지방이 없는, 무지방의
ruin [rúːin] 파멸, 파산, 파괴하다

TUE

This was what people got for loving each other

이것이 인간이 사랑해서 얻게 되는 결과구나

Poor, poor dear Cat. And this was the price you paid for sleeping together. This was the end of the trap. This was what people got for loving each other. Catherine had a good time in the time of pregnancy. It wasn't bad. She was hardly ever sick. She was not awfully uncomfortable until toward the last. So now they got her in the end. You never got away with anything. Get away hell!

가엾고 가엾은 내 귀여운 캣! 그래. 이것이 바로 함께 잠을 잔 것에 대한 대가야. 이것이 그 덫의 끝이구나. 이것이 인간이 사랑해서 얻게 되는 결과구나. 캐서린은 임신 중에 정말 건강했어. 임신의 고통도 없었지. 입덧도 거의 없었고. 마지막까지도 전혀 힘들어하지 않았어. 그런데 이제 마침내 그녀가 붙잡힌 거야. 무슨 짓을 해도 벗어날 길이 없어. 벗어나다니, 당치도 않은 소리!

문장분석

Poor, poor dear Cat. And this was (the price) you paid for sleeping together.

This was the end of the trap. This was (what) people got for loving each other.

Catherine had a good time in the time of pregnancy. It wasn't bad. She was

hardly ever sick. She was not awfully uncomfortable until toward the last. So now
거의 …않다

they got her in the end. You never got away with anything. Get away hell!
일반인

price [prais] 가격, 대가(代價), ~에 값을 매기다
trap [træp] 올가미, 함정, 덫
pregnancy [prégnənsi] 임신, 풍부, 풍만

awfully [ɔ́:fli] 아주, 무척, 몹시
uncomfortable [ʌnkʌ́mfərtəbəl] 불쾌한, 기분이
언짢은, 거북한

You never had time to learn

그것에 대해 배울 시간이 없었어

Now Catherine would die. That was what you did. You died. You did not know what it was about. You never had time to learn. They threw you in and told you the rules and the first time they caught you off base they killed you. Or they killed you gratuitously like Aymo. Or gave you the syphilis like Rinaldo. But they killed you in the end.

이제 캐서린은 죽겠지. 내가 바로 그렇게 만든 거야. 인간은 죽는다. 그것이 무엇인지 몰랐어. 그것에 대해 배울 시간이 없었던 거야. 경기장에 던져 놓은 뒤 몇 가지 규칙을 알려주고는 베이스를 벗어나는 순간 공을 던져 잡아 버리거든. 아이모처럼 아무 까닭 없이 죽이거나. 또는 리날디처럼 매독에 걸리게 하지. 하지만 결국에는 모두 죽이고 말지.

문장분석

Now Catherine would die. That was what you did. You died. You did not know what it was about. You never had time to learn. They threw you in and told you the rules and the first time they caught you off base/ they killed you. Or they killed you gratuitously/ like Aymo. Or (they) gave you the syphilis/ like Rinaldo. But they killed you/ in the end.
결국

throw [θrou]
  (threw [θru:] - thrown [θroun]) (내)던지다
through [θru:] …을 지나서, …을 꿰뚫어
thorough [θə́:rou] 철저한, 충분한, 완벽한, 완전한

gratuitous [ɡrətjúːətəs]
  무상의, 이유 없는, 불필요한, 정당성이 없는
syphilis [sífəlis] 매독

When there were enough on the end they fell off into the fire

그들은 끄트머리 쪽에 잔뜩 모여 있다가 불 속으로 뚝뚝 떨어졌다

Once in camp I put a log on top of the fire and it was full of ants. As it commenced to burn, the ants swarmed out and went first toward the centre where the fire was; then turned back and ran toward the end. When there were enough on the end they fell off into the fire. Some got out, their bodies burnt and flattened, and went off not knowing where they were going.

언젠가 캠프를 할 때 나는 모닥불 위에 통나무 하나를 얹어놓은 적이 있다. 통나무에는 개미가 잔뜩 붙어 있었다. 통나무에 불이 붙기 시작하자 개미들은 우글우글 기어 나와 처음에는 불이 있는 한가운데로 기어갔다. 그러다가 나무 끄트머리 쪽으로 돌아갔다. 개미 떼는 끄트머리 쪽에 잔뜩 모여 있다가 불 속으로 뚝뚝 떨어졌다. 그중 몇 마리는 기어 나왔지만 몸이 불에 타서 납작해진 채로 어디로 가는 줄도 모르고 무작정 달아났다.

문장분석

Once in camp/ I put a log/ on top of the fire and it was full of ants. As it

commence to burn, the ants swarmed out and went first toward (the centre)
~하면서

where the fire was; then turned back and ran toward the end. When there were

enough on the end/ they fell off into the fire. Some (ants) got out, their bodies

burnt and flattened, and went off/ not knowing (where they were going).

ant [ænt] 개미
aunt [ænt] 아주머니(이모, 백모, 숙모, 고모)
commence [kəméns] 시작하다, 개시하다

swarm [swɔːrm] 떼, 무리, 때를 짓다, 모여들다
flatten [flǽtn] 평평하게 하다, 고르다, 펴다

I remember thinking at the time that it was the end of the world

나는 그때 바로 이것이야말로 세계의 종말이라고 생각했다

But most of them went toward the fire and then back toward the end and swarmed on the cool end and finally fell off into the fire. I remember thinking at the time that it was the end of the world and a splendid chance to be a messiah and lift the log off the fire and throw it out where the ants could get off onto the ground.

그러나 대부분의 개미들은 불 쪽으로 갔다가 나무 끄트머리 쪽으로 돌아가서 뜨겁지 않은 곳에 모여 있다가 결국은 불 속으로 떨어졌다. 나는 그때 바로 이것이야말로 세계의 종말이라고 생각했다. 구세주가 되어 통나무를 불 속에서 끄집어내어 개미들이 땅바닥으로 달아날 수 있는 곳으로 던져줄 수 있는 절호의 기회라고 생각했다.

문장분석

But most of them went toward the fire and then back toward the end and swarmed on the cool end and finally fell off into the fire. I remember thinking (at the time) that it was the end of the world and a splendid chance to be a messiah and lift the log off the fire and throw it out where the ants could get off onto the ground.

toward [təwɔ́:rd] …쪽으로, …로 향하여
splendid [spléndid]
  빛나는(glorious), 훌륭한, 멋진, 근사한
messiah [misáiə] 메시아, 구세주, 해방자

lift [lift] 들어 올리다
log [lɔ(:)g] 통나무, 원목, 땔나무

Vocabulary Of The Week

MON

exciting [iksáitiŋ]
흥분시키는, 자극적인,
몹시 흥취를 자극하는
excited [iksáitid] 흥분한, 활발한
thin [θin] 얇은, 가는, 홀쭉한
fat-free 지방이 없는, 무지방의

ruin [rúːin] 파멸, 파산, 파괴하다

TUE

price [prais]
가격, 대가(代價), ~에 값을 매기다
trap [træp] 올가미, 함정, 덫
pregnancy [prégnənsi]
임신, 풍부, 풍만
awfully [ɔ́ːfli] 아주, 무척, 몹시

uncomfortable [ʌnkʌ́mfərtəbəl]
불쾌한, 기분이 언짢은, 거북한

WED

throw [θrou]
(threw [θruː] - thrown [θroun])
(내)던지다
through [θruː]
…을 지나서, …을 꿰뚫어

thorough [θə́ːrou]
철저한, 충분한, 완벽한, 완전한
gratuitous [grətjúːətəs]
무상의, 이유 없는, 불필요한,
정당성이 없는
syphilis [sífəlis] 매독

THU

ant [ænt] 개미
aunt [ænt]
아주머니(이모, 백모, 숙모, 고모)
commence [kəméns]
시작하다, 개시하다

swarm [swɔːrm]
떼, 무리, 때를 짓다, 모여들다
flatten [flǽtn]
평평하게 하다, 고르다, 펴다

FRI

toward [təwɔ́ːrd]
…쪽으로, …로 향하여
splendid [spléndid]
빛나는(glorious), 훌륭한, 멋진, 근사한
messiah [misáiə]
메시아, 구세주, 해방자

lift [lift] 들어 올리다
log [lɔ(ː)g] 통나무, 원목, 땔나무

MON

I'll do anything for you if you won't let her die

만약 그녀를 죽지 않게 해 주신다면 당신을 위해 무슨 일이라도 하겠습니다

I sat outside in the hall. Everything was gone inside of me. I did not think. I could not think. I knew she was going to die and I prayed that she would not. Don't let her die. Oh, God, please don't let her die. I'll do anything for you if you won't let her die.

나는 복도에 앉아 있었다. 몸속에서 모든 것이 빠져나가는 것 같았다. 아무것도 생각나지 않았다. 아무것도 생각할 수 없었다. 지금 그녀가 죽어가고 있다는 것을 알았고, 그래서 제발 죽지 않게 해 달라고 기도를 드렸다. 그녀가 죽지 않게 해주소서. 아, 하느님. 제발 그녀가 죽지 않게 해 주소서. 만약 그녀를 죽지 않게 해 주신다면 당신을 위해 무슨 일이라도 하겠습니다.

I sat outside in the hall. (Everything) inside of me was gone. I did not think. I could

not think. I knew she was going to die and I prayed that she would not (die).

Don't let her die. Oh, God, please don't let her die. I'll do anything for you/ if you

won't let her die.
will not

pray [prei] 기도하다
prayer [prɛər] 빌기, 기도
prayer [préiər] 기도하는 사람

aisle [ail]
(좌석의 사이·건물·열차내 따위의) 통로, 복도
ail [eil] …을 괴롭히다, 고통을 주다, 앓다

You took the baby but don't let her die

당신은 갓난아기를 데려가셨습니다, 하지만 그녀만은 제발 죽지 않게 해 주소서

Please, please, please, dear God, don't let her die. Dear God, don't let her die. Please, please, please don't let her die. God please make her not die. I'll do anything you say if you don't let her die. You took the baby but don't let her die. That was all right but don't let her die. Please, please, dear God, don't let her die.

자비하신 하느님. 그녀가 죽지 않게 해 주소서. 부디, 부디, 부디 그녀가 죽지 않게 해 주소서. 만약 그녀를 죽지 않게 해주신다면, 당신이 시키는 일은 무엇이든지 다 하겠습니다. 당신은 갓난아기를 데려가셨습니다. 하지만 그녀만은 제발 죽지 않게 해 주소서. 어린것을 데려가신 건 괜찮습니다. 하지만 그녀만은 죽지 않게 해주소서. 부디, 부디 인자하신 하느님, 그녀만은 죽지 않게 해주옵소서.

문장분석

Please, please, please, dear God, don't let her die. Dear God, don't let her die. Please, please, please don't let her die. God please make her not die. I'll do anything you say if you don't let her die. You took the baby but don't let her die. That was all right but don't let her die. Please, please, dear God, don't let her die.

implore [implɔ́:r] 간청하다, 애원하다, 탄원하다
stillbirth 사산(死産), 사산아
still [stil] 정지(靜止)한, 움직이지 않는, 말이 없는

abort [əbɔ́:rt] 유산하다(miscarry), 임신을 중절하다
pregnant [prégnənt] 임신한, 풍부한

I'm not afraid. I just hate it

나는 하나도 두렵지 않아요, 다만 죽음이 미울 뿐이에요

"You'll be all right, Cat. I know you'll be all right."
"I meant to write you a letter to have if anything happened, but I didn't do it."
"Do you want me to get a priest or any one to come and see you?"
"Just you," she said. Then a little later, "I'm not afraid. I just hate it."

"곧 완쾌될 거야, 캣. 반드시 일어날 거야."
"만일을 위해 당신에게 편지를 써 두려고 했는데 그러지 못했어요."
"신부님이나 누구, 와 달라고 할까?"
"당신만 있으면 돼요." 그녀가 대답했다. 조금 있다가 다시 말을 이었다. "나는 하나도 두렵지 않아요, 다만 죽음이 미울 뿐이에요."

문장분석

"You'll be all right, Cat. I know you'll be all right."

"I meant to write you a letter to have if anything happened, but I didn't do it."

"Do you want me to get a priest or any one to come and see you?"

"Just you," she said. Then a little later, "I'm not afraid. I just hate it."
Only

meant [ment]
   mean(의미·의도·계획·예정하다)의 과거·과거분사
priest [priːst] 성직자

a little/ a few 약간 있는(긍정)
little/ few 거의 없는(부정)
hatred [héitrid] 증오, 원한, 혐오

You won't do our things with another girl, will you?

우리가 하던 일을 다른 여자하고 똑같이 하지 않을 거지?

"Do you want me to do anything, Cat? Can I get you anything?"
Catherine smiled, "No." Then a little later, "You won't do our things with another girl, or say the same things, will you?"
"Never."
"I want you to have girls, though."
"I don't want them."

"내가 해 줄 건 없어, 캣? 뭘 갖다줄까?"
캐서린이 미소를 지었다. "없어." 그러고 나서 조금 있다가 다시 말을 이었다.
"우리가 하던 일을 다른 여자하고 똑같이 하지 않을 거지? 우리가 하던 말을 다
른 여자하고 똑같이 나누지 않을 거야, 그렇지?"
"물론 안 하고말고."
"하지만 당신에게 여자가 생겼으면 해."
"난 그런 거 필요 없어."

문장분석

"Do you want me to do anything, Cat? Can I get you anything?"

Catherine smiled, "No." Then a little later, "You won't do our things with another
        will not

girl, or say the same things, will you?"

"Never."

"I want you to have girls, though."
                        하지만, 그래도

"I don't want them."

thou [ðau]
  (인칭대명사 2인칭·단수·주격) 너(는),
  그대(는), 당신(은)
though [ðou] (~이기는) 하지만

thought [θɔːt] 생각하기, 사색, 사고
amour [əmúər] (F.) 정사(情事), 바람기, 연애 (사건)
amour fou [F. amuːrfu] 미친 듯한 사랑

After a while I left the hospital and walked back to the hotel in the rain

잠시 뒤 나는 병원을 나와 비를 맞으며 호텔을 향해 발걸음을 옮겼다

"You can't come in yet."
"You get out," I said. "The other one too."
But after I had got them out and shut the door and turned off the light it wasn't any good. It was like saying good-by to a statue. After a while I went out and left the hospital and walked back to the hotel in the rain.

"아직 들어오시면 안 됩니다."
"당신이나 나가요. 다른 분들도요." 내가 소리를 질렀다.
그러나 간호사들을 내보내고 문을 닫고 전등을 꺼도 소용이 없었다. 마치 동상에게 마지막 작별 인사를 하는 것 같았다. 잠시 뒤 나는 병실 밖으로 나와 병원을 뒤로 한 채 비를 맞으며 호텔을 향해 발걸음을 옮겼다.

문장분석

"You can't come in/ yet."

"You, get out," I said. "The other one, too."

But after I had got them out and shut the door and turned off the light/ it wasn't
any good. It was like saying good-by to a statue. After a while/ I went out and left
쓸모 있는
the hospital and walked back to the hotel in the rain.

statue [stǽtʃuː] 상(像), 조상(彫像)   whine [hwain]
static [stǽtik] 정적(靜的)인, 고정된, 정지상태의   애처로운 소리로 울다, 흐느껴 울다, 낑낑거리다
while [hwail] 동안, 시간, 잠시, …하는 동안   rain forest 다우림(多雨林), 열대 우림

Vocabulary Of The Week

MON

pray [prei] 기도하다
prayer [prɛər] 빌기, 기도
prayer [préiər] 기도하는 사람
aisle [ail]
(좌석의 사이·건물·열차내 따위의)
통로, 복도

ail [eil]
…을 괴롭히다, 고통을 주다, 앓다

TUE

implore [implɔ́:r]
간청하다, 애원하다, 탄원하다
stillbirth 사산(死産), 사산아
still [stil]
정지(靜止)한, 움직이지 않는,
말이 없는

abort [əbɔ́:rt]
유산하다(miscarry), 임신을 중절하다
pregnant [prégnənt] 임신한, 풍부한

WED

meant [ment]
mean(의미·의도·계획·예정하다)
의 과거·과거분사
priest [pri:st] 성직자
a little/ a few 약간 있는(긍정)
little/ few 거의 없는(부정)

hatred [héitrid] 증오, 원한, 혐오

THU

thou [ðau]
(인칭대명사 2인칭·단수·주격)
너(는), 그대(는), 당신(은)
though [ðou] (~이기는) 하지만
thought [θɔ:t] 생각하기, 사색, 사고

amour [əmúər]
(F.) 정사(情事), 바람기, 연애 (사건)
amour fou [F. amu:rfu]
미친 듯한 사랑

FRI

statue [stǽtʃu:] 상(像), 조상(彫像)
static [stǽtik]
정적(靜的)인, 고정된, 정지상태의
while [hwail]
동안, 시간, 잠시, …하는 동안

whine [hwain]
애처로운 소리로 울다, 흐느껴 울다,
낑낑거리다
rain forest
다우림(多雨林), 열대 우림

MON

No one has explained what the leopard was seeking at that altitude

이 표범이 무엇을 찾아 그 높은 곳까지 왔는지 아무도 그 이유를 모른다

Kilimanjaro is a snow-covered mountain 19,710 feet high, and is said to be the highest mountain in Africa. Its western summit is called the Masai "Ngaje Ngai," the House of God. Close to the western summit there is the dried and frozen carcass of a leopard. No one has explained what the leopard was seeking at that altitude.

킬리만자로는 해발 19,710피트 높이의 눈 덮인 산으로, 아프리카에서 가장 높다고 한다. 그 서쪽 봉우리는 마사이어로 '응가예 응가이', 즉 '신의 집'이라고 부른다. 서쪽 봉우리 가까운 곳에 얼어서 말라붙은 표범 사체가 있다. 이 표범이 무엇을 찾아 그 높은 곳까지 왔는지 아무도 그 이유를 모른다.

문장분석

Kilimanjaro is a snow-covered mountain (that is) 19,710 feet high, and is said to
━━━━━━━━━━━━━━ ~라고 말해진다

be the highest mountain in Africa. Its western summit is called the Masai "Ngaje
━━━━━━━━━━ ~로 불린다

Ngai," the House of God. Close to the western summit/ there is the dried and

frozen carcass of a leopard. No one has explained what the leopard was seeking

at that altitude.

summit [sʌ́mit]
　정상, 꼭대기, 절정
summit conference(meeting/ talks)
　정상 회담

carcass [kɑ́ːrkəs] (짐승의) 시체, 송장
leopard [lépərd] 표범
altitude [ǽltətjùːd] 높이, 고도

TUE

All he felt now was a great tiredness and anger that this was the end of it

이제 그가 느끼는 것이라곤 끝을 알리는 피로와 분노뿐이었다

Since the gangrene started in his right leg he had no pain and with the pain the horror had gone and all he felt now was a great tiredness and anger that this was the end of it. For this, that now was coming, he had very little curiosity. For years it had obsessed him; but now it meant nothing in itself. It was strange how easy being tired enough made it.

오른쪽 다리에 괴저가 시작된 이후로 그는 아무런 통증을 느끼지 못했고, 통증과 함께 공포도 사라졌다. 이제 그가 느끼는 것이라곤 끝을 알리는 피로와 분노뿐이었다. 지금 다가오고 있는 이것에 그는 호기심이 거의 없었다. 오랫동안 이것에 대한 강박에 사로잡혀 있었지만, 이제 이것은 그 자체로는 아무런 의미가 없었다. 그냥 적당히 피로해지는 것만으로도 쉽게 이렇게 될 수 있다니 신기했다.

문장분석

Since the gangrene started in his right leg/ he had no pain and with the pain/ the horror had gone and all he felt now was a great tiredness and anger that this was the end of it. For this, that now was coming, he had very little curiosity. For years/ it had obsessed him; but now it meant nothing in itself. It was strange how easy being tired enough made it.

그 자체는

gangrene [gǽŋɡriːn] 괴저(壞疽), (도덕적) 부패
curiosity [kjùəriάsəti] 호기심
obsess [əbsés]
 (귀신·망상 따위가) 들리다, 사로잡히다, 괴롭히다

little(few) 거의 없는(부정)
a little(a few) 조금, 약간(긍정)

May 133

What have we done to have that happen to us?

우리가 무슨 짓을 했다고 이런 일이 일어나는 거야?

"It[Money] was always yours as much as mine. I left everything and I went wherever you wanted to go and I've done what you wanted to do. But I wish we'd never come here."

"You said you loved it."

"I did when you were all right. But now I hate it. I don't see why that had to happen to your leg. What have we done to have that happen to us?"

돈은 내 돈인 동시에 언제나 당신 돈이기도 해. 나는 모든 걸 버렸고, 당신이 가고 싶어 하는 곳은 어디든 갔고, 당신이 하고 싶어 하는 건 뭐든 했어. 하지만 여기는 오지 않았으면 좋았어."

"당신이 여기를 사랑한다고 했잖아."

"당신이 괜찮을 때는 그랬지. 하지만 이제는 싫어. 왜 당신 다리에 이런 일이 일어나야 했는지 모르겠어. 우리가 무슨 짓을 했다고 이런 일이 일어나는 거야?

문장분석

"It[Money] was always yours as much as mine. I left everything and I went
　　　　　　　　　　　　　　　　　　　만큼
(wherever) you wanted to go and I've done (what) you wanted to do. But I wish

we'd never come here."

"You said you loved it."

"I did when you were all right. But now I hate it. I don't see (why) that had to
　loved　　　　　　　　　　　　　　　　　　　　　　　　　　이유

happen to your leg. What have we done/ to (have) that (happen) to us?"

hatred [héitrid] 증오, 원한, 혐오　　　　　lap [læp]
regret [rigrét] 유감, 후회(하다)　　　　　　무릎(의자에 앉았을 때 허리에서 무릎까지의 부분)
thigh [θai] 넓적다리　　　　　　　　　　　knee [ni:] 무릎, 정강이 뼈

You're out of your head
당신 머리가 어떻게 되었나 봐

"I loved you. That's not fair. I love you now. I'll always love you. Don't you love me?"
"No," said the man. "I don't think so. I never have."
"Harry, what are you saying? You're out of your head."
"No. I haven't any head to go out of."

"나는 당신을 사랑했어. 그런 말은 부당해. 나는 지금도 당신을 사랑해. 앞으로도 늘 당신을 사랑할 거야. 당신은 나를 사랑하지 않아?"
"그래, 사랑하지 않아. 한 적도 없어."
"해리, 무슨 소리를 하는 거야? 당신 머리가 어떻게 되었나 봐."
"아니. 나는 애초에 어떻게 될 머리가 없는 놈이야."

문장분석

"I loved you. That's not fair. I love you now. I'll always love you. Don't you love me?"

"No," said the man. "I don't think so. I never have (loved you)."

"Harry, what are you saying? You're out of your head."
미쳐서, 열중하여

"No. I haven't any head to go out of."

fair [fɛər] 공평한, 공정한, 올바른
frenzy [frénzi] 격앙시키다, 격노시키다
abnormal [æbnɔ́ːrməl] 보통과 다른, 정상이 아닌

sane [sein] 제정신의, 온건한, 건전한, 분별 있는
insane [inséin] 미친, 발광한, 광기의

It's trying to kill to keep yourself alive, I imagine

내 생각에 그건 자기가 계속 살아 있으려고 남을 죽이려 드는 것과 같아

"Do you think that it is fun to do this? I don't know why I'm doing it. It's trying to kill to keep yourself alive, I imagine. I was all right when we started talking. I didn't mean to start this, and now I'm crazy as a coot and being as cruel to you as I can be. Don't pay any attention, darling, to what I say. I love you, really. You know I love you. I've never loved any one else the way I love you."

"이러는 게 재미있을 거라고 생각해? 내가 왜 이러는지 나도 모르겠어. 내 생각에 그건 자기가 계속 살아 있으려고 남을 죽이려 드는 것과 같아. 처음에 이야기를 시작할 때는 괜찮았어. 나도 이런 걸 시작하려던 건 아니었거든. 그런데 지금나는 얼간이처럼 맛이 가서, 당신한테 있는 대로 잔인하게 굴고 있어. 내가 하는말에 신경 쓰지 마, 응? 사랑해, 정말로. 내가 당신을 사랑하는 거 알잖아. 당신을 사랑하는 것처럼 사랑한 사람은 아무도 없어."

문장분석

"Do you think that it is fun to do this? I don't know why I'm doing it. It's trying to kill (people)/ to keep yourself alive, I imagine. I was all right when we started talking. I didn't mean to start this, and now I'm crazy as a coot and being as cruel to you as I can be. Don't pay any attention, darling, to what I say. I love you, really. You know I love you. I've never loved any one else/ the way I love you."
방식으로

alive [əláiv] 살아 있는, 생존해 있는
coot [kuːt] 큰물닭, 검둥오리, 얼간이
cruel [krúːəl] 잔혹한, 잔인한, 무자비한

attention [əténʃən] 주의, 유의
attendance [əténdəns]
출석(상황), 출근(상황), 참석

136

MON

summit [sʌ́mit]
정상, 꼭대기, 절정
summit conference(meeting/ talks)
정상 회담
carcass [kɑ́ːrkəs]
(짐승의) 시체, 송장

leopard [lépərd] 표범
altitude [ǽltətjùːd] 높이, 고도

TUE

gangrene [gǽŋgriːń]
괴저(壞疽), (도덕적) 부패
curiosity [kjùəriɑ́səti] 호기심
obsess [əbsés]
(귀신·망상 따위가) 들리다,
사로잡히다, 괴롭히다

little(few) 거의 없는(부정)
a little(a few) 조금, 약간(긍정)

WED

hatred [héitrid] 증오, 원한, 혐오
regret [rigrét] 유감, 후회(하다)
thigh [θai] 넓적다리
lap [læp]
무릎(의자에 앉았을 때 허리에서
무릎까지의 부분)

knee [niː] 무릎, 정강이 뼈

THU

fair [fɛər] 공평한, 공정한, 올바른
frenzy [frénzi]
격앙시키다, 격노시키다
abnormal [æbnɔ́ːrməl]
보통과 다른, 정상이 아닌

sane [sein]
제정신의, 온건한, 건전한, 분별 있는
insane [inséin] 미친, 발광한, 광기의

FRI

alive [əláiv] 살아 있는, 생존해 있는
coot [kuːt] 큰물닭, 검둥오리, 얼간이
cruel [krúːəl]
잔혹한, 잔인한, 무자비한
attention [əténʃən] 주의, 유의

attendance [əténdəns]
출석(상황), 출근(상황), 참석

June

06

**You make your own luck, Gig.
You know what makes a good loser?
Practice.**

네 운은 스스로 만들렴, 지그.
무엇이 훌륭한 패배자를 만드는지 아니? 연습이야.

MON

I don't like to leave things behind

뒤에 아무것도 남겨두고 싶지 않아

"You bitch," he said. "You rich bitch. That's poetry. I'm full of poetry now. Rot and poetry. Rotten poetry."
"Stop it. Harry, why do you have to turn into a devil now?"
"I don't like to leave anything," the man said. "I don't like to leave things behind."

"나쁜 년. 돈 많은 부자 년. 이건 시야. 지금 나는 시로 가득해. 헛소리와 시로. 헛소리 같은 시로."
"그만. 해리, 왜 지금 꼭 악마로 바뀌어야 하는 건데?"
"아무것도 남겨두고 싶지 않으니까. 뒤에 아무것도 남겨두고 싶지 않아."

"You bitch," he said. "You rich bitch. That's poetry. I am full of poetry now. Rot and
<u>~로 가득하다</u>

poetry. Rotten poetry."

"Stop it. Harry, why do you have to turn into a devil now?"
<u>바뀌다, 변하다</u>

"I don't like to leave anything," the man said. "I don't like to leave things behind."

bitch [bitʃ]
암컷(개·이리·여우 따위의), 심술궂은 여자,
음란한 여자
poetry [póuitri] 시(poem), 시집

rot [rɑt] 썩음, 부패, 부식
rotten [rɑ́tn] 썩은, 부패한, 더러운
devil [dévl] 악마, (the D-) 마왕, 사탄(Satan)

His lies were more successful with women than when he had told them the truth

그는 진실을 말하는 것보다 거짓을 말하는 것이 더 잘 먹히는 편이었다

It was not her fault that when he went to her he was already over. How could a woman know that you meant nothing that you said; that you spoke only from habit and to be comfortable? After he no longer meant what he said, his lies were more successful with women than when he had told them the truth.

그녀에게 다가갔을 때 그가 이미 끝장난 남자였던 것은 그녀의 잘못이 아니었다. 남자가 하는 말이 전혀 진심이 아니라는 것을, 오로지 습관 때문에, 편해지려고 하는 말일 뿐이라는 것을 여자가 어떻게 알 수 있겠는가? 사실 진심을 말하지 않게 된 이후로, 그는 진실을 말하는 것보다 거짓을 말하는 것이 더 잘 먹히는 편이었다.

문장분석

It was not her fault that when he went to her/ he was already over. How could
가짜 주어   진짜 주어   끝나
a woman know that you meant nothing that you said; that you spoke only from

habit and to be comfortable? After he no longer meant what he said, his lies
                                        더 이상~않다
were more successful with women than when he had told them the truth.

fault [fɔːlt] 과실, 잘못(mistake)
habit [hǽbit] 습관, 버릇, 습성(custom)
habitual [həbítʃuəl]
　습관적인(customary), 습성적인, 버릇의

habitat [hǽbətæt]
　서식 환경, (특히 동식물의) 서식지, 거주지
comfortable [kʌ́mfərtəbəl]
　기분좋은, 편한, 위안의

It was not so much that he lied as that there was no truth to tell

그는 딱히 거짓말을 한다기보다는 말할 진실이 없는 쪽이었다

It was not so much that he lied as that there was no truth to tell. He had had his life and it was over and then he went on living it again with different people and more money, with the best of the same places, and some new ones.

그는 딱히 거짓말을 한다기보다는 말할 진실이 없는 쪽이었다. 그는 자신의 삶을 살았지만 그 삶은 끝이 났으며, 그런 다음에는 다른 사람들과 더불어 더 많은 돈으로, 똑같은 장소 중 가장 좋은 곳에서, 그리고 가끔 새로운 곳에서, 그 삶을 계속 다시 살아갔을 뿐이었다.

문장분석

It was not so much that he lied as that there was no truth to tell. He had had his

life and it was over and then he went on living it again with different people and
　　　　　　끝나다　　　　　　　　　　계속하다

more money, with the best of the same places, and some new ones.
　　　　　　　　　　　　　　　　　　　　　　　　　　　places

not so much A as B A보다는 오히려 B　　　　　truce [tru:s] 정전, 휴전(협정), 쉼, 휴지, 일시적 중지
truth [tru:θ] 진리(眞理), 참　　　　　　　　　false [fɔ:ls] 그릇된, 틀린, 부정확한, 잘못된
moment of truth
　운명의 순간, 결정적 순간, 최후의 일격을 가하는 순간

Africa was where he had been happiest in the good time of his life

아프리카는 그의 삶의 좋았던 시절에 가장 행복하게 지낸 곳이었다

Africa was where he had been happiest in the good time of his life, so he had come out here to start again. They had made this safari with the minimum of comfort. There was no hardship; but there was no luxury and he had thought that he could get back into training that way. That in some way he could work the fat off his soul the way a fighter went into the mountains to work and train in order to burn it out of his body.

아프리카는 그의 삶의 좋았던 시절에 가장 행복하게 지낸 곳이었고, 그래서 다시 시작해보려고 이곳으로 온 것이었다. 그들은 안락을 최소한으로 줄여 이 사파리를 계획했다. 그렇다고 고난을 겪은 것은 아니었다. 하지만 사치도 없었고 그는 그런 식으로 다시 훈련에 들어갈 수 있을 거라고 생각했다. 권투선수가 지방을 태우기 위해 산에 들어가 몸을 쓰고 훈련하는 것과 마찬가지로 그도 어떻게든 노력으로 자신의 영혼의 지방을 벗겨내 버릴 수 있다고 생각한 것이다.

문장분석

Africa was where he had been happiest in the good time of his life, so he had
come out here/ to start again. They had made this safari/ with the minimum of
준비하다
comfort. There was no hardship; but there was no luxury and he had thought
that he could get back into training/ that way. (He had thought) That in some way
그런 방식으로   어떤 방식으로든
he could work the fat off his soul/ the way a fighter went into the mountains/ to
work and train (in order to) burn it out of his body.
~하기 위해서

safari [səfά:ri] (사냥·탐험 등의) 원정 여행, 사파리   comfort [kΛ́mfərt] 위로, 위안
minimum [mínəməm] 최소, 최소(최저)한도   hardship [hά:rdʃip] 고난, 고초
maximum [mǽksəməm]
　최대, 최대한(도), 최대량, 최고치

He had felt the illusion of returning strength of will to work

그는 다시 일할 의지력이 돌아온다는 착각에 빠졌다

She had liked it. She said she loved it. She loved anything that was exciting, that involved a change of scene, where there were new people and where things were pleasant. And he had felt the illusion of returning strength of will to work.

그녀도 좋아했다. 사랑한다고 말했다. 그녀는 흥분할 수 있는 일, 장면전환이 일어나 새로운 사람들이 있고 분위기가 유쾌한 곳에 가게 되는 일이면 무엇이든 사랑했다. 그리고 그는 다시 일할 의지력이 돌아온다는 착각에 빠졌다.

문장분석

She had liked it. She said she loved it. She loved (anything) that was exciting, that involved (a change of scene,) where there were new people and where things were pleasant. And he had felt (the illusion) of returning strength of will to work.

excited [iksáitid] 흥분한, 활발한
exciting [iksáitiŋ] 흥분시키는, 자극적인
involve [inválv] 연루시키다, 포함하다

pleasant [pléznt] 즐거운, 기분좋은, 유쾌한
illusion [ilú:ʒən] 환영(幻影), 환각, 환상, 망상

Vocabulary Of The Week

MON

bitch [bitʃ]
암컷(개·이리·여우 따위의),
심술궂은 여자, 음란한 여자
poetry [póuitri] 시(poem), 시집
rot [rɑt] 썩음, 부패, 부식
rotten [rɑ́tn] 썩은, 부패한

devil [dévl]
악마, (the D-) 마왕, 사탄(Satan)

TUE

fault [fɔːlt] 과실, 잘못(mistake)
habit [hǽbit]
습관, 버릇, 습성(custom)
habitual [həbítʃuəl]
습관적인(customary),
습성적인, 버릇의

habitat [hǽbətæt]
서식 환경, (특히 동식물의) 서식지,
거주지
comfortable [kʌ́mfərtəbəl]
기분좋은, 편한, 위안의

WED

not so much A as B
A보다는 오히려 B
truth [truːθ] 진리(眞理), 참
moment of truth
운명의 순간, 결정적 순간,
최후의 일격을 가하는 순간

truce [truːs]
정전, 휴전(협정), 쉼, 휴지, 일시적 중지
false [fɔːls]
그릇된, 틀린, 부정확한, 잘못된

THU

safari [səfáːri]
(사냥·탐험 등의) 원정 여행, 사파리
minimum [mínəməm]
최소, 최소(최저)한도
maximum [mǽksəməm]
최대, 최대한(도), 최대량, 최고치

comfort [kʌ́mfərt] 위로, 위안
hardship [háːrdʃip] 고난, 고초

FRI

excited [iksáitid] 흥분한, 활발한
exciting [iksáitiŋ]
흥분시키는, 자극적인
involve [inválv]
연루시키다, 포함하다

pleasant [pléznt]
즐거운, 기분좋은, 유쾌한
illusion [ilúːʒən]
환영(幻影), 환각, 환상, 망상

MON

If he lived by a lie he should try to die by it

거짓말로 살아왔다면 거짓말로 죽어야 할 것이다

Now if this was how it ended, and he knew it was, he must not turn like some snake biting itself because its back was broken. It wasn't this woman's fault. If it had not been she it would have been another. If he lived by a lie he should try to die by it. He heard a shot beyond the hill.

그러나 이제 이렇게 끝나는 것이라면 – 그는 이렇게 끝난다는 것을 알고 있었는데 – 등뼈가 부러졌다는 이유로 자신을 물어버린 어떤 뱀처럼 굴어서는 안 되는 것이었다. 그것은 이 여자의 잘못이 아니었다. 이 여자가 아니었다면 다른 여자였을 것이다. 거짓말로 살아왔다면 거짓말로 죽어야 할 것이다. 언덕 너머에서 총소리가 들렸다.

문장분석

Now if this was how it ended, and he knew it was, he must not turn like some
되게 하다
snake biting itself because its back was broken. It wasn't this woman's fault. If it

had not been she/ it would have been another (woman). If he lived by a lie/ he

should try to die by it. He heard a shot/ beyond the hill.
lie

bite [bait] 물다, 물어뜯다   backache [bǽkèik] 요통, 등의 아픔
fault [fɔːlt] 과실, 잘못(mistake)   spine [spain] 등뼈, 척주
false [fɔːls] 그릇된, 틀린, 부정확한, 잘못된

He had destroyed his talent by not using it

그는 사용하지 않음으로써 자신의 재능을 파괴해버렸다

He had destroyed his talent by not using it, by betrayals of himself and what he believed in, by drinking so much that he blunted the edge of his perceptions, by laziness, by sloth, and by snobbery, by pride and by prejudice, by hook and by crook.

그는 재능을 사용하지 않음으로써, 자기 자신과 자신이 믿는 것을 배반함으로써, 술을 너무 마셔 지각의 날을 무디게 함으로써, 게으름으로, 태만으로, 속물 근성으로, 자만심과 편견으로, 어떤 식으로든 기어코 자신의 재능을 파괴해버렸다.

문장분석

He had destroyed his talent/ by not using it, by betrayals of himself and what he
~하는 것
believed in, by drinking so much that he blunted the edge of his perceptions, by
너무~해서   ~하다
laziness, by sloth, and by snobbery, by pride and by prejudice, by hook and by
무슨 짓을 해서라도, 어떻게 해서라도
crook.

betrayal [bitréiəl] 배신, 밀고, 내통
blunt [blʌnt]
 무디게 하다, 날이 안 들게 하다, 무딘, 둔감한
perception [pərsépʃən] 지각(작용), 인식

sloth [slouθ] 마음이 내키지 않음, 게으름, 나태
snobbery [snάbəri] 속물 근성, 신사인 체하기
prejudice [prédʒədis] 편견, 선입관
crook [kruk] 굽은 것, 갈고리

It was a talent but instead of using it, he had traded on it

재능은 재능이었지만 그는 그걸 제대로 사용하지 않고 악용했다

It was a talent all right but instead of using it, he had traded on it. It was never what he had done, but always what he could do. And he had chosen to make his living with something else instead of a pen or a pencil.

그래, 재능은 재능이었지만 그는 그걸 제대로 사용하지 않고 악용했다. 그의 재능은 실제로 그가 해낸 것이었던 적은 한 번도 없고, 늘 그가 앞으로 할 수 있는 어떤 것이었다. 그는 펜이나 연필이 아닌 다른 것으로 생계를 유지하는 쪽을 택했다.

문장분석

It was a talent all right but instead of using it, he had traded on it. It was never
악용하다, 기회로 삼다
what he had done, but always what he could do. And he had chosen to make his
생계를 꾸려 나가다
living with something else instead of a pen or a pencil.
그밖의, 다른

talent [tǽlənt] (타고난) 재주, 재능
gift [gift] 선물, 은혜, (타고난) 재능, 적성(talent)
aptitude [ǽptitùːd]
경향, 습성, 버릇, 기질, 성질, 소질, 재능

instead [instéd] 그 대신에, 그보다도
trade [treid] 장사하다, 매매하다, 거래하다

It was strange that he should be able to give her more for her money

여자에게 여자의 돈을 대가로 많은 것을 줄 수 있다는 것은 이상한 일이었다

It was strange, too, wasn't it, that when he fell in love with another woman, that woman should always have more money than the last one? But when he no longer was in love, when he was only lying, as to this woman, now, it was strange that he should be able to give her more for her money than when he had really loved.

그가 다른 여자를 사랑하게 될 때, 그 여자는 늘 지난번 여자보다 돈이 많다는 것도 이상한 일이었다, 안 그런가? 하지만 그가 더는 사랑을 하지 않게 되었을 때, 거짓말만 하게 되었을 때, 지금, 이 여자에게처럼, 여자에게 여자의 돈을 대가로 많은 것을 줄 수 있다는 것, 정말로 사랑했던 때보다 더 많은 것을 줄 수 있다는 것도 이상한 일이었다.

문장분석

It was strange, too, wasn't it, that when he fell in love with another woman, that
가짜 주어　　　　　　　　　진짜 주어

woman should always have more money than the last one? But when he no
　　　　　　　　　　　　　　　　　　　　　　　　　　　　　　woman

longer was in love, when he was only lying, as to this woman, now, it was strange
더이상~아닌　　　　　　　　　　　　~처럼

that he should be able to give her more for her money than when he had really
　　　　　~할 수 있다

loved.

marriage of convenience
지위·재산을 노린 결혼, 정략결혼

convenience [kənví:njəns] 편리, 편의, 편익

dowry [dáuəri] 지참금, 천부의 재능, 혼수

prenuptial agreement
결혼 전의 약속(합의 내용)

cheat [tʃiːt]
기만하다, 속이다, 바람피우다, 부정행위, 속임수

However you make your living is where your talent lies

무엇을 해서 먹고살든, 거기에 네 재능이 있는 거야

We must all be cut out for what we do, he thought. However you make your living is where your talent lies. He had sold vitality, in one form or another, all his life and when your affections are not too involved you give much better value for the money. He had found that out but he would never write that, now, either. No, he would not write that, although it was well worth writing.

우리 모두 우리가 하고 있는 일에 가장 잘 맞게 태어난 게 분명해, 그는 생각했다. 무엇을 해서 먹고살든, 거기에 네 재능이 있는 거야. 그는 평생 이런 형태로든 저런 형태로든 생명력을 팔아먹었다. 너무 애착을 갖지 않을 때 오히려 돈값을 훨씬 잘할 수 있어. 그는 그 사실을 깨달았지만, 이제는 그것도 결코 쓰지 않을 것이다. 그래, 그것은 정말 쓸 만한 가치가 있었지만, 쓰지 않을 것이다.

문장분석

We must all be cut out for what we do, he thought. However you make your
　　　　　　　　　　　　　　　　　　　　　　　어떤 방식으로 …하더라도　　생계를 꾸리다

living is where your talent lies. He had sold vitality, in one form or another (form),

all his life and when your affections are not too involved/ you give much better
　　　평생　　　　　　　　　　　　　　　　　　　　　　　　　　　　　　　　훨씬

value for the money. He had found that out but he would never write that, now,

either. No, he would not write that, although it was well worth writing.
　　　　　　　　　　　　　　　　　　…이긴 하지만

vitality [vaitǽləti] 생명력, 활력, 생기, 원기　　　value [vǽlju:] 가치, 유용성, 진가, 쓸모
affection [əfékʃən] 애정, 호의　　　　　　　　worth [wəːrθ]
involve [inválv]　　　　　　　　　　　　　　　…의 가치가 있는, …할 만한 가치가 있는
　　말아 넣다, 싸다, 감싸다, 연관시키다

150

Vocabulary Of The Week

MON

bite [bait] 물다, 물어뜯다
fault [fɔːlt] 과실, 잘못(mistake)
false [fɔːls]
　그릇된, 틀린, 부정확한, 잘못된
backache [bǽkèik] 요통, 등의 아픔
spine [spain] 등뼈, 척주

TUE

betrayal [bitréiəl] 배신, 밀고, 내통
blunt [blʌnt]
　무디게 하다, 날이 안 들게 하다,
　무딘, 둔감한
perception [pərsépʃən]
　지각(작용), 인식

sloth [slouθ]
　마음이 내키지 않음, 게으름, 나태
snobbery [snɑ́bəri]
　속물 근성, 신사인 체하기
prejudice [prédʒədis] 편견, 선입관
crook [kruk] 굽은 것, 갈고리

WED

talent [tǽlənt] (타고난) 재주, 재능
gift [gift]
　선물, 은혜, (타고난) 재능, 적성(talent)
aptitude [ǽptitùːd]
　경향, 습성, 버릇, 기질, 성질, 소질, 재능
instead [instéd] 그 대신에, 그보다도

trade [treid]
　장사하다, 매매하다, 거래하다

THU

marriage of convenience
　지위·재산을 노린 결혼, 정략결혼
convenience [kənvíːnjəns]
　편리, 편의, 편익
dowry [dáuəri]
　지참금, 천부의 재능, 혼수

prenuptial agreement
　결혼 전의 약속(합의 내용)
cheat [tʃiːt]
　기만하다, 속이다, 바람피우다,
　부정행위, 속임수

FRI

vitality [vaitǽləti]
　생명력, 활력, 생기, 원기
affection [əfékʃən] 애정, 호의
involve [invɑ́lv]
　말아 넣다, 싸다, 감싸다, 연관시키다

value [vǽljuː]
　가치, 유용성, 진가, 쓸모
worth [wəːrθ]
　…의 가치가 있는,
　…할 만한 가치가 있는

She liked what he wrote and she had always envied the life he led

그녀는 그가 쓴 것을 좋아했으며 늘 그가 사는 것을 부러워했다

It had begun very simply. She liked what he wrote and she had always envied the life he led. She thought he did exactly what he wanted to. The steps by which she had acquired him and the way in which she had finally fallen in love with him were all part of a regular progression in which she had built herself a new life and he had traded away what remained of his old life.

둘 사이는 아주 단순하게 시작되었다. 그녀는 그가 쓴 글을 좋아했으며 늘 그가 사는 것을 부러워했다. 그녀는 그가 자신이 원하는 대로 하는 사람이라고 생각했다. 그녀가 그를 얻어간 단계들과 그녀가 마침내 그를 사랑하게 된 방식은 모두 그녀가 자신을 위해 새로운 삶을 구축해가고 그는 자신의 옛 삶 가운데 남은 것을 팔아버리는 질서 정연한 과정의 일부였다.

문장분석

It had begun very simply. She liked what he wrote and she had always envied (the life) he led. She thought (that) he did exactly what he wanted to. (The steps) by which she had acquired him and (the way) in which she had finally fallen in love with him were all part of a regular (progression) in which she had built herself a new life and he had traded away what remained of his old life.

envy [énvi] 부러워하다, 질투, 부러움
exactly [igzǽktli] 정확하게, 엄밀히
acquire [əkwáiər] 손에 넣다, 획득하다

progression [prəgréʃən] 전진, 진행, 연속, 진보, 발달
remain [riméin] 남다, 남아 있다

152

You don't know the fun it's been to shoot with you

당신하고 같이 사냥하는 게 나한테 얼마나 재미있는 일이었는지 당신은 모를 거야

"I love it. I've loved Africa. Really. If you're all right it's the most fun that I've ever had. You don't know the fun it's been to shoot with you. I've loved the country."

"난 사냥을 사랑해. 나는 아프리카를 사랑했어. 정말로. 당신만 괜찮으면 이게 나한테 평생 가장 재미있는 거야. 당신하고 같이 사냥하는 게 나한테 얼마나 재미있는 일이었는지 당신은 모를 거야. 나는 이 땅을 사랑했어."

문장분석

"I love it. I've loved Africa. Really. If you're all right/ it's (the most fun) that I've ever had. You don't know (the fun) it's been to shoot with you. I've loved the country."

poach [poutʃ]
침입하다, 밀렵하다, 도용하다, 빼내다

poacher [póutʃər]
남의 땅을 침입한 자, 찜통, 밀렵자

fowl [faul] 닭, 가금, 조류
avian influenza 조류인플루엔자
avian [éiviən] 조류의

Just then it occurred to him that he was going to die

바로 그때 그는 자신이 지금 죽음 가까이 다가서고 있다는 생각에 사로잡혔다

She was very good to him. He had been cruel and unjust in the afternoon. She was a fine woman, marvellous really. And just then it occurred to him that he was going to die. It came with a rush; not as a rush of water nor of wind; but of a sudden, evil-smelling emptiness and the odd thing was that the hyena slipped lightly along the edge of it.

그녀는 정말이지 그에게 아주 잘해 주었다. 오후에 그는 잔인했고 부당했다. 그녀는 좋은 여자였다. 정말 굉장한 여자였다. 바로 그때 그는 자신이 지금 죽음 가까이 다가서고 있다는 생각에 사로잡혔다. 그 생각은 빠르게 들이닥쳤다. 그러나 물이나 바람처럼 들이닥치는 것이 아니라, 갑자기 악취를 풍기는 공허처럼 들이닥쳤다. 묘한 것은 하이에나가 그 공허의 가장자리를 따라 가볍게 미끄러지듯 달려갔다는 것이다.

문장분석

She was very good to him. He had been cruel and unjust/ in the afternoon. She was a fine woman, marvellous really. And just then/ it occurred to him that he was going to die. It came with a rush; not as a rush of water nor of wind; but of a sudden, evil-smelling emptiness and the odd thing was that the hyena slipped lightly along the edge of it.

바로 그때 가짜 주어 / 진짜 주어 / …도 또한 …아닌 / ~를 따라서

cruel [krúːəl] 잔혹한, 무자비한
marvelous [máːrvələs] 불가사의한, 이상한, 놀라운, 훌륭한, 굉장한

occur [əkɔ́ːr] (사건 따위가) 일어나다, 생기다
odd [ɑd] 묘한, 이상한
edge [edʒ] 끝머리, 테두리, 가장자리

154

He had loved too much, demanded too much, and he wore it all out

그는 너무 많이 사랑했고, 너무 많이 요구했고, 결국 모두 닳아 없어지게 만들었다

He had never quarrelled much with this woman, while with the women that he loved he had quarrelled so much they had finally, always, with the corrosion of the quarrelling, killed what they had together. He had loved too much, demanded too much, and he wore it all out.

사실 이 여자와는 싸움을 많이 하지 않았다. 반면 예전에 그가 사랑한 여자들과는 싸움을 너무 하는 바람에 결국에는 싸움의 부식력 때문에 그들이 공유했던 것들이 죽고 말았다. 늘 그랬다. 그는 너무 많이 사랑했고, 너무 많이 요구했고, 결국 모두 닳아 없어지게 만들었다.

문장분석

He had never quarrelled much with this woman, while with the women that
he loved/ he had quarrelled so much (that) they had finally, (always, with the
너무~해서 ~하다
corrosion of the quarrelling), killed what they had together. He had loved too
much, demanded too much, and he wore it all out.

quarrel [kwɔ́:rəl] 싸움, 말다툼, 싸우다
squirrel [skwə́:rəl] 다람쥐
corrosion [kəróuʒən] 부식(작용), 침식

demand [dimǽnd]
요구하다, 청구하다, 필요로 하다
wear [wɛər] (wore-worn) 닳게 하다, 써서 낡게 하다

Why had they always quarrelled when he was feeling best?

왜 그들은 늘 그가 가장 기분이 좋을 때 싸웠을까?

He remembered the good times with them all, and the quarrels. They always picked the finest places to have the quarrels. And why had they always quarrelled when he was feeling best? He had never written any of that because, at first, he never wanted to hurt any one and then it seemed as though there was enough to write without it.

그는 그 여자들 모두와 좋았던 시절을 기억했고, 그 여자들과 벌인 싸움을 기억했다. 그들은 언제나 싸우기에 가장 좋은 장소를 골랐다. 왜 그들은 늘 그가 가장 기분이 좋을 때 싸웠을까? 그는 그것에 관해서는 전혀 쓴 적이 없는데, 그것은 우선 누구에게도 상처를 주고 싶지 않았기 때문이고, 두 번째는 그것 말고도 쓸 것이 충분한 것 같았기 때문이다.

문장분석

He remembered the good times with them all, and the quarrels. They always picked (the finest places) to have the quarrels. And why had they always quarrelled when he was feeling best? He had never written any of that because, at first, he
~할 때
never wanted to hurt any one and then it seemed as though there was enough
그 다음에는   마치 …인 것처럼
to write without it.

hurt [hə:rt] 상처 내다, …을 다치게 하다
wound [wu:nd] 부상, 상처, 해치다, 상처 내다
wounded [wú:ndid]
　상처 입은, 부상당한, (마음을) 상한
wind [waind]
　(wound [waund]) (강·길이) 꼬불꼬불 구부러지다,
　굽이치다, 감다, 돌리다

argue [á:rgju:]
　논하다, 논의하다, 논쟁하다, 말다툼하다

156

Vocabulary Of The Week

MON

envy [énvi] 부러워하다, 질투, 부러움
exactly [igzǽktli] 정확하게, 엄밀히
acquire [əkwáiər]
손에 넣다, 획득하다
progression [prəgréʃən]
전진, 진행, 연속, 진보, 발달

remain [riméin] 남다, 남아 있다

TUE

poach [poutʃ]
침입하다, 밀렵하다, 도용하다, 빼내다
poacher [póutʃər]
남의 땅을 침입한 자, 찜통, 밀렵자
fowl [faul] 닭, 가금, 조류
avian influenza 조류인플루엔자

avian [éiviən] 조류의

WED

cruel [krú:əl] 잔혹한, 무자비한
marvelous [má:rvələs]
불가사의한, 이상한, 놀라운,
훌륭한, 굉장한
occur [əkə́:r]
(사건 따위가) 일어나다, 생기다

odd [ɑd] 묘한, 이상한
edge [edʒ] 끝머리, 테두리, 가장자리

THU

quarrel [kwɔ́:rəl]
싸움, 말다툼, 싸우다
squirrel [skwə́:rəl] 다람쥐
corrosion [kəróuʒən]
부식(작용), 침식

demand [dimǽnd]
요구하다, 청구하다, 필요로 하다
wear [wɛər]
(wore-worn) 닳게 하다,
써서 낡게 하다

FRI

hurt [hə:rt]
상처 내다, …을 다치게 하다
wound [wu:nd]
부상, 상처, 해치다, 상처 내다
wounded [wú:ndid]
상처 입은, 부상당한, (마음을) 상한

wind [waind]
(wound [waund]) (강·길이) 꼬불꼬불
구부러지다, 굽이치다, 감다, 돌리다
argue [á:rgju:]
논하다, 논의하다, 논쟁하다,
말다툼하다

He had seen the world change

그는 세상이 바뀌는 것을 보았다

He had seen the world change; not just the events; although he had seen many of them and had watched the people, but he had seen the subtler change and he could remember how the people were at different times. He had been in it and he had watched it and it was his duty to write of it; but now he never would.

그는 세상이 바뀌는 것을 보았다. 사건들만이 아니었다. 물론 많은 사건을 보았고, 또 사람들을 지켜보기도 했지만. 그러나 그는 더 미묘한 변화를 보았고, 사람들이 시대마다 어떻게 달랐는지 기억할 수 있었다. 그는 그 변화 속에 있었으며, 그것을 지켜보았고, 그것에 관해 쓰는 것이 그의 의무였다. 그러나 이제 그는 결코 쓰지 못할 것이었다.

문장분석

He had seen the world change; not just the events; although he had seen many
…이긴 하지만
of them and had watched the people, but he had seen the subtler change and
he could remember how the people were at different times. He had been in it
change
and he had watched it and it was his duty to write of it; but now he never would
가짜 주어   진짜 주어
(write of it).

subtle [sʌtl] 미묘한, 포착하기 힘든, 난해한   duty [djúːti] 의무, 본분, 조세, 관세
shuttle [ʃʌtl] 왕복 운행   duty-free 세금 없는, 면세의
space shuttle 우주 왕복선

So this was how you died, in whispers that you did not hear

그러니까 이렇게 죽는 것이다. 귀에 들리지 않는 소곤거림 속에서

As he looked and saw her well-known pleasant smile, he felt death come again in. This time there was no rush. It was a puff, as of a wind that makes a candle flicker and the flame go tall. So this was how you died, in whispers that you did not hear.

그는 그녀를 보다가 그녀 특유의 유쾌한 미소가 눈에 들어오자 다시 죽음이 다가오고 있다고 느꼈다. 이번에는 빠른 속도로 들이닥치지 않았다. 그냥 한 번 획부는 정도였다. 촛불을 일렁이게 하여 불을 키우는 바람처럼. 그러니까 이렇게 죽는 것이다. 귀에 들리지 않는 소곤거림 속에서.

문장분석

As he looked and saw her well-known pleasant smile, he felt death come again
When   잘 알려진

in. This time/ there was no rush. It was a puff, as of a wind that makes a candle
             like

flicker and the flame go tall. So this was how you died, in whispers that you did

not hear.

pleasant [pléznt] 즐거운, 기분좋은, 유쾌한   flame [fleim] 불길, 불꽃, 화염
puff [pʌf] 훅 불기, 한 번 획 불기   whisper [hwispər] 속삭이다, 속삭임
flicker [flikər] 명멸하다, 깜박이다, 흔들리다

He lay still and death was not there

그는 가만히 누워 있었고, 거기에 죽음은 없었다

Too tired. He was going to sleep a little while. He lay still and death was not there. It must have gone around another street. It went in pairs, on bicycles, and moved absolutely silently on the pavements.

그는 피곤했다. 너무 피곤했다. 잠시 눈을 붙일 생각이었다. 그는 가만히 누워 있었고, 거기에 죽음은 없었다. 다른 거리로 간 것이 틀림없었다. 죽음은 짝을 이뤄 다녔다. 자전거를 타고. 소리 하나 내지 않고 포장도로 위를 움직이고 있었다.

문장분석

Too tired. He was going to sleep a little while. He lay still and death was not there.
　　　　　　　　　　　　　　　　　잠깐 동안　　　　　　　　　　motionless
It must have gone around another street. It went/ in pairs, on bicycles, and
　~했음에 틀림없다
moved absolutely silently on the pavements.

lie [lai] (lay-lain) 눕다, (물건이) 놓여 있다
lay [lei] (p., pp. laid [leid]) 눕히다, (물건을) 놓다
absolutely [æbsəlúːtli] 절대적으로, 무조건, 정말로

pavement [péivmənt] 포장도로, 인도
pave [peiv] (도로를) 포장하다

He thought the very rich were a special glamourous race

그는 부자들이 특별히 매혹적인 부류라고 생각했다

He remembered poor Julian and his romantic awe of them and how he had started a story once that began, "The very rich are different from you and me." And how some one had said to Julian, Yes, they have more money. But that was not humorous to Julian. He thought they were a special glamourous race and when he found they weren't it wrecked him just as much as any other thing that wrecked him.

그는 가난한 줄리언을 떠올렸다. 줄리언은 부자들에 대한 낭만적인 경외감을 갖고 있었고, 한때 "큰 부자들은 너와 나하고는 다르다"는 말로 시작되는 소설에 착수했던 적도 있었다. 그러자 무슨 이유에선지 어떤 사람이 줄리언에게 말했다. 그래, 그 사람들은 돈이 더 많지. 하지만 줄리언에게는 그 말이 재미있게 들리지 않았다. 줄리언은 부자들이 특별히 매혹적인 부류라고 생각했으며, 그렇지 않다는 것을 알았을 때 다른 어떤 일보다도 큰 충격을 받고 박살이 나고 말았다.

문장분석

He remembered poor Julian and his romantic awe of them and how he had

started a story once that began, "The very rich are different from you and me."

And how some one had said to Julian, Yes, they have more money. But that was

not humorous to Julian. He thought (that) they were a special glamourous race

and when he found (that) they weren't (a special glamourous race)/ it wrecked

him/ just as much as any other (thing) that wrecked him.
　　　　　　　　　　다른 어떤 것 못지않게

awe [ɔː] 경외(敬畏), 두려움
awesome [ɔ́ːsəm]
두려운, 무서운, 경외케 하는, 인상적인, 멋진, 근사한

glamorous [ɡlǽmərəs] 매력에 찬, 매혹적인
race [reis] 인종, 종족, 인류
wreck [rek] (배의) 난파, 파괴하다

You know the only thing I've never lost is curiosity

있잖아, 내가 한 번도 잃지 않은 건 딱 하나, 호기심뿐이야

He had just felt death come by again.

"You know the only thing I've never lost is curiosity," he said to her.

"You've never lost anything. You're the most complete man I've ever known."

"Christ," he said. "How little a woman knows. What is that? Your intuition?"

Because, just then, death had come and rested its head on the foot of the cot and he could smell its breath.

그는 막 죽음이 다시 오는 것을 느꼈다. "있잖아, 내가 한 번도 잃지 않은 건 딱 하나, 호기심뿐이야." 그가 그녀에게 말했다.

"당신은 아무것도 잃은 적이 없어. 당신은 내가 아는 가장 완전한 사람이야."

"맙소사, 여자는 정말 아는 게 없어. 그게 뭐야? 당신 직관이야?"

바로 그때 죽음이 와서 침상 발치에 머리를 내려놓았기 때문에 그는 그 숨 냄새를 맡을 수 있었다.

문장분석

He had just felt death come by again.

"You know/ the only thing I've never lost is curiosity," he said to her.

"You've never lost anything. You're the most complete man (whom) I've ever known."

"Christ," he said. "How little a woman knows. What is that? Your intuition?"

거의~않다
Because, just then, death had come and rested its head on the foot of the cot and he could smell its breath.

---

curiosity [kjùəriὰsəti] 호기심
complete [kəmplíːt]
　완전한, 완벽한, 흠잡을 데 없는

intuition [intjuíʃən] 직관(력), 직감
cot [kɑt] 간이 침대, 보조 침대
breath [breθ] 숨, 호흡

Vocabulary Of The Week

MON

subtle [sʌtl]
　미묘한, 포착하기 힘든, 난해한
shuttle [ʃʌtl] 왕복 운행
space shuttle 우주 왕복선
duty [djúːti] 의무, 본분, 조세, 관세
duty-free 세금 없는, 면세의

TUE

pleasant [pléznt]
즐거운, 기분좋은, 유쾌한
puff [pʌf] 훅 불기, 한 번 휙 불기
flicker [flíkər]
　명멸하다, 깜박이다, 흔들리다
flame [fleim] 불길, 불꽃, 화염

whisper [hwíspər] 속삭이다, 속삭임

WED

lie [lai] (lay-lain)
　눕다, (물건이) 놓여 있다
lay [lei]
　(p., pp. laid [leid]) 눕히다,
　(물건을) 놓다

absolutely [æbsəlúːtli]
　절대적으로, 무조건, 정말로
pavement [péivmənt]
　포장도로, 인도
pave [peiv] (도로를) 포장하다

THU

awe [ɔː] 경외(敬畏), 두려움
awesome [ɔ́ːsəm]
　두려운, 무서운, 경외케 하는,
　인상적인, 멋진, 근사한
glamorous [glǽmərəs]
　매력에 찬, 매혹적인

race [reis] 인종, 종족, 인류
wreck [rek] (배의) 난파, 파괴하다

FRI

curiosity [kjùəriɑ́səti] 호기심
complete [kəmplíːt]
　완전한, 완벽한, 흠잡을 데 없는
intuition [ìntjuíʃən] 직관(력), 직감
cot [kɑt] 간이 침대, 보조 침대
breath [breθ] 숨, 호흡

July
07

***Being against evil
doesn't make you good.***

악에 맞선다고 해서 당신이 선한 것은 아니다.

MON

A brave man is always frightened three times by a lion

용감한 남자는 사자 때문에 반드시 세 번 겁을 먹는다

He could hear his wife breathing quietly, asleep. There was no one to tell he was afraid, nor to be afraid with him, and, lying alone, he did not know the Somali proverb that says a brave man is always frightened three times by a lion; When he first sees his track, when he first hears him roar and when he first confronts him.

그는 아내가 조용히 숨을 쉬며 자고 있음을 알 수 있었다. 두렵다고 말할 사람도 함께 두려워할 사람도 없었다. 혼자 누운 그는 이런 소말리아 속담이 있다는 것을 알지 못했다. 용감한 남자는 사자 때문에 반드시 세 번 겁을 먹는다. 처음 사자의 발자국을 볼 때, 처음 사자가 울부짖는 소리를 들을 때, 처음 사자와 마주할 때.

문장분석

He could hear his wife breathing quietly, asleep. There was no one to tell (that) he was afraid, nor (one) to be afraid with him, and, lying alone, he did not know the Somali proverb that says a brave man is always frightened three times by a lion; When he first sees his track, when he first hears him roar and when he first confronts him.

breathe [briːð] 호흡하다, 숨을 쉬다
proverb [právəːrb] 속담, 격언
frighten [fráitn] 두려워하게 하다

roar [rɔːr] (짐승 따위가) 으르렁거리다, 포효하다
confront [kənfránt] …에 직면하다, …와 만나다

That was one of the few things that he really knew

그것은 그가 진정으로 알고 있는 몇 안 되는 것들 가운데 하나였다

His wife had been through with him before but it never lasted. He was very wealthy, and would be much wealthier, and he knew she would not leave him ever now. That was one of the few things that he really knew.

아내는 전에도 그와 끝을 낸 적이 있지만 결코 오래가지는 않았다. 그는 큰 부자였고, 더 큰 부자가 될 것이었기 때문이다. 그는 그녀가 이번에도 자신을 영영 떠나지는 않을 것임을 알았다. 그것은 그가 진정으로 알고 있는 몇 안 되는 것들 가운데 하나였다.

문장분석

His wife had been through with him before but it never lasted. He was very
~와 끝내다
wealthy, and would be much wealthier, and he knew she would not leave him
훨씬
ever now. That was one of the few things that he really knew.
영원히

through [θru:] …을 통하여, …을 꿰뚫어　　wealthy [wélθi] 넉넉한, 유복한, 풍부한
thorough [θə́:rou] 철저한, 충분한, 완벽한　　wealth [welθ] 부(富), 재산
last [læst] 지속하다, 끝다

Fear gone like an operation. Something else grew in its place

마치 수술을 해서 잘라낸 것처럼 공포가 사라졌다. 대신 그 자리에 다른 어떤 것이 들어섰다

Fear gone like an operation. Something else grew in its place. Main thing a man had. Made him into a man. Women knew it too. No bloody fear.

마치 수술을 해서 잘라낸 것처럼 공포가 사라졌다. 대신 그 자리에 다른 어떤 것이 들어섰다. 남자들이 가지고 있는 중요한 것. 그것이 그들을 남자로 만들어주었다. 여자들도 그것을 알았다. 빌어먹을 공포가 그들에게서 사라졌다는 것을.

문장분석

Fear gone like an operation. Something else grew in its place. (Main thing) (that) a
그 외에, 다른
man had. (The main thing) Made him into a man. Women knew it too. No bloody
변화된 결과   change
fear.

fear [fiər] 두려움, 무서움, 공포
operation [ὰpəréiʃən] 수술, 조작, 작동, 운전
bloody [blʌ́di]
  피나는, 어처구니없는, 지독한(damned)

blood [blʌd] 피, 혈액
bleed [bliːd]
  (bled [bled]) 출혈하다, (⋯에서) 피가 흐르다

It was all a nothing and a man was a nothing too

모든 게 허무였고, 사람 또한 허무였다

What did he fear? It was not a fear or dread, It was a nothing that he knew too well. It was all a nothing and a man was a nothing too. It was only that and light was all it needed and a certain cleanness and order. Some lived in it and never felt it but he knew it all was nada y pues nada y nada y pues nada.

그는 뭘 두려워하는 걸까? 두려움이나 걱정은 아니었다. 그가 너무나 잘 알고 있는 허무였다. 모든 게 허무였고, 사람 또한 허무였다. 다만 그것뿐이었기에, 필요한 것은 오직 빛, 그리고 약간의 깨끗함과 질서뿐이었다. 어떤 사람들은 허무 안에 살면서도 결코 그것을 느끼지 못했지만, 그는 그 모두가 나다 이 푸에스 나다 이 나다 이 푸에스 나다임을 알았다.

What did he fear? It was not a fear or dread, It was a nothing that he knew too well. It was all a nothing and a man was a nothing too. It was only that and light was all it needed and a certain cleanness and order. Some lived in it and never felt it but he knew it all was nada y pues nada y nada y pues nada.

dread [dred] 공포, 불안, 두려워하다, 무서워하다
order [ɔ́ːrdər] 명령, 지휘, 질서
certain [sə́ːrtən]
　확신하는, 일정한, 어떤, 어느 정도의

nada [nάːdə] 아무 것도 없음, 무(nothing)
nada y pues nada y nada y pues nada
　(Sp.) 허무 그리고 허무 그리고 허무

He smiled at the face in the mirror and it grinned back at him

그가 거울 속의 얼굴을 향해 웃음을 짓자, 그 얼굴도 그를 보며 싱긋 웃었다

On his way back to the living room he passed a mirror in the dining room and looked in it. His face looked strange. He smiled at the face in the mirror and it grinned back at him. He winked at it and went on. It was not his face but it didn't make any difference.

그는 거실로 돌아오는 길에 다이닝룸의 거울을 지나다 자신의 모습을 보았다. 얼굴이 낯설어 보였다. 그가 거울 속의 얼굴을 향해 웃음을 짓자, 그 얼굴도 그를 보며 싱긋 웃었다. 그는 거울 속의 얼굴을 향해 한쪽 눈을 찡긋한 다음 다시 걸었다. 그의 얼굴이 아니었지만 아무 상관 없었다.

문장분석

On his way back to the living room/ he passed a mirror/ in the dining room and
　　～로 돌아오는 길에
looked in it. His face looked strange. He smiled at the face in the mirror and it
　　　　　　　～처럼 보이다
grinned back at him. He winked at it and went on. It was not his face but it did
　　　　　　　　　　　　　　　　　　　계속
not make any difference.
전혀 차이가 없다, 문제가 안 되다

mirror [mírər] 거울　　　　　　　giggle [gígəl] 킥킥 웃다
dine [dain] 식사하다　　　　　　 wink [wiŋk] 눈을 깜박이다(blink), 눈으로 신호하다
grin [grin] 씩 웃다

Vocabulary Of The Week

MON

breathe [bri:ð] 호흡하다, 숨을 쉬다
proverb [prάvə:rb] 속담, 격언
frighten [fráitn] 두려워하게 하다
roar [rɔ:r]
(짐승 따위가) 으르렁거리다, 포효하다

confront [kənfrʌ́nt]
···에 직면하다, ···와 만나다

TUE

through [θru:]
···을 통하여, ···을 꿰뚫어
thorough [θə́:rou]
철저한, 충분한, 완벽한
last [læst] 지속하다, 끌다

wealthy [wélθi]
넉넉한, 유복한, 풍부한
wealth [welθ] 부(富), 재산

WED

fear [fiər] 두려움, 무서움, 공포
operation [άpəréiʃən]
수술, 조작, 작동, 운전
bloody [blʌ́di]
피나는, 어처구니없는,
지독한(damned)

blood [blʌd] 피, 혈액
bleed [bli:d]
(bled [bled]) 출혈하다,
(···에서) 피가 흐르다

THU

dread [dred]
공포, 불안, 두려워하다, 무서워하다
order [ɔ́:rdər] 명령, 지휘, 질서
certain [sə́:rtən]
확신하는, 일정한, 어떤, 어느 정도의

nada [nά:də]
아무 것도 없음, 무(nothing)
nada y pues nada y nada y
pues nada
(Sp.) 허무 그리고 허무 그리고 허무

FRI

mirror [mírər] 거울
dine [dain] 식사하다
grin [grin] 씩 웃다
giggle [gígəl] 킥킥 웃다

wink [wiŋk]
눈을 깜박이다(blink),
눈으로 신호하다

MON

And therefore never send to know for whom the bell tolls; it tolls for thee

그러니 누구를 위하여 종이 울리는지 알아보려 하지 말라, 그것은 곧 너 자신을 위하여 울리는 것이므로

No man is an island, entire of itself; every man is a piece of the continent, a part of the main. If a clod be washed away by the sea, Europe is the less, as well as if a promontory were, as well as if a manor of they friends's or of thine own were. Any man's death diminishes me, because I am involved in mankind. And therefore never send to know for whom the bell tolls; it tolls for thee.   - John Donne

아무도 자신만으로 완전한 섬이 되지는 않는 것은 모든 사람이 대륙의 한 조각, 본토의 한 부분이기 때문이라. 한 줌 흙이 바닷물에 씻겨 나간다면 유럽은 그만큼 더 작아진다. 이는 하나의 곶이 씻겨 나가고 그대 친구의 혹은 그대의 영지가 씻겨 나갈 때에도 마찬가지이리라. 나는 이 인류에 속해 있으니, 모든 사람의 죽음은 곧 내가 작아지는 것이리라. 그러니 누구를 위하여 종이 울리는지 알아보려 하지 말라. 그것은 곧 너 자신을 위하여 울리는 것이므로.

문장분석

No man is an island, entire of itself; every man is a piece of the continent, a part of the main. If a clod be washed away by the sea, Europe is the less, as well as if a
···뿐만 아니라, 또한
promontory were (washed away), as well as if a manor of thy friends's or of thine
너의 (것)
own were. Any man's death diminishes me, because I am involved in mankind.
Every
And therefore never send to know for whom the bell tolls; it tolls for thee.
you

continent [kántənənt] 대륙, 육지
clod [klɑd] 흙(덩어리)
promontory [práməntɔ̀:ri] 곶, 갑(岬), 융기, 돌기

manor [mǽnər] 장원(莊園), 영지, 소유지
diminish [diminiʃ] 줄이다, 작아지다
involve [inválv] 감싸다, 연루시키다, 관련시키다

Do not try to trap me into thinking

날 꾀어 생각하게 만들려 말라

Golz had said and filled up the glasses again. "You never think about only girls. I never think at all. Why should I? I am Général Sovietique. I never think. Do not try to trap me into thinking."

골스는 말하며 두 사람의 잔에 다시 술을 따랐다. "자네는 오로지 여자에 대해서만 생각을 안 한다고 했지? 난 생각 자체를 안 해. 생각할 필요가 뭐가 있어? 나는 소비에트의 장군이야. 결코 생각 따위는 하지 않지. 그러니 날 꾀어 생각하게 만들려 말게."

Golz had said and filled up the glasses again. "You never think about only girls. I never think at all. Why should I (think)? I am Général Sovietique. I never think. Do not try to trap me into thinking."

general [dʒénərəl] 대장, 장군, 일반의, 보통의
admiral [ǽdmərəl] 해군 대장, (함대) 사령관, 제독
sergeant [sáːrdʒənt] 병장, 부사관

colonel [kə́ːrnəl] 대령, 연대장
trap [træp] 올가미, 함정, 덫을 놓다

Every time Robert Jordan looked at her he could feel a thickness in his throat

로버트 조던은 그녀를 볼 때마다 목구멍이 꽉 막혀 오는 것을 느꼈다

She sat down opposite him and looked at him. He looked back at her and she smiled and folded her hands together over her knees. Her legs slanted long and clean from the open cuffs of the trousers as she sat with her hands across her knees and he could see the shape of her small up-tilted breasts under the gray shirt. Every time Robert Jordan looked at her he could feel a thickness in his throat.

그녀는 맞은편에 앉아서 그를 쳐다보았다. 그도 함께 그녀를 쳐다보았다. 그러자 그녀는 미소를 지으며 무릎 위에다 두 손을 얌전히 포개어 놓았다. 그녀가 무릎 위에 두 손을 가지런히 놓고 앉자 바지의 열린 아랫단으로 길고 깔끔한 다리가 비스듬히 드러나 보였다. 그리고 회색 셔츠 밑으로는 자그마하게 위로 치켜 올라간 가슴이 그 윤곽을 드러냈다. 로버트 조던은 그녀를 볼 때마다 목구멍이 꽉 막혀 오는 것을 느꼈다.

문장분석

She sat down/ opposite him and looked at him. He looked back at her and she smiled and folded her hands together/ over her knees. Her legs slanted long and clean from the open cuffs of the trousers/ as she sat with her hands across her knees and he could see the shape of her small up-tilted breasts/ under the gray shirt. <u>Every time</u> Robert Jordan looked at her/ he could feel a thickness in his throat.
Whenever

knee [niː] 무릎
slant [slænt] 경사, 비탈, 기울다, 경사지다
breast [brest] 가슴, 옷가슴

thickness [θíknis] 두께, 두꺼움, 굵음
throat [θrout] 목

But I feel nothing against it when it is necessary

그러나 필요할 때는 난 그것에 반대하지 않아요

"You like to hunt?"

"Yes, man. More than anything. We all hunt in my village. You do not like to hunt?" "No," said Robert Jordan. "I do not like to kill animals."

"With me it is the opposite," the old man said.

"I do not like to kill men."

"Nobody does except those who are disturbed in the head," Robert Jordan said. But I feel nothing against it when it is necessary. When it is for the cause."

"사냥을 좋아하세요?" 로버트 조던이 물었다.

"그럼요. 그 어떤 것보다도 좋아해요. 우리 동네에서는 모두들 사냥에 열심입니다. 사냥을 싫어하나요?"

"싫어해요. 동물을 죽이는 것이 싫어요."

"난 그 반대요. 난 사람을 죽이는 게 싫어요." 노인이 말했다.

"머리가 이상한 사람을 빼놓고는 다 마찬가지지요. 그러나 필요할 때는 사람을 죽여도 아무런 느낌이 없습니다. 정의를 위해서라면 말입니다." 로버트 조던이 말했다.

문장분석

"You like to hunt?"

"Yes, man. (I like) More than anything. We all hunt in my village. You do not like to hunt?"

"No," said Robert Jordan. "I do not like to kill animals."

"With me/ it is the opposite," the old man said.

"I do not like to kill men."

"Nobody does except (those) who are disturbed in the head," Robert Jordan said.
likes

"But I feel nothing against it when it is necessary. When it is for the cause."
반대하여

opposite [ápəzit]
반대 위치에, 마주보고 있는, 반대쪽의

disturb [distə́:rb] 방해하다, …에게 폐를 끼치다

necessary [nésəsèri] 필요한, 없어서는 안 될

necessity [nisésəti] 필요, 필요성

cause [kɔːz] 원인, 근거, 주장, 주의, 대의명분

If there were God, never would He have permitted what I have seen with my eyes

만약 신이 있다면 내 눈으로 목격한 일이 벌어지지 않았을 겁니다

"Since we do not have God here any more, neither His Son nor the Holy Ghost, who forgives? I do not know."
"You have not God any more?"
"No. Man. Certainly not. If there were God, never would He have permitted what I have seen with my eyes. Let them have God."
"They claim Him."
"Clearly I miss Him, having been brought up in religion. But now a man must be responsible to himself."

"여긴 이미 신도 없고 신의 아들도 없고 또 성령도 없으니까, 누가 누구를 용서해 주는지는 모르겠어요."
"여기 이미 신이 없다고요?"
"그래요. 없는 게 확실해요. 만약 신이 있다면 내 눈으로 목격한 일이 벌어지지 않았을 겁니다. 사람들에게 이제 신이 있었으면 해요."
"사람들은 모두 이게 신의 뜻이라고 주장하는데요."
"나도 신자로 자랐기 때문에 신의 간섭을 간절히 바랍니다. 하지만 지금은 인간이 자신의 행위에 대해 책임을 져야 할 때인 것 같아요."

문장분석

"Since we do not have God here any more, neither His Son nor the Holy Ghost,
Because
who forgives? I do not know."

"You have not God any more?"

"No. Man. Certainly not. If there were God, never would He have permitted what

I have seen with my eyes. Let them have God."

"They claim Him."

"Clearly I miss Him, having been brought up in religion. But now a man must be
기르다, 양육하다
responsible to himself."

ghost [goust] 유령, 영혼
permit [pəːrmít] 허락하다, 허가하다, 인가하다
claim [kleim]
　(당연한 권리로서) 요구하다, 제 것이라고 주장하다

religion [rilídʒən] 종교
responsible [rispánsəbəl]
　책임 있는, 책임을 져야 할, 원인이 되는

Vocabulary Of The Week

MON

continent [kάntənənt] 대륙, 육지
clod [klɑd] 흙(덩어리)
promontory [prάməntɔ̀:ri]
곶, 갑(岬), 융기, 돌기
manor [mǽnər]
장원(莊園), 영지, 소유지

diminish [dimíniʃ] 줄이다, 작아지다
involve [inválv]
감싸다, 연루시키다, 관련시키다

TUE

general [dʒénərəl]
대장, 장군, 일반의, 보통의
admiral [ǽdmərəl]
해군 대장, (함대) 사령관, 제독
sergeant [sά:rdʒənt] 병장, 부사관
colonel [ká:rnəl] 대령, 연대장

trap [træp] 올가미, 함정, 덫을 놓다

WED

knee [ni:] 무릎
slant [slænt]
경사, 비탈, 기울다, 경사지다
breast [brest] 가슴, 옷가슴
thickness [θíknis] 두께, 두꺼움, 굵음
throat [θrout] 목

THU

opposite [άpəzit]
반대 위치에, 마주보고 있는, 반대쪽의
disturb [distə́:rb]
방해하다, …에게 폐를 끼치다
necessary [nésəsèri]
필요한, 없어서는 안 될

necessity [nisésəti] 필요, 필요성
cause [kɔ:z]
원인, 근거, 주장, 주의, 대의명분

FRI

ghost [goust] 유령, 영혼
permit [pə:rmít]
허락하다, 허가하다, 인가하다
claim [kleim]
(당연한 권리로서) 요구하다,
제 것이라고 주장하다

religion [rilídʒən] 종교
responsible [rispάnsəbəl]
책임 있는, 책임을 져야 할,
원인이 되는

MON

It is necessary to drink much of that for me to seem beautiful

술 취한 눈에는 제가 더 예뻐 보일 거예요

Maria filled his cup with wine. "Drink that," she said. "It will make me seem even better. It is necessary to drink much of that for me to seem beautiful." "Then I had better stop," Robert Jordan said. "Already thou seemest beautiful and more." "That's the way to talk," the woman said. "You talk like the good ones. What more does she seem?" "Intelligent," Robert Jordan said lamely.

마리아가 그의 잔에 와인을 따라 주며 말했다. "이걸 마셔요. 술 취한 눈에는 제가 더 예뻐 보일지도 모르니까." "그렇다면 마시지 말아야겠군. 당신은 이미 아름다워 보이니까." "그럼요. 그렇게 말해야죠. 당신은 여자한테 말하는 법을 알고 있군요. 또 어떻게 보여요?" 필라르가 물었다. "똑똑해 보여요." 로버트 조던은 다소 수줍은 듯 말했다.

문장분석

Maria filled his cup with wine. "Drink that," she said. "It will make me seem even better.
훨씬
It is necessary to drink much of that for me to seem beautiful." "Then I
의미상 주어
had better stop," Robert Jordan said. "Already thou seemest beautiful and more."
you
"That's the way to talk," the woman said. "You talk like the good ones. What more
일반인
does she seem?" "Intelligent," Robert Jordan said lamely.

thou [ðau] 너(you)
thee [ðiː] 너에게(you), 너를(you)
thine [ðain] 너의(your), 너의 것(yours)

intelligent [intélədʒənt] 지적인, 지성을 갖춘
lame [leim]
절름발이의, 절룩거리는, 어설픈, 서투른, 약한

I care much for jokes but not in the form of address

난 농담을 좋아하지만 사람을 부를 때는 농담을 하지 않아요

"I don't joke that way," Robert Jordan said. "In the joking commences a rottenness."

"Thou art very religious about thy politics," the woman teased him. "Thou makest no jokes?"

"Yes. I care much for jokes but not in the form of address. It is like a flag."

"I could make jokes about a flag. Any flag," the woman laughed. "The old flag of yellow and gold we called pus and blood. The flag of the Republic with the purple added we call blood, pus and permanganate."

"난 그런 식으로 농담을 하지 않아요. 농담을 하다 보면 부패가 시작되는 법입니다."

"당신은 정치를 아주 진지하게 생각하는군요. 그래, 그 때문에 전혀 농담을 하지 않나요?" 필라르가 놀리듯이 말했다.

"물론 합니다. 또 좋아하고요. 그러나 사람을 부를 때는 농담을 하지 않아요. 사람의 이름은 깃발 같은 것이니까요."

"난 깃발에 대해서도 농담을 할 수 있어요. 노란 바탕에 황금이 그려진 옛날 깃발은 고름과 피라고 불렀고, 그 옛날 깃발에 자주색이 가미된 공화국 깃발을 보고 피, 고름 그리고 석류(石榴)라고 불렀지."

문장분석

"I don't joke that way," Robert Jordan said. "In the joking/ commences (a rottenness)."
그런 식으로

"Thou art very religious about thy politics," the woman teased him. "Thou makest
You are   your
no jokes?"

"Yes. I care much for jokes but not in the form of address. It is like a flag."
            like much

"I could make jokes about a flag. Any flag," the woman laughed. "The old flag

of yellow and gold/ we called pus and blood. The flag of the Republic with the

purple added/ we call blood, pus and permanganate."

commence [kəméns] 시작하다, 개시하다
rotten [rátn] 썩은, 부패한, 타락한
tease [tiːz]
　집적거리다, 애타게 하다, 괴롭히다, 희롱하다

address [ədrés] 응대, 말하는 태도, 주소
pus [pʌs] 고름
permanganate [pəːrmǽŋɡənèit]
　석류(돌처럼 단단하게 된 혹)

Now I know why I have felt as I have

이제야 내가 왜 그런 기분을 느꼈는지 그 이유를 알 것 같아요

"Now I know why I have felt as I have," Maria said. "Now it is clear."
"Qué va,"
Robert Jordan said and reaching over, he ran his hand over the top of her head. He had been wanting to do that all day and now he did it, he could feel his throat swelling.

"이제야 내가 왜 그런 기분을 느꼈는지 그 이유를 확실히 알 것 같아요. 이제 분명해졌어요." 마리아가 말했다.
"뭐죠?"
로버트 조던은 그렇게 말하면서 손을 뻗어 그녀의 머리를 쓰다듬었다. 그는 하루 종일 그렇게 하고 싶었고 이제 그렇게 해보니 다시 목이 메었다.

문장분석

"Now I know why I have felt as I have," Maria said. "Now it is clear."

"Qué va,"

Robert Jordan said and reaching over, he ran his hand over the top of her head.

He had been wanting to do that/ all day and now he did it, he could feel his
온종일
throat swelling.

---

qué va (Sp.) 뭔데?　　　　　　　　　choke [tʃouk]
throat [θrout] 목(구멍)　　　　　　　　질식시키다, …을 숨막히게 하다, 막다, 메우다
swell [swel] 복받치다, 부풀다, 팽창하다, 부어오르다　inhale [inhéil] 빨아들이다, 흡입하다

I wanted you to do that all day

당신이 그렇게 해주기를 온종일 기다렸어요

She moved her head under his hand and smiled up at him and he felt the thick but silky roughness of the cropped head rippling between his fingers. Then his hand was on her neck and then he dropped it. "Do it again," she said. "I wanted you to do that all day."

그녀는 머리를 부드럽게 움직여 그를 올려다보며 미소를 지었다. 부드러우면서도 뻣뻣한 짧은 머리가 그의 손가락에 느껴졌다. 그는 잠시 그녀의 목을 쓰다듬다가 손을 내렸다. "다시 한번 해줘요. 당신이 그렇게 해주기를 온종일 기다렸어요." 그녀가 말했다.

문장분석

She moved her head under his hand and smiled up at him and he felt the thick but silky roughness of the cropped head rippling between his fingers. Then his hand was on her neck and then he dropped it. "Do it again," she said. "I wanted you to do that/ all day."

thick [θik] 두꺼운, 굵은, 진한
silky [silki] 비단 같은, 보드라운, 매끄러운(smooth)
rough [rʌf] 거친, 거칠거칠한, 껄껄한

crop [krɑp]
(끝을) 잘라내다, …의 털을 깎다, 농작물이 나다
ripple [ripəl] 잔물결이 일다, 물결 모양이 되다

Where do the noses go? I always wondered where the noses would go

코는 어떻게 해요? 코를 어디다 둬야 하는지 늘 궁금했어요

"Kiss me a little."
"I do not know how."
"Just kiss me." She kissed him on the cheek.
"No."
"Where do the noses go? I always wondered where the noses would go."
"Look, turn thy head,"

"살짝 키스해 줘요."
"어떻게 하는지 몰라요."
"그저 키스하면 돼요." 그녀는 뺨에다 키스했다.
"아니야."
"코는 어느 쪽으로 해요? 코를 어디로 둬야 하는지 늘 궁금했어요."
"고개를 돌리면 돼요."

문장분석

"Kiss me a little." "I do not know how (to kiss)." "Just kiss me." She kissed him on
조금, 약간
the cheek. "No." "Where do the noses go? I always wondered where the noses
would go." "Look, turn thy head,"
                           your

cheek [tʃiːk] 뺨, 볼
wonder [wʌ́ndər] 놀라다, 궁금하다
collarbone [kɑ́lərbòun] 쇄골, 빗장뼈

nape [neip] 목덜미
nasal [néizəl] 코의, 콧소리의, 비음의

Vocabulary Of The Week

MON

thou [ðau] 너(you)
thee [ði:] 너에게(you), 너를(you)
thine [ðain]
  너의(your), 너의 것(yours)
intelligent [intéləʤənt]
  지적인, 지성을 갖춘

lame [leim]
  절름발이의, 절룩거리는, 어설픈,
  서투른, 약한

TUE

commence [kəméns]
  시작하다, 개시하다
rotten [rátn] 썩은, 부패한, 타락한
tease [ti:z]
  집적거리다, 애타게 하다, 괴롭히다,
  희롱하다

address [ədrés]
  응대, 말하는 태도, 주소
pus [pʌs] 고름
permanganate [pəːrmǽŋgənèit]
  석류(돌처럼 단단하게 된 혹)

WED

qué va (Sp.) 뭔데?
throat [θrout] 목(구멍)
swell [swel]
  복받치다, 부풀다, 팽창하다,
  부어오르다

choke [tʃouk]
  질식시키다, …을 숨막히게 하다, 막다,
  메우다
inhale [inhéil] 빨아들이다, 흡입하다

THU

thick [θik] 두꺼운, 굵은, 진한
silky [sílki]
  비단 같은, 보드라운,
  매끄러운(smooth)
rough [rʌf] 거친, 거칠거칠한, 껄껄한

crop [krɑp]
  (끝을) 잘라내다, …의 털을 깎다,
  농작물이 나다
ripple [rípəl]
  잔물결이 일다, 물결 모양이 되다

FRI

cheek [tʃi:k] 뺨, 볼
wonder [wʌ́ndər] 놀라다, 궁금하다
collarbone [kɑ́lərbòun]
  쇄골, 빗장뼈
nape [neip] 목덜미
nasal [néizəl] 코의, 콧소리의, 비음의

MON

In mountains there are only two directions, down and up

산에는 방향이 두 군데밖에 없어. 위로 올라가거나 내려가거나

"So do I like the pines, but we have been too long in these pines. Also I am tired of the mountains. In mountains there are only two directions. Down and up and down leads only to the road and the towns of the Fascists."

"나도 소나무를 좋아하기는 해. 하지만 이 소나무 숲에 너무 오래 있었어. 그리고 산이라면 이제 지긋지긋해. 산에는 방향이 두 군데밖에 없어. 위로 올라가거나 내려가거나 둘 중 하나야. 그런데 아래로 내려가면 도로가 나오는데 파시스트들이 사는 마을로 가는 길이지."

문장분석

"So do I like the pines, but we have been too long in these pines. Also I am tired
　　　　　　　　　　　　　　　　　　　　　　　　　　　　　　　　　　~에 질리다
of the mountains. In mountains/ there are only two directions. Down and up/
and down leads only to the road and the towns of the Fascists."

pine [pain] 솔, 소나무(~ tree)	direction [dirékʃən] 지도, 지시, 사용법, 방향
tired of	so 동사 주어 too(동의)
지긋지긋한(fed up with, sick of, sick and tired of)	so 주어 동사 really(강조)

TUE

Do you know how an ugly woman feels?

당신은 못생긴 여자의 마음을 알아요?

"Thou art not ugly."
"Vamos, I'm not ugly. I was born ugly. All my life I have been ugly. You, Inglés, who know nothing about women. Do you know how an ugly woman feels? Do you know what it is to be ugly all your life and inside to feel that you are beautiful? It is very rare."

"당신은 못생기지 않았어요."
"하긴, 내가 못생긴 건 아니지. 다만 그렇게 태어났을 뿐이지. 평생 동안 이런 얼굴이었지. 이봐요, 영국 양반, 당신은 여자에 대해서 잘 모르지요? 당신은 못생긴 여자의 마음을 알아요? 평생 동안 못생긴 얼굴을 하고 다녔으면서도 속으로는 자신이 아름답다고 생각하는 게 어떤 건지 알아? 그건 아주 이상한 거예요."

문장분석

"Thou art not ugly."
　　You are

"Vamos, I'm not ugly. I was born ugly. All my life/ I have been ugly. You, Inglés,
(Sp.) 이런!, 야!　　　　　　　　　　　　　　　한평생

who know nothing about women. Do you know how an ugly woman feels?

Do you know what it is to be ugly all your life and inside/ to feel that you are

beautiful? It is very rare."

inglés (Sp.) 영국 태생의, 영국의, 영어
rare [rɛər] 드문, 진기한, 유례없는
rarely [rɛ́ərli] 드물게, 좀처럼 …하지 않는(seldom)

art [ɑːrt] are(thou를 주어로)
enchant [entʃǽnt]
매혹하다, 황홀케 하다, …의 마음을 호리다

July 185

Yet one has a feeling within one that blinds a man while he loves you

그러나 남자의 사랑을 받으면 여자의 내부에서는 남자를 눈멀게 하는 감정이 생겨요

"Yet one has a feeling within one that blinds a man while he loves you. You, with that feeling, blind him, and blind yourself. Then one day, for no reason, he sees you ugly as you really are and he is not blind any more and then you see yourself as ugly as he sees you and you lose your man and your feeling."

"그러나 남자의 사랑을 받으면 여자의 내부에서는 남자를 눈멀게 하는 감정이 생겨요. 그런 감정으로 남자를 눈멀게 하고 심지어 자기 자신도 눈멀게 하지. 그러다가 어느 날 갑자기 남자는 그 눈먼 상태에서 깨어나 여자가 정말로 못생겼다는 것을 보게 되는 거죠. 그러면 여자는 남자를 잃게 되고 그 황홀한 기분도 사라지고 말아요."

문장분석

"Yet one has a feeling (within one) that blinds a man while he loves you. You, with
일반인
that feeling, blind him, and blind yourself. Then one day, for no reason, he sees
이유 없이
you ugly as you really are (ugly) and he is not blind any more and then you see

yourself as ugly as he sees you and you lose your man and your feeling."

blind [blaind] 눈멀게 하다, 눈먼
reason [ríːzən] 이유(cause), 까닭, 이성, 판단력
lose [luːz] 잃다, 놓쳐버리다

loss [lɔ(ː)s] 잃음, 분실, 상실
loose [luːs] 매지 않은, 풀린, 흐트러진

Now I think I am past it, but it still might come

이제 내 나이는 그럴 때가 지났지만 그런 일이 다시 올 수도 있어요

"After a while, when you are as ugly as I am, as ugly as women can be, then, as I say, after a while the feeling, the idiotic feeling that you are beautiful, grows slowly in one again. It grows like a cabbage. And then, when the feeling is grown, another man sees you and thinks you are beautiful and it is all to do over. Now I think I am past it, but it still might come. You are lucky, guapa, that you are not ugly."

"그러나 시간이 한참 지나면 말이에요, 나처럼 못생긴 여자도 자신이 못생겼다는 그런 생각이 서서히 사라지고 자신이 다시 아름다워졌다는 바보 같은 생각이 다시 꽃피는 거예요. 마치 양배추처럼. 그리고 그런 감정이 풍성해지고 다른 남자가 그런 상태의 여자를 눈여겨보게 되면 다시 사랑이 시작되는 거죠. 이제 내 나이는 그럴 때가 지났지만 그런 일이 다시 올 수도 있어요. 이쁜이, 넌 못생기지 않아서 얼마나 다행이야."

문장분석

"After a while, when you are as ugly as I am, as ugly as women can be, then, as I say, after a while the feeling, (the idiotic feeling) that you are beautiful, grows
한참 후
slowly in one again. It grows like a cabbage. And then, when the feeling is grown,
일반인
another man sees you and thinks you are beautiful and it is all to do over. Now I
다시 하다
think (that) I am past it, but it still might come. You are lucky, guapa, that you are
not ugly."

guapa (Sp.) 잘생긴, 예쁜 (여성용 형용사) idiom [ídiəm] 숙어, 관용구
idiotic [idiátik] 백치의, 천치의   cabbage [kǽbidʒ] 양배추
idiot [ídiət] 천치, 바보

There is nothing that I cannot hear

어떤 얘기라도 들을 수 있어요

"And what happened?"

"Much," the woman said. "Much. And all of it ugly. Even that which was glorious."

"Tell me about it," Robert Jordan said. "It is brutal," the woman said. "I do not like to tell it before the girl."

"Tell it," said Robert Jordan. "And if it is not for her, that she should not listen."

"I can hear it," Maria said.

She put her hand on Robert Jordan's. "There is nothing that I cannot hear."

"It isn't whether you can hear it," Pilar said. "It is whether I should tell it to thee and make thee bad dreams."

"그래, 그다음은 어떤 일이 벌어졌나요?"

"많은 일이 벌어졌지. 죄다 추악한 일뿐이었어요. 한때 영광스러웠던 것조차 말이에요. 모두 끔찍한 일이에요. 마리아 앞에서는 그 얘기를 하고 싶지 않아요."

"말해 보세요. 마리아는 자기와 관계없는 얘기라면 안 들으면 됩니다."

"괜찮아요. 어떤 얘기라도 들을 수 있어요." 마리아가 로버트 조던의 손을 잡으며 말했다.

"물론 들을 수 없는 것은 아니지. 괜히 그런 얘기를 듣고서 꿈자리가 뒤숭숭하게 만들까 봐 그러는 거지."

문장분석

"And what happened?"

"Much," the woman said. "Much. And all of it ugly. Even that which was glorious."
심지어

"Tell me about it," Robert Jordan said. "It is brutal," the woman said. "I do not like

to tell it/ before the girl."

"Tell it," said Robert Jordan. "And if it is not for her, she should not listen that." "I

can hear it," Maria said.

She put her hand on Robert Jordan's (hand). "There is nothing that I cannot hear."

"It isn't whether you can hear it," Pilar said. "It is whether I should tell it to thee
you

and make thee bad dreams."

glorious [glɔ́:riəs] 영광스러운, 명예로운
brutal [brú:tl] 잔인한, 짐승의
brute [bru:t] 짐승, 금수

whether [hwéðər] …인지 어떤지
weather [wéðər] 일기, 기후, 기상, 날씨

Vocabulary Of The Week

July
WEEK 4

MON

pine [pain] 솔, 소나무(~ tree)
tired of
　지긋지긋한(fed up with, sick of,
　sick and tired of)
direction [dirékʃən]
　지도, 지시, 사용법, 방향

so 동사 주어 too(동의)
so 주어 동사 really(강조)

TUE

inglés
　(Sp.) 영국 태생의, 영국의, 영어
rare [rɛər] 드문, 진기한, 유례없는
rarely [réərli]
　드물게, 좀처럼 …하지 않는(seldom)
art [ɑːrt] are(thou를 주어로)

enchant [entʃǽnt]
　매혹하다, 황홀케 하다,
　…의 마음을 호리다

WED

blind [blaind] 눈멀게 하다, 눈먼
reason [ríːzən]
　이유(cause), 까닭, 이성, 판단력
lose [luːz] 잃다, 놓쳐버리다
loss [lɔ(ː)s] 잃음, 분실, 상실
loose [luːs] 매지 않은, 풀린, 흐트러진

THU

guapa
　(Sp.) 잘생긴, 예쁜 (여성용 형용사)
idiotic [ìdiɑ́tik] 백치의, 천치의
idiot [ídiət] 천치, 바보
idiom [ídiəm] 숙어, 관용구
cabbage [kǽbidʒ] 양배추

FRI

glorious [glɔ́ːriəs]
　영광스러운, 명예로운
brutal [brúːtl] 잔인한, 짐승의
brute [bruːt] 짐승, 금수
whether [hwéðər] …인지 어떤지

weather [wéðər]
　일기, 기후, 기상, 날씨

August
08

When you start to live outside yourself,
it's all dangerous.

당신을 벗어난 삶을 살기 시작했다면 그건 모두 위험한 일이다.

All his life he would remember the curve of her throat

그는 한평생 그녀 목덜미의 곡선을 기억할 것이다

Then there was the smell of heather crushed and the roughness of the bent stalks under her head and the sun bright on her closed eyes and all his life he would remember the curve of her throat with her head pushed back into the heather roots and her lips that moved smally and by themselves and the fluttering of the lashes on the eyes tight closed against the sun and against everything.

그는 뭉개진 히스의 냄새와 마리아의 머리 아래서 꺾어진 거친 풀 줄기를 느낄 수 있었다. 햇빛이 그녀의 감은 눈 위로 쏟아졌다. 그는 한평생 이 순간을 기억할 것이다. 히스의 뿌리 사이로 그녀의 뒤로 젖혀진 머리가 파묻혔을 때, 부드러운 그녀의 목덜미가 위로 드러나고 자그마한 입술이 저절로 움직이고 그녀의 두 눈은 햇빛도 그 무엇도 보지 않으려는 듯 감겨져 있는 그 순간을.

문장분석

Then there was the smell of (heather) (that was) crushed and the roughness of

the bent stalks under her head and the sun bright on her closed eyes and all his
한평생
life/ he would remember the curve of (her throat) with her head pushed back into

the heather roots and (her lips) that moved smally and by themselves and the
저절로
fluttering of (the lashes on the eyes) (that were) tight closed against the sun and

against everything.

heather [héðər] 히스(heath)속(屬)의 식물
crush [krʌʃ] 눌러서 뭉개다, 짓밟다, 으깨다
stalk [stɔːk] 줄기, 대, 잎자루

flutter [flʌtər]
퍼덕거리다, 날개 치며 날다, 떨리다, 실룩거리다
lash [læʃ] 속눈썹(eyelash)

For her everything was red, orange, gold-red from the sun on the closed eyes

눈 감은 그녀에게는 모든 것이 붉은색, 오렌지색, 황금색이었다

For her everything was red, orange, gold-red from the sun on the closed eyes, and it all was that color, all of it, the filling, the possessing, the having, all of that color, all in a blindness of that color.

눈 감은 그녀에게는 모든 것이 붉은색, 오렌지색, 황금색이었다. 사랑은 모두 그 색깔이었다. 그 모든 것, 충만, 소유 등이 모두 그 색깔이었으며 혹은 그 색깔의 맹목적인 현란함이었다.

For her/ everything was red, orange, gold-red from the sun on the closed eyes, and (it all) was that color, all of it, the filling, the possessing, the having, all of that color, all in a blindness of that color.

possess [pəzés] 소유하다, 지니다
blindness [bláindnis] 맹목, 무분별
indigo [índigòu] 쪽(물감), 남색

violet [váiəlit] 보랏빛
ultraviolet 자외선(의)

He felt the earth move out and away from under them

그는 두 사람 밑에서 땅이 움직이더니 쑥 꺼져 버리는 느낌을 받았다

For him it was a dark passage which led to nowhere, then to nowhere, then again to nowhere, once again to nowhere, always and forever to nowhere. They were both there, time having stopped and he felt the earth move out and away from under them.

그에게 있어서 사랑은 아무리 그 어떤 곳에 이르고자 하여도 도저히 도달할 수 없는, 그리하여 그 어느 곳에도 영원히 이르지 못할 것 같은 어두운 통로였다. 그들은 함께 동시에 그런 상태에 도달했고 시간은 완전히 정지해 버렸다. 그는 두 사람 밑에서 땅이 움직이더니 쑥 꺼져 버리는 느낌을 받았다.

문장분석

For him/ it was (a dark passage) which led to nowhere, then to nowhere, then again to nowhere, once again to nowhere, always and forever to nowhere. They were both there, time having stopped and he felt the earth (move) out and away from under them.

passage [pǽsidʒ] 통행, 통과, 통로, 악절, 부분
reach [riːtʃ] ⋯에 도착하다, ⋯에 도달하다
leech [liːtʃ] 거머리

earth [əːrθ] 흙, 땅 지구(the ~)
earthen [ə́ːrθən] 흙으로 만든, 흙의

But do not tell any one else that, he thought

그러나 이건 누구에게도 말해서는 안 된다고 생각했다

What were his politics then? He had none now, he told himself. But do not tell any one else that, he thought. Don't ever admit that. And what are you going to do afterwards? I am going back and earn my living teaching Spanish as before, and I am going to write a true book. I'll bet, he said. I'll bet that will be easy.

그럼 네 정치적 신념은 무엇인가? 현재로서는 그런 신념이 없지. 그는 혼잣말을 했다. 그러나 이건 누구에게도 말해서는 안 된다고 생각했다. 그런 건 인정조차 하지 말아야 해. 그럼 나중엔 뭘 할 거지? 전처럼 스페인어 강사로 생계를 꾸려 나가게 되겠지. 그리고 진실한 책을 쓰겠지. 장담하건대, 지금 생각으로는 책을 쓰는 일이 그렇게 어려울 것 같지 않아.

What were his politics then? He had none now, he told himself. But do not tell any one else that, he thought. Don't ever admit that. And what are you going to
혹시라도
do afterwards? I am going back and earn my living teaching Spanish as before,
생계를 유지하다
and I am going to write a true book. I'll bet, he said. I'll bet that will be easy.
확신하건대

politics [pálitiks] 정치, 정치학
politician [pàlətíʃən] 정치가
asylum [əsáiləm] (보호) 시설, 피난처, 도피처

admit [ædmít] 허가하다, 인정하다
afterwards [ǽftərwərdz]
나중에, 그후(afterward)

To be bigoted you have to be absolutely sure that you are right

독선적인 사람이 되기 위해서는 먼저 자기 자신이 절대로 옳다는 확신이 있어야
한다

Bigotry is an odd thing. To be bigoted you have to be absolutely sure that you are right and nothing makes that surety and righteousness like continence. Continence is the foe of heresy.

독선이란 참으로 이상한 것이다. 독선적인 사람이 되기 위해서는 먼저 자기 자
신이 절대로 옳다는 확신이 있어야 한다. 그리고 절제만큼 그런 확신과 독선을
가능하게 해 주는 것도 없다. 금욕은 이단자들의 적이다.

문장분석

Bigotry is an odd thing. To be bigoted/ you <u>have to</u> be absolutely sure that you

_{must}

are right and (nothing) makes that surety and righteousness (like continence).

Continence is the foe of heresy.

bigotry [bígətri] 편협, 독선
bigoted [bígətid] 편협한, 고집불통의
odd [ɑd] 이상한, 묘한

continence [kántənəns] 자제, 절제, 금욕
heresy [hérəsi] 이교, 이단, 이교 신앙
foe [fou] 적, 원수

MON

heather [héðər]
히스(heath)속(屬)의 식물
crush [krʌʃ]
눌러서 뭉개다, 짓밟다, 으깨다
stalk [stɔːk] 줄기, 대, 잎자루

flutter [flʌ́tər]
퍼덕거리다, 날개 치며 날다, 떨리다,
실룩거리다
lash [læʃ] 속눈썹(eyelash)

TUE

possess [pəzés] 소유하다, 지니다
blindness [blaindnis] 맹목, 무분별
indigo [índigòu] 쪽(물감), 남색
violet [váiəlit] 보랏빛
ultraviolet 자외선(의)

WED

passage [pǽsidʒ]
통행, 통과, 통로, 악절, 부분
reach [riːtʃ]
…에 도착하다, …에 도달하다
leech [liːtʃ] 거머리
earth [əːrθ] 흙, 땅 지구(the ~)

earthen [ə́ːrθən] 흙으로 만든, 흙의

THU

politics [pálitiks] 정치, 정치학
politician [pàlətíʃən] 정치가
asylum [əsáiləm]
(보호) 시설, 피난처, 도피처
admit [ædmít] 허가하다, 인정하다

afterwards [ǽftərwərdz]
나중에, 그후(afterward)

FRI

bigotry [bígətri] 편협, 독선
bigoted [bígətid] 편협한, 고집불통의
odd [ɑd] 이상한, 묘한
continence [kántənəns]
자제, 절제, 금욕
heresy [hérəsi] 이교, 이단, 이교 신앙

foe [fou] 적, 원수

MON

You have it now and that is all your whole life is; now

넌 지금 그걸 가지고 있고 그게 바로 네 인생의 전부야, 지금이

You have it now and that is all your whole life is; now. There is nothing else than now. There is neither yesterday, certainly, nor is there any tomorrow. How old must you be before you know that? There is only now, and if now is only two days, then two days is your life and everything in it will be in proportion. This is how you live a life in two days.

넌 지금 그걸 가지고 있고 그게 바로 네 인생의 전부야, 지금이. 지금 이외에는 아무것도 없는 거야. 어제라는 것도 내일이라는 것도 존재하지 않아. 얼마나 더 나이가 들어야 이 엄연한 진실을 깨달을 수 있겠어? 오직 지금이 있을 뿐이며 그 지금이 고작 이틀에 불과하다면 네 인생이 이틀뿐이라고 생각하면 그만이야. 그러면 그 이틀의 시간 안에 있는 모든 것은 적절히 균형을 이루게 되겠지. 이것이 이틀이라는 인생을 살아가는 방법이야.

문장분석

You have it now and that is all your whole life is; now. There is nothing else than now. There is neither yesterday, certainly, nor is there any tomorrow. How old must you be/ before you know that? There is only now, and if now is only two days, then two days is your life and everything in it will be in proportion. This is
균형을 잡아, 어울리게
how you live a life in two days.

certainly [sə́ːrtənli]
확실히, 꼭, 의심 없이, 반드시, 정말
absolutely [æ̀bsəlúːtli] 절대적으로, 정말로
proportion [prəpɔ́ːrʃən] 비(比), 비율, 조화, 균형

neither [níːðər]
(둘 중에서) 어느 쪽의 —도 …아니다(~nor)
nor [nɔːr]
(neither 또는 not과 상관적으로) …도 또한 …않다

198

A good life is not measured by any biblical span

좋은 인생은 성경에 나오는 인생의 길이로 결정되는 것이 아니야

And if you stop complaining and asking for what you never will get, you will have a good life. A good life is not measured by any biblical span. So now do not worry, take what you have, and do your work and you will have a long life and a very merry one. Hasn't it been merry lately?

공연히 불평하는 것을 그만두고, 얻을 수도 없는 것을 요구하는 짓 따위도 그만 둬. 그게 좋은 인생의 시작이야. 좋은 인생은 성경에 나오는 인생의 길이로 측 정되는 것이 아니야. 자, 그러니 걱정 따위는 집어치우고 즐길 수 있는 것을 마음껏 취하도록 해. 그리고 주어진 일을 열심히 하다 보면 오래 살게 되고 인생이 즐겁게 돼. 요새 재미있지 않았나?

문장분석

And if you stop complaining and asking for (what) you never will get, you will
요구하다

have a good life. A good life is not measured by any biblical span. So now do not

worry, take (what) you have, and (do) your work (and) you will have a long life and a
~하는 것

very merry one. Hasn't it been merry lately
life

complain [kəmpléin] 불평하다, 우는소리하다
measure [méʒər] 재다, 측정하다
biblical [bíblikəl]
  성경의, 성경에서 인용한, 성경에 관한

span [spæn] 길이, 기간
lately [léitli] 요즈음, 최근(of late)

What are you complaining about? That's the thing about this sort of work

도대체 뭘 불평하는 거야? 이런 일이란 다 그런 거야

What are you complaining about? That's the thing about this sort of work, he told himself, and was very pleased with the thought, it isn't so much what you learn as it is the people you meet. He was pleased then because he was joking and he came back to the girl. "I love you, rabbit," he said to the girl. "What was it you were saying?"

도대체 뭘 불평하는 거야? 이런 일이란 다 그런 거야. 그는 중얼거렸다. 그는 그런 생각에 기분이 좋아졌다. 늘 사람을 괴롭게 하는 것은 인생에 대한 어떤 지식이라기보다는 어쩔 수 없이 만나야 하는 사람들인 것이다. 그는 그런 생각을 하다 보니 기분이 좋아졌다. 그는 또다시 마리아에게 말을 걸었다. "사랑해, 토끼. 당신이 무슨 말을 하다 말았지?"

문장분석

What are you complaining about? That's the thing about this sort of work, he

told himself, and was very pleased with the thought, it isn't not so much what you
　　　　　　　　　　　　　　　　　　　　　　　　　　　　　　…보다는 오히려

learn as it is the people you meet. He was pleased then because he was joking
　　　　　　　　　　　　　　　　　　　　　　　　　그리고 나서

and he came back to the girl. "I love you, rabbit," he said to the girl. "What was it

you were saying?"

complaint [kəmpléint]
　불평, 찡찡거림, 우는소리, 불평거리, 고충

whine [hwain]
　흐느껴 울다, 우는 소리를 하다, 푸념하다, 투덜대다

please [pliːz]
　기쁘게 하다, 만족시키다(satisfy), …의 마음에 들다

thought [θɔːt] 생각하기, 사색, 사고

taught [tɔːt] teach(가르치다)의 과거·과거분사

It was part of being an insider but it was a very corrupting business

그것은 내부자가 되기 위한 일부였지만 그것은 매우 타락한 행위였다

He had learned that. If a thing was right fundamentally the lying was not supposed to matter. There was a lot of lying though. He did not care for the lying at first. He hated it. Then later he had come to like it. It was part of being an insider but it was a very corrupting business.

그는 그것을 터득했다. 어떤 일이 근본적으로 옳은 일이라면 그것을 위해서는 거짓말을 할 수도 있다는 걸. 그렇지만 거짓말이 너무 난무했다. 처음에 그는 거짓말을 하고 싶은 생각이 들지 않았다. 그는 거짓을 싫어했다. 그런데 나중에는 거짓이 좋아졌다. 그것은 내부자가 되기 위한 일부였지만 그것은 매우 타락한 행위였다.

문장분석

He had learned that. If a thing was right fundamentally/ the lying was not

supposed to matter. There was a lot of lying though. He did not care for the lying
<u>중요하다, 문제가 되다</u>   <u>하지만</u>   <u>like</u>

at first. He hated it. Then later/ he had come to like it. It was part of being an
<u>처음에는</u>   <u>become</u>

insider but it was a very corrupting business.

fundamentally [fʌ̀ndəméntəli]
본질적(근본적)으로

suppose [səpóuz]
가정하다(assume), 상상하다, 추측하다

though [ðou] (…이긴) 하지만

corrupt [kərʌ́pt]
부정한, 뇌물이 통하는, 타락한, 퇴폐한

corruption [kərʌ́pʃən] 타락, 퇴폐, 부패(행위)

And if thou dost not love me, I love thee enough for both

당신이 저를 사랑하지 않는다면 저 혼자서라도 두 사람 몫의 사랑을 하겠어요

"Good. I go. And if thou dost not love me, I love thee enough for both."
He looked at her and smiled through his thinking.
"When you hear firing," he said, "come with the horses. Aid the Pilar with my sacks. It is possible there will be nothing. I hope so."

"좋아요. 가겠어요. 당신이 저를 사랑하지 않는다면 저 혼자서라도 두 사람 몫의 사랑을 하겠어요."
그는 그녀를 쳐다보았다. 그리고 마음속에 떠오르는 따뜻한 생각으로 미소를 지었다.
"총소리가 나면 말을 데리고 와. 내 배낭을 옮기는 필라르를 도와줘. 아무 일 없을지도 몰라. 그러길 바라야지."

문장분석

"Good. I go. And if <u>thou dost</u> not love me, I love <u>thee</u> enough for both." He looked
         you do   you

at her and smiled through his thinking. "When you hear firing," he said, "come

with the horses. Aid the Pilar with my sacks. It is possible there will be nothing. I

hope so."

horse [hɔːrs] 말
hoarse [hɔːrs] 목쉰, 쉰 목소리의, 귀에 거슬리는
sack [sæk] 마대, 자루, 부대

saddle [sǽdl] 안장
possibility [pὰsəbíləti]
   가능성, 실현성, 있을 수 있음

Vocabulary Of The Week

MON

certainly [sə́ːrtənli]
확실히, 꼭, 의심 없이, 반드시, 정말
absolutely [æ̀bsəlúːtli]
절대적으로, 정말로
proportion [prəpɔ́ːrʃən]
비(比), 비율, 조화, 균형

neither [níːðər]
(둘 중에서) 어느 쪽의 —도
…아니다(~nor)
nor [nɔːr]
(neither 또는 not과 상관적으로)
…도 또한 …않다

TUE

complain [kəmpléin]
불평하다, 우는소리하다
measure [méʒər] 재다, 측정하다
biblical [bíblikəl]
성경의, 성경에서 인용한, 성경에 관한
span [spæn] 길이, 기간

lately [léitli] 요즈음, 최근(of late)

WED

complaint [kəmpléint]
불평, 찡찡거림, 우는소리, 불평거리,
고충
whine [hwain]
흐느껴 울다, 우는 소리를 하다,
푸념하다, 투덜대다

please [pliːz]
기쁘게 하다, 만족시키다(satisfy),
…의 마음에 들다
thought [θɔːt] 생각하기, 사색, 사고
taught [tɔːt]
teach(가르치다)의 과거·과거분사

THU

fundamentally [fʌ̀ndəméntəli]
본질적(근본적)으로
suppose [səpóuz]
가정하다(assume), 상상하다,
추측하다
though [ðou] (…이긴) 하지만

corrupt [kərʌ́pt]
부정한, 뇌물이 통하는, 타락한, 퇴폐한
corruption [kərʌ́pʃən]
타락, 퇴폐, 부패(행위)

FRI

horse [hɔːrs] 말
hoarse [hɔːrs]
목쉰, 쉰 목소리의, 귀에 거슬리는
sack [sæk] 마대, 자루, 부대
saddle [sǽdl] 안장

possibility [pàsəbíləti]
가능성, 실현성, 있을 수 있음

MON

But for the Maria and me it means that we must live all of our life in this time

그렇지만 마리아와 나에게는 이 시간 안에 두 사람의 삶을 모두 살아야 한다는 거야

"It is because of the lack of time that there has been informality. What we do not have is time. Tomorrow we must fight. To me that is nothing. But for the Maria and me it means that we must live all of our life in this time."
"And a day and a night is little time," Agustín said.
"Yes. But there has been yesterday and the night before and last night."

"우리에게 가장 모자라는 것은 시간이야. 내일은 전투를 벌여야 해. 나 한 사람에게는 그 전투가 아무 문제도 아니야. 그렇지만 마리아와 나에게는 이 시간 안에 두 사람의 삶을 모두 살아야 한다는 거야."
"하룻낮과 하룻밤은 짧은 시간인데." 아구스틴이 말했다.
"그래. 하지만 어제, 그리고 그제 밤과 어젯밤이 있었지."

문장분석

(What) we do not have is time. Tomorrow/ we must fight. To me/ that is nothing.

But for the Maria and me/ it means that we must live all of our life/ in this time."

"And a day and a night is little time," Agustín said. "Yes. But there has been

yesterday and the night before (last) and last night."
　　　　　　　　　　그저께 밤

lack [læk] 부족(want), 결핍, 결여, 없음
lag [læg] 처지다, 꾸물거리다, 지연, 지체
informality [infɔːrmǽləti] 비공식, 약식(행위)
formality [fɔːrmǽləti]
　형식에 구애됨, 딱딱함, 격식을 차림

formidable [fɔːrmədəbl]
　무서운, 만만찮은, 얕잡을 수 없는

You have no right to forget anything

무슨 일이든 잊어버릴 수 있는 권리는 네게 없다

But I won't keep a count of people I have killed as though it were a trophy record or a disgusting business like notches in a gun, he told himself. I have a right to not keep count and I have a right to forget them. No, himself said. You have no right to forget anything. You have no right to shut your eyes to any of it nor any right to forget any of it nor to soften it nor to change it.

하지만 내가 죽인 사람의 숫자를 마치 상패의 숫자라도 되는 것처럼 세거나, 총에다 무슨 표시를 새기는 비열한 짓을 하는 건 싫다, 하고 그는 생각했다. 그것을 세지 않았던 것은 나의 권리이며 숫자를 잊어버리는 것도 나의 권리이다. 아니다. 그는 자신에게 말했다. 무슨 일이든 잊어버릴 수 있는 권리는 네게 없다. 무슨 일에서나 눈을 감아 버리거나 잊어버리거나 약화시키거나 변경하거나 할 권리는 없다.

문장분석

But I won't keep a count of (people) I have killed/ as though it were a trophy
　　　will not　　수를 계속 기록하다　　　　　　　　　　마치~처럼

record or a disgusting business like notches in a gun, he told himself. I have a
　　　　　　　　　　　　　　~처럼

right to not keep count and I have a right to forget them. No, himself said. You
　권리

have no right to forget anything. You have no right to shut your eyes to any of it

nor any right to forget any of it nor to soften it nor to change it.
and also not

disgusting [disgʌ́stiŋ]　　　　　　　soften [sɔ́(:)fən, sɑ́fən]
　구역질나는, 정떨어지는, 지겨운　　　　부드럽게(연하게) 하다, 약하게 하다

disgusted [disgʌ́stid]　　　　　　　harden [hɑ́:rdn]
　정떨어진, 욕지기나는, 화나는　　　　　굳히다, 딱딱(단단)하게 하다, 단련하다

notch [nɑtʃ] (V 자 모양의) 새김눈, 벤자리

Don't ever kid yourself with too much dialectics

너무 많은 변증법으로 자신을 속이지 마

You're not a real Marxist and you know it. You believe in Liberty, Equality and Fraternity. You believe in Life, Liberty and the Pursuit of Happiness. Don't ever kid yourself with too much dialectics. They are for some but not for you. You have to know them in order not to be a sucker.

너는 진짜 마르크스주의자가 아니야. 그건 너도 알고 있어. 넌 자유, 평등, 박애를 믿는 자이며 생명, 자유, 행복을 추구하는 자야. 너무 많은 변증법으로 자신을 속이지 마. 변증법은 다른 누군가를 위한 것이지 너를 위한 것은 아니야. 단지 바보 취급을 받지 않을 정도로만 그걸 알고 있으면 되는 거야.

문장분석

You're not a real Marxist and you know it. You believe in Liberty, Equality and

Fraternity. You believe in Life, Liberty and the Pursuit of Happiness. Don't ever kid
                                                                          혹시라도.
yourself with too much dialectics. They are for some but not for you. You have to
                                                      어떤 사람들   must
know them in order not to be a sucker.
         ~않기 위해서

liberty [líbərti] 자유(freedom)   dialectic [dàiəléktik] 변증(법)적인, 방언의, 변증법
fraternity [frətə́:rnəti] 형제의 사이, 동포애, 우애   sucker [sʌ́kər] 빠는 사람, 젖먹이, 속기 쉬운 사람
pursuit [pərsúːt] 추적, 추격, 추구

THU

If this war is lost all of those things are lost

전쟁에서 진다면 그 모든 것을 잃게 되지

You have put many things in abeyance to win a war. If this war is lost all of those things are lost. But afterwards you can discard what you do not believe in. There is plenty you do not believe in and plenty that you do believe in.

이 전쟁에 이기기 위해서는 많은 것들을 유보 상태로 남겨 둬야 해. 이 전쟁에서 진다면 그 모든 것을 잃게 돼. 그렇지만 전쟁이 끝나면 네가 믿지 않는 것은 버릴 수 있어. 네가 믿지 않는 것도 엄청나게 많지만 진정으로 믿는 것도 엄청나게 많아.

문장분석

You have put many things in abeyance/ to win a war. If this war is lost/ all of those things are lost. But afterwards/ you can discard what you do not believe in. There is plenty you do not believe in and plenty that you do believe in.
강조

abeyance [əbéiəns] 중지, 중절, 정지, 미정
truce [tru:s] 휴전, 정전(협정)
obey [oubéi] …에 복종하다, …에 따르다

discard [diskáːrd] 버리다, 처분하다
plenty [plénti] 많음, 가득, 풍부, 다량, 충분

Don't ever kid yourself about loving some one

어떤 사람을 사랑하는 문제와 관련해서는 절대 농담을 하지 마

And another thing. Don't ever kid yourself about loving some one. It is just that most people are not lucky enough ever to have it. You never had it before and now you have it. What you have with Maria, whether it lasts just through today and a part of tomorrow, or whether it lasts for a long life is the most important thing that can happen to a human being.

그리고 또 한 가지. 어떤 사람을 사랑하는 문제와 관련해서는 절대 농담을 하지 마. 사랑한다는 것, 이거야말로 아무에게나 찾아오는 행운이 아니야. 너도 지금까지 한 번도 가져 보지 못했다가 이제 간신히 얻게 되었잖아. 마리아와 함께 누리고 있는 것, 그것이 오늘까지, 그리고 내일의 일부 동안만 계속될 수 있는 것이든, 평생 동안 지속되는 것이든, 사람에게 일어나는 일 중에서 가장 중요한 사건은 사랑이야.

문장분석

And another thing. Don't ever kid yourself about loving some one. It is just that most people are not lucky/ enough ever to have it. You never had it before and now you have it. What you have with Maria, whether it lasts just through today and a part of tomorrow, or whether it lasts for a long life/ is the most important
동사
thing that can happen to a human being.

kid [kid] 조롱하다, 농담을 하다
last [læst] 계속(지속, 존속)하다, 끌다
whether [hwéðər] …인지 어떤지

weather [wéðər] 일기, 기후, 기상, 날씨
thorough [θə́:rou] 철저한, 충분한, 완벽한, 완전한

Vocabulary Of The Week

MON

lack [læk]
부족(want), 결핍, 결여, 없음
lag [læg]
처지다, 꾸물거리다, 지연, 지체
informality [ìnfɔːrmǽləti]
비공식, 약식(행위)

formality [fɔːrmǽləti]
형식에 구애됨, 딱딱함, 격식을 차림
formidable [fɔ́ːrmədəbl]
무서운, 만만찮은, 얕잡을 수 없는

TUE

disgusting [disgʌ́stiŋ] 구
역질나는, 정떨어지는, 지겨운
disgusted [disgʌ́stid]
정떨어진, 욕지기나는, 화나는
notch [nɑtʃ]
(V 자 모양의) 새김눈, 벤자리

soften [sɔ́(ː)fən, sɑ́fən]
부드럽게(연하게) 하다, 약하게 하다
harden [hɑ́ːrdn]
굳히다, 딱딱(단단)하게 하다,
단련하다

WED

liberty [líbərti] 자유(freedom)
fraternity [frətə́ːrnəti]
형제의 사이, 동포애, 우애
pursuit [pərsúːt] 추적, 추격, 추구
dialectic [dàiəléktik]
변증(법)적인, 방언의, 변증법

sucker [sʌ́kər]
빠는 사람, 젖먹이, 속기 쉬운 사람

THU

abeyance [əbéiəns]
중지, 중절, 정지, 미정
truce [truːs] 휴전, 정전(협정)
obey [oubéi]
…에 복종하다, …에 따르다
discard [diskɑ́ːrd] 버리다, 처분하다

plenty [plénti]
많음, 가득, 풍부, 다량, 충분

FRI

kid [kid] 조롱하다, 농담을 하다
last [læst] 계속(지속, 존속)하다, 끌다
whether [hwéðər] …인지 어떤지
weather [wéðər]
일기, 기후, 기상, 날씨

thorough [θə́ːrou]
철저한, 충분한, 완벽한, 완전한

MON

You are lucky even if you die tomorrow

넌 내일 죽을지라도 운이 좋은 거야

There will always be people who say it does not exist because they cannot have it. But I tell you it is true and that you have it and that you are lucky even if you die tomorrow.

물론 자신들이 소유하지 못했기 때문에 그런 건(사랑) 이 세상에 존재하지 않는다고 말하는 사람은 어느 시대에나 있었어. 하지만 넌 그것을 소유하고 있어. 그걸 자신 있게 말할 수 있어. 그렇기 때문에 넌 내일 죽을지라도 운이 좋은 사내인 거야.

문장분석

There will always be (people) who say it does not exist/ because they cannot have

it. But I tell you (that) it is true and (tell you) that you have it and (tell you) that you

are lucky/ even if you die tomorrow.
　　　　　　　~할지라도

exist [igzíst] 존재하다
existence [igzístəns] 존재, 실재
own [oun] 소유하다, 자기 자신의

envy [énvi] 질투, 부러움, 부러워하다
envious [énviəs] …을 부러워하는, 질투심이 강한

Dying was nothing and he had no fear of it in his mind

그에게 있어 죽음이란 하찮은 일에 불과했고 마음속에 두려움도 없었다

If one must die, he thought, and clearly one must, I can die. But I hate it. Dying was nothing and he had no picture of it nor fear of it in his mind. But living was a field of grain blowing in the wind on the side of a hill. Living was a hawk in the sky. Living was an earthen jar of water in the dust of the threshing with the grain flailed out and the chaff blowing.

사람이 꼭 죽어야 한다면 나도 죽을 수 있다. 하지만 죽는 건 싫다. 그는 죽음에 대한 뚜렷한 모습도, 마음속에 두려움도 없었다. 그러나 언덕 한 귀퉁이에서 바람에 흔들리고 있는 낟 알갱이도 살아 있다. 하늘의 매도 살아 있다. 탈곡장 옆에 놓인 흙으로 만든 물동이도 낟 알갱이와 왕겨 가루를 뒤집어쓴 채 살아 있다.

문장분석

If one must die, he thought, and clearly one must,/ I can die. But I hate it. Dying
일반인
was nothing and he had no picture of it nor fear of it in his mind. But living was
and also not
a field of grain blowing in the wind on the side of a hill. Living was a hawk in the
주어
sky. Living was an earthen jar of water in the dust of the threshing with the grain
주어   주어
flailed out and the chaff blowing.

grain [grein] 낟알, 곡물, 알곡
blow [blou] 불다, (바람이) 불다
thresh [θreʃ] (곡식을) 도리깨질하다, 탈곡하다

trash [træʃ] 쓰레기, 페물
chaff [tʃæf] 왕겨, 여물

WED

I love thee as I love all that we have fought for

우리가 싸워서 얻고자 했던 모든 것과 마찬가지로 난 당신을 사랑해

"I love thee as I love all that we have fought for. I love thee as I love liberty and dignity and the rights of all men to work and not be hungry. I love thee as I love Madrid that we have defended and as I love all my comrades that have died. And many have died. Many. Many. Thou canst not think how many."

"우리가 싸워서 얻고자 했던 모든 것과 마찬가지로 난 당신을 사랑해. 자유와 숭고함과, 모든 인간이 가진 일하고 배곯지 않을 권리만큼이나 당신을 사랑해. 우리가 지켰던 마드리드를 사랑하듯 당신을 사랑하고, 죽은 내 전우들을 사랑하듯이 당신을 사랑해. 많은 전우들이 죽었어. 너무나 많이. 너무나. 얼마나 많은지 당신은 모를 거야."

문장분석

"I love thee/ as I love all that we have fought for. I love thee/ as I love liberty and
　　　　you　~처럼
dignity and the rights of all men to work and not be hungry. I love thee/ as I love
Madrid that we have defended and as I love all my comrades that have died. And
many have died. Many. Many. Thou canst not think (that) how many (died).
　　　　　　　　　　　　　　　　　　You can

fought [fɔːt] fight(싸우다)의 과거·과거분사
liberty [líbərti] 자유(freedom)
dignity [dígnəti] 존엄, 위엄, 품위
comrade [kάmræd] 동료, 동지, 친구

co-worker
　함께 일하는 사람, 협력자, 동료(fellow worker)

But I say this now to tell thee a little

지금 말하고 있는 건 일부에 불과해

"But I love thee as I love what I love most in the world and I love thee more. I love thee very much, rabbit. More than I can tell thee. But I say this now to tell thee a little. I have never had a wife and now I have thee for a wife and I am happy."

"하지만 나는 세상에 있는 모든 것을 사랑하는 것처럼 당신을 사랑해. 아니, 그보다 더 많이 사랑해. 난 이렇게 당신을 사랑하고 있어. 말로 표현하기 힘들 정도야. 지금 말하고 있는 건 일부에 불과해. 나에게 아내가 있었던 적이 없어. 이제 당신은 나의 아내이고 난 그 때문에 행복하다고."

문장분석

But I love thee/ as I love what I love most in the world and I love thee more. I love
      you   ~처럼

thee very much, rabbit. More than I can tell thee. But I say this now to tell thee a

little. I have never had a wife and now I have thee for a wife and I am happy."

rabbit [ræbit] 집토끼
hare [hɛər] 산토끼
a little/ a few 약간, 조금 있는(긍정)

little/ few 거의 없는(부정)
confide [kənfáid] 털어놓다, 신뢰하다

I would not wish to bring either a son or a daughter into this world

난 딸이든 아들이든 태어나게 하고 싶지 않아

"Then I would not wish to bring either a son or a daughter into this world as this world is. And also you take all the love I have to give." "I would like to bear thy son and thy daughter," she told him. "And how can the world be made better if there are no children of us who fight against the fascists?"

"난 이런 세상에는 딸이든 아들이든 태어나게 하고 싶지 않아. 그리고 내가 당신에게 모든 사랑을 주고 있잖아." 그가 말했다.

"하지만 난 당신의 딸이나 아들을 낳고 싶어. 그리고 파시스트들과 맞서 싸울 우리의 딸이나 아들이 태어나지 않는다면 어떻게 이 세상이 더 좋아질 수 있겠어?" 마리아가 힘주어 말했다.

문장분석

"Then I would not wish to bring either a son or a daughter into this world as this world is. And also you take all the love I have to give." "I would like to bear thy son and thy daughter," she told him. "And how can the world be made better/ if there are no children of us who fight against the fascists?"

bear [bɛər] (아이를) 낳다
pregnant [prégnənt] 임신한
delivery [dilívəri] 분만, 해산, 배달

premature [priːmətjúər]
조기의, 조산의, 너무 이른, 너무 서두른
ICU intensive care unit(집중 치료실)

Vocabulary Of The Week

August WEEK 4

MON

exist [igzíst] 존재하다
existence [igzístəns] 존재, 실재
own [oun] 소유하다, 자기 자신의
envy [énvi] 질투, 부러움, 부러워하다
envious [énviəs]
　…을 부러워하는, 질투심이 강한

TUE

grain [grein] 낟알, 곡물, 알곡
blow [blou] 불다, (바람이) 불다
thresh [θreʃ]
　(곡식을) 도리깨질하다, 탈곡하다
trash [træʃ] 쓰레기, 폐물
chaff [tʃæf] 왕겨, 여물

WED

fought [fɔːt]
　fight(싸우다)의 과거·과거분사
liberty [líbərti] 자유(freedom)
dignity [dígnəti] 존엄, 위엄, 품위
comrade [kάmræd] 동료, 동지, 친구

co-worker
　함께 일하는 사람, 협력자,
　동료(fellow worker)

THU

rabbit [rǽbit] 집토끼
hare [hɛər] 산토끼
a little/ a few 약간, 조금 있는(긍정)
little/ few 거의 없는(부정)
confide [kənfáid] 털어놓다, 신뢰하다

FRI

bear [bɛər] (아이를) 낳다
pregnant [prégnənt] 임신한
delivery [dilívəri] 분만, 해산, 배달
premature [prìːmətjúər]
　조기의, 조산의, 너무 이른,
　너무 서두른

ICU
Intensive Care Unit(집중 치료실)

September

09

The first and final thing
you have to do in this world is
to last it and not be smashed by it.

이 세상에서 당신이 해야 할 첫 번째이자 마지막 일은
그 일을 지속하는 것이고 그것으로 인해 부서지지 않는 것이다.

MON

Maybe I have had all my life in three days

어쩌면 나는 지난 사흘 동안에 내 전 생애를 살아버렸는지도 몰라

Maybe I have had all my life in three days, he thought. If that's true I wish we would have spent the last night differently. But last nights are never any good. Last nothings are any good. Yes, last words were good sometimes. "Viva my husband who was Mayor of this town" was good.

어쩌면 나는 지난 사흘 동안에 내 전 생애를 살아버렸는지도 몰라. 만일 그게 사실이라면 마지막 밤을 달리 보내고 싶다는 생각도 들었다. 하지만 마지막 밤 이란 어떤 식으로 보내든 기분 좋을 리가 없다. 그래, 아까 (필라르의) 마지막 말은 그런대로 괜찮은 말이었어. "이 마을의 촌장이었던 내 남편 만세"라, 괜 찮았어.

문장분석

Maybe/ I have had all my life/ in three days, he thought. If that's true/ I wish we
　　　　　　　　　한평생
would have spent the last night differently. But last nights are never any good.

Last nothings are any good. Yes, last words were good sometimes. "Viva my

husband who was Mayor of this town" was good.

spend [spend] 쓰다, 소비하다　　　　civic [sívik] 시의, 도시의, 시민의
viva [ví:və] (It.) 만세　　　　　　　differential [difərénʃəl]
mayor [méiər] 시장, 읍장　　　　　　　차별의, 차이를 나타내는, 차별적인

He did not like these people who were like dangerous children

그는 무모한 짓을 저지를 수 있는 아이들 같은 이 사람들이 싫었다

Andrés smelt the foulness the defenders of the hill crest had made all through the bracken on that slope. He did not like these people who were like dangerous children; dirty, foul, undisciplined, kind, loving, silly and ignorant but always dangerous because they were armed. He, Andrés, was without politics except that he was for the Republic.

안드레스는 어둠 속에서 비탈 아무 곳에나 갈긴 지독한 똥 냄새를 맡았다. 그는 무모한 짓을 저지를 수 있는 아이들 같은 이 사람들이 싫었다. 더럽고 추잡스럽고 무식하고 친절하고 사랑할 줄 알고 우둔하고 무지하지만 무기를 들고 있으면 더없이 위험해지는 사람들. 안드레스는 그가 공화당 편이라는 것 말고는 정치에 대해 관심이 없었다.

문장분석

Andrés smelt (the foulness) the defenders of the hill crest had made/ all through the bracken on that slope. He did not like (these people) who were like dangerous children; dirty, foul, undisciplined, kind, loving, silly and ignorant but always dangerous because they were armed. He, Andrés, was without politics/ except
···외에는
that he was for the Republic.
~에 찬성하여

foul [faul] 더러운, 불결한, 냄새 나는
crest [krest] 꼭대기
bracken [brǽkən] 고사리(류의 숲)

discipline [dísəplin] 훈련(하다)
ignorant [ígnərənt] 무지한, 무식한

It is not liberty not to bury the mess one makes

자신이 싼 것을 치우지도 못한다면 그건 자유가 아니다

He had heard these people talk many times and he thought what they said was often beautiful and fine to hear but he did not like them. It is not liberty not to bury the mess one makes, he thought. No animal has more liberty than the cat; but it buries the mess it makes. The cat is the best anarchist. Until they learn that from the cat I cannot respect them.

그는 이런 사람들이 하는 말을 여러 번 들은 적이 있었다. 그들이 말하는 깃을 들으면 때때로 아름답고 훌륭하다고 생각될 때도 있었지만 그들이 좋아지지는 않았다. 자신이 싼 것을 치우지도 못한다면 그건 자유가 아니다. 동물 중에서도 가장 자유롭게 구는 녀석은 고양이다. 하지만 고양이도 제 똥은 묻을 줄 안다. 고양이야말로 최고의 무정부주의자다. 이놈들이 최소한 고양이한테 이런 점을 배울 때까지 난 저들을 존경하지 않을 것이다.

문장분석

He had heard these people talk many times and he thought what they said was
~하는 것
often beautiful and fine to hear but he did not like them. It is not liberty not to
bury the mess one makes, he thought. No animal has more liberty than the cat;
but it buries the mess it makes. The cat is the best anarchist. Until they learn that
from the cat/ I cannot respect them.

mess [mes] 지저분한 모양, 혼란
bury [béri] 묻다,(흙 따위로) 덮다
burial [bériəl] 매장, 매장식

anarchistic [ænərkístik] 무정부주의(자)의
respectable [rispéktəbəl] 존경할 만한, 훌륭한

Today is only one day in all the days that will ever be

오늘은 수많은 날들 중 그저 하루이고, 앞으로도 그럴 것이다

Today is only one day in all the days that will ever be. But what will happen in all the other days that ever come can depend on what you do today. It's been that way all this year. It's been that way so many times. All of this war is that way.

오늘은 수많은 날들 중 그저 하루이고, 앞으로도 그럴 것이다. 하지만 다른 날들에 벌어지는 일은 네가 오늘 뭘 하냐에 달려 있다. 올해 내내 그랬다. 너무 많이 그랬다. 이 전쟁의 모든 것이 그런 식이다.

문장분석

Today is only one day in all the days that will ever be. But what will happen in all the other days that ever come can depend on what you do today. It's been that way/ all this year. It's been that way/ so many times. All of this war is that way.

~에 달려있다 / 그런 식으로

depend [dipénd]
…나름이다, (…에) 달려 있다, 좌우되다
defend [difénd] 막다, 지키다, 방어하다
offend [əfénd] 성나게 하다, 기분을 상하게 하다

offense [əféns]
(규칙·법령 따위의) 위반, 반칙, 불법
impressive [imprésiv]
인상에 남는, 인상적인, 감동을 주는

We will not go to Madrid now but I go always with you wherever thou go

우린 이제 마드리드로 가지 않지만 당신이 가는 곳이라면 어디든지 내가 함께 가는 거야

"Guapa," he said to Maria and took hold of her two hands. "Listen. We will not be going to Madrid—"
Then she started to cry.
"No, guapa, don't," he said. "Listen. We will not go to Madrid now but I go always with thee wherever thou goest. Understand?"
She said nothing and pushed her head against his cheek with her arms around him.

"예쁜이, 우린 이제 마드리드로 같이 가지 못하게 되었어." 그가 마리아의 두 손을 잡으며 말했다.
그러자 그녀가 울기 시작했다.
"울지 마, 마리아. 우린 이제 마드리드로 가지 않아. 그러나 당신이 가는 곳이라면 어디든지 내가 함께 가는 거야, 알겠지?" 그녀는 아무런 대답도 하지 않고 양팔로 그를 껴안으면서 자신의 머리를 그의 뺨에 갖다 댔다.

문장분석

"Guapa," he said to Maria and took hold of her two hands. "Listen. We will not be
~을 잡다, 쥐다

going to Madrid—"

Then she started to cry.

"No, guapa, don't," he said. "Listen. We will not go to Madrid now but I go always

with thee/ wherever thou goest. Understand?"
you go
She said nothing and pushed her head against his cheek with her arms around

him.

cheek [tʃiːk] 뺨, 볼
cheekbone 광대뼈
chin [tʃin] 턱, 턱끝

tear [tiər] 눈물
tear [tɛər] (tore [tɔːr]- torn [tɔːrn]) 찢다, 째다

Vocabulary Of The Week

MON

spend [spend] 쓰다, 소비하다
viva [víːvə] (It.) 만세
mayor [méiər] 시장, 읍장
civic [sívik] 시의, 도시의, 시민의
differential [difərénʃəl]
　차별의, 차이를 나타내는, 차별적인

TUE

foul [faul] 더러운, 불결한, 냄새 나는
crest [krest] 꼭대기
bracken [brǽkən] 고사리(류의 숲)
discipline [dísəplin] 훈련(하다)
ignorant [ígnərənt] 무지한, 무식한

WED

mess [mes] 지저분한 모양, 혼란
bury [béri] 묻다,(흙 따위로) 덮다
burial [bériəl] 매장, 매장식
anarchistic [ænərkístik]
　무정부주의(자)의

respectable [rispéktəbəl]
　존경할 만한, 훌륭한

THU

depend [dipénd]
　…나름이다, (…에) 달려 있다,
　좌우되다
defend [difénd]
　막다, 지키다, 방어하다

offend [əfénd]
　성나게 하다, 기분을 상하게 하다
offense [əféns]
　(규칙·법령 따위의) 위반, 반칙, 불법
impressive [imprésiv]
　인상에 남는, 인상적인, 감동을 주는

FRI

cheek [tʃiːk] 뺨, 볼
cheekbone 광대뼈
chin [tʃin] 턱, 턱끝.
tear [tiər] 눈물
tear [tɛər] (tore [tɔːr]- torn [tɔːrn])
　찢다, 째다

MON

As long as there is one of us there is both of us

우리 두 사람 가운데 한 사람이라도 살아 있으면 그건 둘 다 살아 있는 거야

"Listen to this well, rabbit," he said.
He knew there was a great hurry and he was sweating very much, but this had to be said and understood.
"Thou wilt go now, rabbit. But I go with thee. As long as there is one of us there is both of us. Do you understand?"
"Nay, I stay with thee."

"내 말 잘 들이, 토끼."
그는 사정이 매우 급박하다는 것을 잘 알았고 몹시 땀을 흘리고 있었다. 그러나 마리아에게 사정을 설명해 이해시켜야만 했다.
"당신은 이제 가야 해, 토끼. 하지만 나도 당신과 함께 가는 거야. 우리 두 사람 가운데 한 사람이라도 살아 있으면 그건 둘 다 살아 있는 거야, 알겠지?"
"아뇨, 당신과 함께 있겠어요."

문장분석

"Listen to this well, rabbit," he said.

He knew there was a great hurry and he was sweating very much, but this had to be said and understood.

"Thou wilt go now, rabbit. But I go with thee. As long as there is one of us/ there
 You   will   you   ~하는 한
is both of us. Do you understand?"

"Nay, I stay with thee."

sweat [swet] 땀(을 흘리다)　　　　　explain [ikspléin] 설명하다
urgent [ə́ːrdʒənt] 긴급한, 절박한, 매우 위급한　　explanation [èksplənéiʃən] 설명, 해설, 해석
stay [stei] 머무르다, 남다

It is harder for thee, but I am thee also now

당신에게는 어려운 일일 거야, 그러나 나는 이제 당신의 일부가 되었어

"Yes. Therefore go for a favor. Do it for me since it is what thou canst do."
"But you don't understand, Roberto. What about me? It is worse for me to go." "Surely," he said. "It is harder for thee. But I am thee also now."
She said nothing. He looked at her and he was sweating heavily and he spoke now, trying harder to do something than he had ever tried in all his life.

"물론 그렇겠지. 그렇지만 나를 봐서라도 가줘. 나를 위해 당신이 할 수 있는 일을 해줘."
"싫어요, 로베르토. 난 어떻게 해요? 난 가고 싶지 않아요."
"물론 그렇겠지. 당신에게는 어려운 일일 거야. 그러나 나는 이제 당신의 일부가 되었어."
그녀는 아무런 대답도 하지 않았다. 그는 땀을 흘리면서 그녀를 쳐다보았다. 그것은 그가 일생 동안 해온 일 중에서 가장 어려운 일이었다.

문장분석

"Yes. Therefore go for a favor. Do it for me since it is what thou canst do."
                                      because
"But you don't understand, Roberto. What about me? It is worse for me to go."
                                                    가짜 주어   행위자 진짜 주어
"Surely," he said. "It is harder for thee. But I am thee also now."
                                       you
She said nothing. He looked at her and he was sweating heavily and he spoke

now, trying harder to do something than he had ever tried in all his life.
                                                    한평생, 전 생애

favor [féivər] 호의, 친절   worse [wəːrs]
favorable [féivərəbəl]   (bad, ill의 비교급) 보다 나쁜, (병이) 악화된
  호의를 보이는, 찬성의(approving), 유리한   worsen [wəːrsən] 악화하다, 악화시키다
favorite [féivərit] 마음에 드는 (것)

Now you are going well and fast and far and we both go in thee

이제 당신은 안전하게 먼 곳으로 떠나는 거야, 우리 둘은 당신 속에서 함께 가는 거야

"Now you are going well and fast and far and we both go in thee. Now put thy hand here. Now put thy head down. Nay, put it down. That is right. Now I put my hand there. Good. Thou art so good. Now do not think more. Now art thou doing what thou should."

"이제 당신은 안전하게 즉시 먼 곳으로 떠나는 거야. 우리 둘은 당신 속에서 함께 가는 것이지. 이제 당신 손을 여기에 갖다 대라고. 그리고 고개를 숙여. 아냐, 고개를 숙이라니까. 그래, 됐어. 이제 내가 머리에 손을 댈게. 좋아, 당신은 참으로 착한 여자야. 이제 더 이상 다른 생각은 하지 마. 당신은 해야 할 일을 하는 거야."

문장분석

"Now you are going well and fast and far and we both go in thee. Now put thy (you / your) hand here. Now put thy head down. Nay, put it down. That is right. Now I put my hand there. Good. Thou art (You are) so good. Now do not think more. Now art thou doing what thou should (do)."

thumb [θʌm] 엄지손가락
index finger 집게손가락
middle finger 가운뎃손가락

ring finger (왼손의) 약손가락
pinkie [píŋki] 새끼손가락

The me in thee

당신 안에 내가 있어

"Now thou art obeying. Not me but us both. The me in thee. Now you go for us both. Truly. We both go in thee now. This I have promised thee. Thou art very good to go and very kind. We will go to Madrid another time, rabbit. Truly. Now stand up and go and we both go. Stand up. See?"

"No," she said and held him tight around the neck.

"이제 당신은 자신의 뜻이 아니라 우리 두 사람의 뜻을 따르고 있는 거야. 당신 안에 내가 있어. 이제 당신은 우리 둘을 위해 가는 거야. 우리 둘은 이제 당신 속에서 가는 거야. 이건 내가 당신에게 약속했던 거야. 당신은 착하고 온순한 사람이니까 이제 떠나는 거야. 마드리드는 다음에 가자고, 토끼. 이제 일어나서 우리 둘을 위해 가줘. 자, 일어서."

"싫어요." 그녀가 그의 목을 감싸 안으며 말했다.

문장분석

"Now thou art obeying. Not me but us both. The me in thee. Now you go for us
<u>you are</u>   <u>you</u>

both. Truly. We both go in thee now. I have promised thee (This). Thou art very

good to go and very kind. We will go to Madrid/ another time, rabbit. Truly. Now

stand up and go and we both go. Stand up. See?"

"No," she said and held him tight around the neck.

obey [oubéi] …에 복종하다, …에 따르다
obedience [oubíːdiəns] 복종, 순종
promise [prámis] 약속, 계약

promising [práməsiŋ] 가망 있는, 유망한, 믿음직한
tighten [táitn] (바짝) 죄다, 팽팽하게 치다, 단단하게 하다

There is no good-by, guapa, because we are not apart

작별 인사도 할 필요가 없어. 우린 헤어지는 게 아니니까

"There is no good-by, guapa, because we are not apart. That it should be good in the Gredos. Go now. Go good. Nay,"
He spoke now still calmly and reasonably as Pilar walked the girl along.
"Do not turn around. Put thy foot in. Yes. Thy foot in. Help her up," he said to Pilar.
"Get her in the saddle. Swing up now."

"작별 인사도 할 필요가 없어, 이쁜이. 우린 헤어지는 게 아니니까. 그레도스에 선 일이 잘 풀려나갈 거야. 자, 이제 가. 정말 가라니까."

그는 마리아가 필라르와 함께 걸음을 떼어 놓는 것을 보면서 조용하고 침착한 목소리로 말했다.

"돌아보지 마. 걸어 나가. 그렇지. 자, 어서 발을 떼어 놓아." 그는 다시 필라르 에게 말했다. "일으켜 세워 줘요. 그녀를 안장에 태워요, 이제 훌쩍 올려놓아 요."

문장분석

"There is no good-by, guapa, because we are not apart. That it should be good in
···이라는 것
the Gredos. Go now. Go good."
잘
He spoke now still calmly and reasonably as Pilar walked the girl along.
함께, ···을 따라
"Do not turn around. Put thy foot in. Yes. Thy foot in. Help her up," he said to
돌아서   your
Pilar.

"Get her in the saddle. Swing up now."

apart [əpάːrt]
떨어져서, 갈라져서, 따로따로, 뿔뿔이
calmly [kάːmli]
온화하게, 침착히, 냉정히, 태연스레

reasonable [ríːzənəbəl]
분별 있는, 사리를 아는, 온당한
saddle [sǽdl] 안장
swing [swiŋ] 휙 치켜 올리다

Vocabulary Of The Week

MON

sweat [swet] 땀(을 흘리다)
urgent [ə́:rdʒənt]
　긴급한, 절박한, 매우 위급한
stay [stei] 머무르다, 남다
explain [ikspléin] 설명하다

explanation [èksplənéiʃən]
　설명, 해설, 해석

TUE

favor [féivər] 호의, 친절
favorable [féivərəbəl]
　호의를 보이는, 찬성의(approving),
　유리한
favorite [féivərit] 마음에 드는 (것)

worse [wə:rs]
　(bad, ill의 비교급) 보다 나쁜,
　(병이) 악화된
worsen [wə́:rsən]
　악화하다, 악화시키다

WED

thumb [θʌm] 엄지손가락
index finger 집게손가락
middle finger 가운뎃손가락
ring finger (왼손의) 약손가락
pinkie [píŋki] 새끼손가락

THU

obey [oubéi]
　…에 복종하다, …에 따르다
obedience [oubí:diəns] 복종, 순종
promise [prámis] 약속, 계약
promising [práməsiŋ]
　가망 있는, 유망한, 믿음직한

tighten [táitn]
　(바짝) 죄다, 팽팽하게 치다,
　단단하게 하다

FRI

apart [əpá:rt]
　떨어져서, 갈라져서, 따로따로, 뿔뿔이
calmly [ká:mli]
　온화하게, 침착히, 냉정히, 태연스레
reasonable [rí:zənəbəl]
　분별 있는, 사리를 아는, 온당한

saddle [sǽdl] 안장
swing [swiŋ] 휙 치켜 올리다

MON

The world is a fine place and worth the fighting for

이 세상은 아름다운 곳이고 그것을 지키기 위해서라면 싸워 볼 만한 가치가 있어

I have fought for what I believed in for a year now. If we win here we will win everywhere. The world is a fine place and worth the fighting for and I hate very much to leave it. And you had a lot of luck, he told himself, to have had such a good life. You've had just as good a life as grandfather's though not as long.

나는 소신을 위해 1년 동안 싸워 왔어. 우리가 여기서 이긴다면 모든 곳에서 다 이기는 거야. 이 세상은 아름다운 곳이고 그것을 지키기 위해서라면 싸워 볼 만 한 가치가 있어. 아, 정말 이 세상을 떠나기가 싫구나. 그러나 지금까지 보람 있 는 인생을 살았으니 그걸로 행운이라고 할 수 있지. 비록 돌아가신 할아버지처 럼 오래 살지는 못했지만 보람 있는 인생이었어.

문장분석

I have fought for (what) I believed in for a year now. If we win here/ we will win everywhere. The world is a fine place and worth the fighting for and I hate very much to leave it. And you had a lot of luck, he told himself, to have had such a
　　　　　　　　　　　　　　　　　　많은
good life. You've had just (as) good a life (as) grandfather's (life)/ though not as long.

worth [wəːrθ]
　…의 가치가 있는, …할 만한 가치가 있는
worthwhile [wə́ːrθhwáil]
　할 보람이 있는, 시간을 들일 만한

worthy [wə́ːrði]
　훌륭한, 존경할 만한, (…에) 어울리는,
hatred [héitrid] 증오, 원한, 혐오
though [ðou] …이긴 하지만, …이지만

You do not want to complain when you have been so lucky

그렇게 운이 좋았으니 불평할 건 없겠지

You've had as good a life as any one because of these last days. You do not want to complain when you have been so lucky. I wish there was some way to pass on what I've learned, though. Christ, I was learning fast there at the end.

지난 며칠 때문에 그 어떤 사람에게도 부끄럽지 않은 보람찬 인생을 보낼 수 있었어. 그렇게 운이 좋았으니 불평할 건 없겠지. 그렇지만 내가 터득한 이 지혜를 다음 사람들에게 전달할 수 있었으면 좋았을 텐데. 그래 생각해 보니 인생의 막판에 와서야 많은 것을 단시간 내에 배운 것 같아.

문장분석

You've had as good a life as any one/ because of these last days. You do not want
life

to complain/ when you have been so lucky. I wish (that) there was some way to

pass on what I've learned, though. Christ, I was learning fast there at the end.
물려주다   last days

complain [kəmpléin]
불평하다, 우는소리하다, 한탄하다
complaint [kəmpléint] 불평, 찡찡거림, 불평거리
fortunate [fɔ́ːrtʃənit] 운이 좋은, 행운의, 복받은

regret [rigrét] 유감, 후회(하다)
regretful [rigrétfəl]
유감으로 생각하는, 후회하는, 불만스러운

There's no one thing that's true, it's all true

단 한 가지만 진실한 건 아냐, 모든 게 진실인 거야

That part is just as true as Pilar's old women drinking the blood down at the slaughter-house. There's no one thing that's true. It's all true. The way the planes are beautiful whether they are ours or theirs. The hell they are, he thought.

그래, 그건 필라르가 말한 늙은 여인들이 도살장에서 소의 피를 벌컥벌컥 마시는 것처럼 실감 나는 진실이야. 단 한 가지만 진실한 건 아냐. 사실은 모든 게 진실인 거야. 저 들판이 우리 것이든 아니든 아름답다는 사실은 진실이야. 저 들판은 정말 아름답구나.

문장분석

That part is just as true as Pilar's old women drinking the blood down at the slaughterhouse. There's no one thing that's true. It's all true. The way the planes are beautiful/ whether they are ours or theirs. (The hell) they are (beautiful), he thought.
···처럼 / 강조

blood [blʌd] 피, 혈액
bleed [bliːd] 피가 나다, 피를 흘리다
slaughter [slɔ́ːtər] 도살(butchering)
butcher [bútʃər] 푸주한, 정육점 주인, 도살하다
plane [plein] 평면, 면, 수평면

232

It is only missing it that's bad

나쁜 건 인생을 떠나야 한다는 것이지

Who do you suppose has it easier? Ones with religion or just taking it straight? It comforts them very much but we know there is no thing to fear. It is only missing it that's bad. Dying is only bad when it takes a long time and hurts so much that it humiliates you. That is where you have all the luck, see? You don't have any of that.

죽음을 앞에 놓으면 어느 쪽이 더 유리할까? 종교를 믿는 사람과 객관적으로 받아들이는 사람 중에. 종교가 있으면 위안은 많이 되겠지만 그렇지 않다고 하더라도 두려워할 것은 아무것도 없어. 나쁜 건 인생을 떠나야 한다는 것이지. 죽는데 시간이 너무 많이 걸리고 또 고통이 너무 심해 괴롭다면 그 죽음은 비참한 거지. 그런데 넌 그렇지는 않으니 행운이잖아? 적어도 그런 건 없으니까 말이야.

문장분석

Who (do you suppose) has it easier? Ones with religion or people just taking it
　　　　　　　　　　　　　　　　People
straight? It comforts them very much but we know there is no thing to fear. It is
　　　　　　　　　　　　　　　　　　　　　　　　　　　　　　　　　　　강조 구문
only missing it that is bad. Dying is only bad when it takes a long time and hurts
　　　　　　　　　　　　　　　　　　　　　　　~할 때
so much that it humiliates you. That is where you have all the luck, see? You don't
너무~해서　~하다
have any of that.

suppose [səpóuz] 가정하다(assume), 상상하다
religion [rilídʒən] 종교
comfort [kʌ́mfərt] 위로, 위안, 위로하다

hurt [həːrt] 상처 내다, …을 다치게 하다
humiliate [hjuːmílièit]
　욕보이다, 창피를 주다, 굴복시키다

He could feel his heart beating against the pine needle floor of the forest

숲속의 솔잎 바닥에 몸을 착 깔고 엎드렸을 때 그는 심장이 마구 뛰는 것을 느꼈다

Robert Jordan lay behind the tree, holding onto himself very carefully and delicately to keep his hands steady. He was waiting until the officer reached the sunlit place where the first trees of the pine forest joined the green slope of the meadow. He could feel his heart beating against the pine needle floor of the forest.

로버트 조던은 나무 뒤에 숨어 몸가짐을 바르게 잡으면서 손이 떨리지 않게 하려고 애썼다. 그는 그 장교가 해가 비치는 곳까지 오기를 기다렸다. 그곳은 소나무 숲이 목초지의 푸른 등성이와 연결되는 바로 그 지점이었다. 숲속의 솔잎 바닥에 몸을 착 깔고 엎드렸을 때 그는 심장이 마구 뛰는 것을 느꼈다.

문장분석

Robert Jordan lay behind the tree, holding onto himself very carefully and
                                    (잡다, 유지하다)
delicately to keep his hands steady. He was waiting/ until the officer reached
the sunlit place where the first trees of the pine forest joined the green slope of
the meadow. He could feel his heart beating against the pine needle floor of the
forest.

lie [lai] (lay [lei]- lain [lein]) 눕다, (물건이) 놓여있다
delicate [délikət] 섬세한, 우아한, 고운(fine)
sunlight [sʌ́nlit] 햇볕에 쬐인, 볕이 드는, 희망에 찬

meadow [médou] 풀밭, 목초지
needle [níːdl] 바늘, (침엽수의) 잎

Vocabulary Of The Week

MON

worth [wəːrθ]
…의 가치가 있는,
…할 만한 가치가 있는
worthwhile [wə́ːrθhwáil]
할 보람이 있는, 시간을 들일 만 한

worthy [wə́ːrði]
훌륭한, 존경할 만한, (…에) 어울리는,
hatred [héitrid] 증오, 원한, 혐오
though [ðou]
…이긴 하지만, …이지만

TUE

complain [kəmpléin]
불평하다, 우는소리하다, 한탄하다
complaint [kəmpléint]
불평, 찡찡거림, 불평거리
fortunate [fɔ́ːrtʃənit]
운이 좋은, 행운의, 복받은

regret [rigrét] 유감, 후회(하다)
regretful [rigrétfəl]
유감으로 생각하는, 후회하는,
불만스러운

WED

blood [blʌd] 피, 혈액
bleed [bliːd] 피가 나다, 피를 흘리다
slaughter [slɔ́ːtər] 도살(butchering)
butcher [bútʃər]
푸주한, 정육점 주인, 도살하다
plane [plein] 평면, 면, 수평면

THU

suppose [səpóuz]
가정하다(assume), 상상하다
religion [rilídʒən] 종교
comfort [kʌ́mfərt]
위로, 위안, 위로하다

hurt [həːrt]
상처 내다, …을 다치게 하다
humiliate [hjuːmílièit]
욕보이다, 창피를 주다, 굴복시키다

FRI

lie [lai]
(lay [lei]- lain [lein]) 눕다,
(물건이) 놓여있다
delicate [délikət]
섬세한, 우아한, 고운(fine)

sunlight [sʌ́nlit]
햇볕에 쬐인, 볕이 드는, 희망에 찬
meadow [médou] 풀밭, 목초지
needle [níːdl] 바늘, (침엽수의) 잎

He was an old man who fished alone in a skiff in the Gulf Stream

그는 멕시코 만류에서 조각배를 타고 홀로 고기잡이하는 노인이었다

He was an old man who fished alone in a skiff in the Gulf Stream and he had gone eighty-four days now without taking a fish. In the first forty days a boy had been with him.

그는 멕시코 만류에서 조각배를 타고 홀로 고기잡이하는 노인이었다. 여든 날 하고도 나흘이 지나도록 고기 한 마리 낚지 못했다. 처음 사십 일 동안은 소년이 함께 있었다.

He was an old man who fished alone in a skiff in the Gulf Stream and he had
멕시코 만류

gone eighty-four days now/ without taking a fish. In the first forty days/ a boy

had been with him.

alone [əlóun] 다만 홀로, 혼자서
lone [loun] 짝이 없는, 외로운, 고독을 좋아하는
skiff [skif] 소형 보트, 소형 범선

gulf [gʌlf] 만(폭에 비해 안 길이가 길다)
stream [stri:m] 시내, 개울, 흐름, 조류

TUE

The boy's parents called the old man salao, the worst form of unlucky

소년의 부모는 노인을 가장 운이 없는 사람, '살라오'라고 불렀다

But after forty days without a fish the boy's parents had told him that the old man was now definitely and finally salao, which is the worst form of unlucky, and the boy had gone at their orders in another boat which caught three good fish the first week.

그러나 사십일이 지나도록 고기 한 마리 잡지 못하자 소년의 부모는 그에게 이제 노인이 누가 뭐래도 틀림없이 '살라오'가 되었다고 말했다. '살라오'란 스페인 말로 가장 운이 없는 사람이라는 뜻이다. 소년은 부모가 시키는 대로 다른 배로 옮겨 타게 되었는데, 그 배는 첫 주에 큼직한 고기를 세 마리나 잡았다.

But after forty days without a fish/ the boy's parents had told him that the old man was now definitely and finally salao, which is the worst form of unlucky, and the boy had gone at their orders in another boat which caught three good fish the first week.

parent [péərənt] 어버이(아버지 또는 어머니)
parental [pəréntl] 어버이(로서)의, 어버이다운
definite [défənit]
 (윤곽·한계가) 뚜렷한, 확실한, 명확한

worst [wəːrst] (bad, ill의 최상급) 최악의, 가장 나쁜
unfortunate [ʌnfɔ́ːrtʃənit] 불운한, 불행한

The sail looked like the flag of permanent defeat

돛은 마치 영원한 패배를 상징하는 깃발처럼 보였다

It made the boy sad to see the old man come in each day with his skiff empty and he always went down to help him carry either the coiled lines or the gaff and harpoon and the sail that was furled around the mast. The sail was patched with flour sacks and, furled, it looked like the flag of permanent defeat.

소년은 날마다 노인이 빈 배로 돌아오는 것을 보고 가슴이 아팠다. 그래서 늘 노인을 마중나가 노인이 사려 놓은 낚시 줄이며 갈고리며 작살이며 돛대에 둘둘 말아 놓은 돛 따위를 나르는 일을 도와주었다. 돛은 여기저기 밀가루 부대 조각으로 기워져 있어서 돛대를 높이 펼쳐 올리면 마치 영원한 패배를 상징하는 깃발처럼 보였다.

문장분석

[It] made the boy sad (to see) the old man (come) in each day/ with his skiff empty and he always went down/ to help him carry (either) the coiled lines (or) the gaff and harpoon and the sail that was furled around the mast. The sail was patched with flour sacks and, furled, it looked like the flag of permanent defeat.

gaff [gæf] 작살, 갈고리
harpoon [hɑːrpúːn] (고래잡이용) 작살
furl [fəːrl]
　(돛·기 따위를) 감아 걷다, 개키다, (우산 따위를) 접다

flour [flauər] 밀가루, 분말, 가루
permanent [pə́ːrmənənt]
　영원한, 영속하는, 불변의

His eyes were the same color as the sea and were cheerful and undefeated

그의 두 눈은 바다와 똑같은 빛깔을 띠었으며 기운차고 지칠 줄 몰랐다

The old man was thin and gaunt with deep wrinkles in the back of his neck. His hands had the deep-creased scars from handling heavy fish on the cords. But none of these scars were fresh. Everything about him was old except his eyes and they were the same color as the sea and were cheerful and undefeated.

노인은 깡마르고 여윈 데다 목덜미에는 주름이 깊게 잡혀 있었다. 두 손에는 큰 고기를 잡으면서 밧줄을 다루다가 생긴 상처가 깊게 파여 있었다. 어느 것 하나 새로 생긴 상처는 아니었다. 두 눈을 제외하면 노인의 것은 하나같이 노쇠해 있었다. 오직 두 눈만은 바다와 똑같은 빛깔을 띠었으며 기운차고 지칠 줄 몰랐다.

문장분석

The old man was thin and gaunt/ with deep wrinkles in the back of his neck.

His hands had the deep-creased scars/ from handling heavy fish on the cords.

But none of these scars were fresh. Everything about him was old/ except his

eyes and they were the same color as the sea and (they) were cheerful and

undefeated.

thin [θin] 얇은, 두껍지 않은
gaunt [gɔːnt] 수척한, 몹시 여윈
wrinkle [ríŋkəl] (피부·천 따위의) 주름

crease [kriːs] 주름(살), 접은 금
scar [skɑːr] 상처 자국, 흉터

You're with a lucky boat, so stay with them

네가 타는 배는 운이 좋은 배야, 그러니 그 사람들하고 그냥 있어라

"Santiago, I could go with you again. We've made some money."
"No, you're with a lucky boat. Stay with them."
"It was papa made me leave. I am a boy and I must obey him. He hasn't much faith."
"No," the old man said. "But we have. Haven't we?"

"산티아고 할아버지, 이제 할아버지랑 다시 고기잡이를 할 수 있어요. 우린 돈을 좀 벌었거든요."
"그건 안 돼. 네가 타는 배는 운이 좋은 배야. 그러니 그 사람들하고 그냥 있어라."
"할아버지 곁을 떠나라고 한 건 아버지였어요. 전 아직 나이가 어리니까 아버지 말을 따라야 해요. 그런데 아버지한테는 그다지 신념이라는 게 없어요."
"그건 그렇지. 하지만 우리한테는 신념이 있지. 안 그래?"

문장분석

"Santiago, I could go with you again. We've made some money."

"No, you're with a lucky boat. Stay with them."

"It was papa made me leave. I am a boy and I must obey him. He hasn't much faith."

"No," the old man said. "But we have (faith). Haven't we?"

leave [liːv] (뒤에) 남기다, 남기고 가다, 떠나가다
obey [oubéi] …에 복종하다, …에 따르다
obedience [oubíːdiəns] 복종, 순종

faithful [féiθfəl]
　충실한, 성실한, 믿을 수 있는(reliable)
earn [əːrn] (생활비를) 벌다, 획득하다, 얻다

Vocabulary Of The Week

MON

alone [əlóun] 다만 홀로, 혼자서
lone [loun]
  짝이 없는, 외로운, 고독을 좋아하는
skiff [skif] 소형 보트, 소형 범선
gulf [gʌlf]
  만(폭에 비해 안 길이가 길다)

stream [striːm]
  시내, 개울, 흐름, 조류

TUE

parent [péərənt]
  어버이(아버지 또는 어머니)
parental [pəréntl]
  어버이(로서)의, 어버이다운
definite [défənit]
  (윤곽·한계가) 뚜렷한, 확실한, 명확한

worst [wəːrst]
  (bad, ill의 최상급) 최악의, 가장 나쁜
unfortunate [ʌnfɔ́ːrtʃənit]
  불운한, 불행한

WED

gaff [gæf] 작살, 갈고리
harpoon [hɑːrpún]
  (고래잡이용) 작살
furl [fəːrl]
  (돛·기 따위를) 감아 걷다, 개키다,
  (우산 따위를) 접다

flour [flauər] 밀가루, 분말, 가루
permanent [pə́ːrmənənt]
  영원한, 영속하는, 불변의

THU

thin [θin] 얇은, 두껍지 않은
gaunt [gɔːnt] 수척한, 몹시 여윈
wrinkle [ríŋkəl] (피부·천 따위의) 주름
crease [kriːs] 주름(살), 접은 금
scar [skɑːr] 상처 자국, 흉터

FRI

leave [liːv]
  (뒤에) 남기다, 남기고 가다, 떠나가다
obey [oubéi]
  …에 복종하다, …에 따르다
obedience [oubíːdiəns] 복종, 순종

faithful [féiθfəl]
  충실한, 성실한, 믿을 수 있는(reliable)
earn [əːrn]
  (생활비를) 벌다, 획득하다, 얻다

October
10

Never mistake movement for action.
움직임과 행동을 절대 혼동하지 마라.

MON

His hope and his confidence had never gone

그는 아직 희망과 자신감을 잃지 않고 있었다

"One (sardine)," the old man said.
His hope and his confidence had never gone.
But now they were freshening as when the breeze rises.
"Two," the boy said.
"Two," the old man agreed. "You didn't steal them?"
"I would," the boy said. "But I bought these."

"한 마리면 충분해."
노인은 아직 희망과 자신감을 잃지 않고 있었다. 그리고 미풍이 불어올 때처럼 희망과 자신감이 새롭게 솟구치고 있었다.
"그럼 두 마리 가져올게요." 소년이 말했다.
"좋아, 그럼 두 마리다. 설마 훔친 건 아니겠지?"
"훔칠 수도 있었지만 이건 돈 주고 산 거예요." 소년이 대답했다.

문장분석

"One (sardine)," the old man said.

His hope and his confidence had never gone. But now they were freshening as
~처럼

when the breeze rises.
~할 때

"Two," the boy said.

"Two," the old man agreed. "You didn't steal them?"

"I would (steal them)," the boy said. "But I bought these."

sardine [sɑːrdíːn] 정어리
confidence [kɑ́nfidəns] 신용, 신뢰
freshen [fréʃən]
　새롭게 하다(되다), 원기 왕성해지다

breeze [briːz] 산들바람, 미풍
rise [raiz] (바람이) 세어지다, 일어서다, 일어나다

What do you have to eat?

드실 만한 게 있나요?

"What do you have to eat?" the boy asked.
"A pot of yellow rice with fish. Do you want some?"
"No. I will eat at home. Do you want me to make the fire?"
"No. I will make it later on. Or I may eat the rice cold."

"드실 만한 게 있나요?" 소년이 물었다.
"노란 쌀밥 한 그릇이랑 생선이 있어. 너도 좀 먹을래?"
"아뇨, 전 집에 가서 먹을게요. 불을 피워 드릴까요?"
"괜찮아. 나중에 내가 피우마. 아니면 그냥 찬밥을 먹어도 되고."

문장분석

"What do you have to eat?" the boy asked.

"A pot of yellow rice with fish. Do you want some?"

"No. I will eat at home. Do you want me to make the fire?"
불을 피우다

"No. I will make it later on. Or I may eat the rice cold."
나중에

famine [fǽmin] 기근, 식량 부족
feminine [fémənin] 여성의, 여성스러운
hunger [hʌ́ŋgər] 공복, 배고픔

hunger cure 단식 요법
arson [ɑ́:rsn] 방화(죄)

First you borrow, then you beg

처음엔 돈을 빌리다가 나중엔 구걸하지

"One sheet[lottery]. That's two dollars and a half. Who can we borrow that from?"
"That's easy. I can always borrow two dollars and a half."
"I think perhaps I can too. But I try not to borrow. First you borrow. Then you beg."

"한 장[복권]만 사도록 하자. 2달러 50센트야. 한데 누구한테 그 돈을 꾸지?"
"그건 문제없어요. 2달러 50센트 정도야 저도 언제든지 빌릴 수 있거든요."
"아마 나도 빌릴 순 있을 거야. 하지만 난 될 수 있으면 돈을 빌리지 않고 싶구나. 처음엔 돈을 빌리지. 그러다 나중엔 구걸하게 되는 법이거든."

문장분석

"One sheet[lottery]. That's two dollars and a half. Who(m) can we borrow that from?"

"That's easy. I can always borrow two dollars and a half."

"I think perhaps I can too. But I try not to borrow. First you borrow. Then you beg."

sheet [ʃiːt]
　한 장의 종이, 시트, (침구 따위의) 커버, 홑이불
borrow [bɔ́(ː)rou] 빌리다
lend [lend] 빌려주다

beg [beg]
　(먹고 입을 것·돈·허가·은혜 따위를) 빌다, 구하다
beggar [bégər] 거지

They were strange shoulders, still powerful although very old

비록 늙었지만 그의 어깨는 여전히 이상하리만큼 힘이 넘쳤다

When the boy came back the old man was asleep in the chair and the sun was down. The boy took the old army blanket off the bed and spread it over the back of the chair and over the old man's shoulders. They were strange shoulders, still powerful although very old, and the neck was still strong too and the creases did not show so much when the old man was asleep and his head fallen forward.

소년이 돌아와 보니 노인은 의자에 앉은 채 잠이 들어 있었고 해는 이미 떨어져 있었다. 소년은 침대에서 낡은 군용 담요를 가져와 의자 뒤쪽에서 펴서 노인의 어깨를 덮어 주었다. 비록 늙었지만 그의 어깨는 여전히 이상하리만큼 힘이 넘쳤다. 목에도 여전히 힘이 있었고 고개를 앞쪽으로 떨어뜨리고 잠을 자고 있을 때면 주름살도 별로 눈에 띄지 않았다.

문장분석

When the boy came back/ the old man was asleep in the chair and the sun was
~할 때

down. The boy took the old army blanket off the bed and spread it over the back

of the chair and over the old man's shoulders. They were strange shoulders, still

powerful although very old, and the neck was still strong too and the creases did
비록~이지만

not show so much/ when the old man was asleep and his head fallen forward.

blanket [blǽŋkit] 담요
blank [blæŋk] 공백의, 백지의
shoulder [ʃóuldər] 어깨

crease [kriːs] 주름(살), 접은 금
forward [fɔ́ːrwərd] 앞으로, 전방에

I wanted to take him fishing but I was too timid to ask him

나는 그를 데리고 함께 낚시를 가고 싶었지만, 워낙 소심해서 차마 부탁할 수 없었어

"Do you remember when he[DiMaggio] used to come to the Terrace? I wanted to take him fishing but I was too timid to ask him. Then I asked you to ask him and you were too timid."

"I know. It was a great mistake. He might have gone with us. Then we would have that for all of our lives."

"그 선수[디마지오]가 전에 '테라스'에 찾아오곤 했던 일이 기억나니? 나는 그를 데리고 함께 낚시를 가고 싶었지만, 워낙 소심해서 차마 부탁할 수 없었어. 그래서 네가 부탁해 보라고 했는데 너도 소심했지."

"알고 있어요. 큰 실수였죠. 부탁했더라면 어쩌면 우리와 함께 낚시하러 가 줬을지도 모르는데 말이에요. 그랬더라면 평생을 두고 자랑거리가 되었을 텐데요."

문장분석

"Do you remember when he used to come to the Terrace? I wanted to take him
　　　　　　　　　　　~하곤 했다

fishing but I was too timid to ask him. Then I asked you to ask him and you were

too timid."

"I know. It was a great mistake. He might have gone with us. Then we would

have that for all of our lives."
　　　　　　　평생

timid [tímid] 겁많은, 소심한　　　　　　　be used to 동사 ~하기 위해 사용되다
arrogant [ǽrəgənt] 거드럭거리는, 거만한　　be used to ~ing ~하는 것에 익숙하다
used to 동사 ~하곤 했다(과거의 습관)

Vocabulary Of The Week

MON

sardine [sɑːrdíːn] 정어리
confidence [kɑ́nfidəns] 신용, 신뢰
freshen [fréʃən]
  새롭게 하다(되다), 원기 왕성해지다
breeze [briːz] 산들바람, 미풍

rise [raiz]
(바람이) 세어지다, 일어서다,
일어나다

TUE

famine [fǽmin] 기근, 식량 부족
feminine [fémənin]
  여성의, 여성스러운
hunger [hʌ́ŋgər] 공복, 배고픔
hunger cure 단식 요법
arson [ɑ́ːrsn] 방화(죄)

WED

sheet [ʃiːt]
  한 장의 종이, 시트,
  (침구 따위의) 커버, 홑이불
borrow [bɔ́(ː)rou] 빌리다
lend [lend] 빌려주다

beg [beg]
(먹고 입을 것·돈·허가·은혜 따위를)
빌다, 구하다
beggar [bégər] 거지

THU

blanket [blǽŋkit] 담요
blank [blæŋk] 공백의, 백지의
shoulder [ʃóuldər] 어깨
crease [kriːs] 주름(살), 접은 금
forward [fɔ́ːrwərd] 앞으로, 전방에

FRI

timid [tímid] 겁많은, 소심한
arrogant [ǽrəgənt]
  거드럭거리는, 거만한
used to 동사
  ~하곤 했다(과거의 습관)

be used to 동사
  ~하기 위해 사용되다
be used to ~ing
  ~하는 것에 익숙하다

MON

He was asleep in a short time and he dreamed of Africa

노인은 곧 잠이 들었고, 아프리카에 대한 꿈을 꾸었다

He was asleep in a short time and he dreamed of Africa when he was a boy and the long golden beaches and the white beaches, so white they hurt your eyes, and the high capes and the great brown mountains.

노인은 곧 잠이 들었고, 아직 소년이었을 시절에 본 아프리카에 대한 꿈을 꾸었다. 황금빛으로 빛나는 긴 해변과 눈이 부시도록 새하얀 해안선, 그리고 드높은 갑(岬)과 우뚝 솟은 커다란 갈색 산들이 꿈에 나타났다.

문장분석

He was asleep/ in a short time and he dreamed of (Africa) when he was a boy and

the long golden beaches and the white beaches, (so) white (that) they hurt your

eyes, and the high capes and the great brown mountains.

beach [biːtʃ] 해변, 물가
bitch [bitʃ]
　암컷(개·이리·여우 따위의), 심술궂은 여자
cape [keip] 곶(headland), 갑(岬)

mountaineer [màuntəníər]
　등산가, 산악인, 등산하다
nightmare [náitmèər] 악몽, 가위눌림

He smelled the smell of Africa that the land breeze brought at morning

그는 아침이면 육지 미풍이 싣고 오는 아프리카 대륙의 냄새를 맡았다

He lived along that coast now every night and in his dreams he heard the surf roar and saw the native boats come riding through it. He smelled the tar and oakum of the deck as he slept and he smelled the smell of Africa that the land breeze brought at morning.

그는 매일 밤마다 꿈속에서 이 해안가를 따라 살았고, 꿈속에서 파도가 으르렁거리는 소리를 들었으며, 파도를 헤치며 다가오는 원주민의 배들을 보았다. 그는 잠을 자면서도 갑판의 타르 냄새와 뱃밥 냄새를 코끝으로 맡았으며, 아침이면 육지 미풍이 싣고 오는 아프리카 대륙의 냄새를 맡았다.

문장분석

He lived along that coast now every night and in his dreams/ he heard the surf roar and saw the native boats come riding through it. He smelled the tar and oakum of the deck/ as he slept and he smelled the smell of Africa that the land breeze brought at morning.
사이로
while

coast [koust] 연안, 해안
surf [sə:rf] (해안에) 밀려드는 파도
roar [rɔ:r] 으르렁거리다, 포효하다, 울려 퍼지다

oakum [óukəm]
뱃밥(낡은 밧줄을 푼 것, 누수방지용으로 틈새를 메움)
breeze [bri:z] 산들바람, 미풍

He loved the lions on the beach as he loved the boy

그는 소년을 사랑하듯 해안에 나타나는 사자들을 사랑했다

He no longer dreamed of storms, nor of women, nor of great occurrences, nor of great fish, nor fights, nor contests of strength, nor of his wife. He only dreamed of places now and of the lions on the beach. They played like young cats in the dusk and he loved them as he loved the boy. He never dreamed about the boy.

이제 노인의 꿈에는 폭풍우도, 여자도, 큰 사건도, 큰 고기도, 싸움도, 힘겨루기도, 그리고 죽은 아내의 모습도 나타나지 않았다. 다만 그는 여러 지역과 해안에 나타나는 사자들 꿈만 꿀 뿐이었다. 사자들은 황혼 속에서 마치 새끼 고양이처럼 뛰어놀았고, 그는 소년을 사랑하듯 이 사자들을 사랑했다. 그는 한 번도 소년의 꿈을 꾸어 본 적이 없었다.

문장분석

He no longer dreamed of storms, nor of women, nor of great occurrences, nor of
더이상~아닌   and also not

great fish, nor fights, nor contests of strength, nor of his wife. He only dreamed

of places now and of the lions on the beach. They played like young cats/ in the

dusk and he loved them as he loved the boy. He never dreamed about the boy.
~하듯

storm [stɔːrm] 폭풍(우)
occurrence [əkə́ːrəns] 사건, 생긴 일
strength [streŋkθ] 세기, 힘

dusk [dʌsk] 어둑어둑함, 땅거미, 황혼(twilight)
auspicious [ɔːspíʃəs] 길조의, 경사스런, 상서로운

The old man put his arm across his shoulders and said, "I am sorry."

노인은 한 팔로 소년의 어깨를 감싸며 말했다, "미안하구나."

The old man nodded and the boy took his trousers from the chair by the bed and, sitting on the bed, pulled them on. The old man went out the door and the boy came after him. He was sleepy and the old man put his arm across his shoulders and said, "I am sorry."

노인이 고개를 끄덕이자 소년은 침대 옆 의자에서 바지를 집어 들고 침대에 앉아서 입었다. 노인이 문밖으로 나가자 소년도 그의 뒤를 따랐다. 소년은 아직도 졸렸고, 그래서 노인은 한 팔로 소년의 어깨를 감싸며 말했다. "미안하구나."

문장분석

The old man nodded and the boy took his trousers from the chair by the bed and, sitting on the bed, <u>pulled them on</u>. The old man went out the door and
잡아당겨 입다
the boy came after him. He was sleepy and the old man put his arm across his
~을 따라
shoulders and said, "I am sorry."

nod [nɑd] 끄덕이다
trousers [tráuzərz] (남자의) 바지
pants [pænts] 바지

pant [pænt] 헐떡거리다, 숨차다
shoulder [ʃóuldər] 어깨

The birds have a harder life than we do

새들은 우리 인간보다 더 고달픈 삶을 사는군

He was very fond of flying fish as they were his principal friends on the ocean. He was sorry for the birds, especially the small delicate dark terns that were always flying and looking and almost never finding, and he thought, "The birds have a harder life than we do except for the robber birds and the heavy strong ones."

그는 날치를 무척이나 좋아하여 날치를 바다에서는 가장 친한 친구로 생각했다. 그러나 새들은 가엽다고 생각했는데, 그중에서도 언제나 날아다니면서 먹이를 찾지만 얻는 것이라곤 거의 없는 조그마하고 연약한 제비갈매기를 특히 가엽게 생각했다. 새들은 우리 인간보다 더 고달픈 삶을 사는구나, 하고 생각했다. 물론 강도 새라든가 힘센 새들은 빼놓고 말이지만.

문장분석

He was very fond of flying fish as they were his principal friends on the ocean. He
　　　　～을 매우 좋아하다　　　　　　처럼
was sorry for the birds, especially the small delicate dark terns that were always
　～를 안쓰럽게 여기는
flying and looking and almost never finding, and he thought, "The birds have a

harder life than we do/ except for the robber birds and the heavy strong ones."
　　　　　　　　　　　　　　　　　　　　　　　　　　　　　　　　　　　　birds

fond [fɑnd] 좋아서(liking), 사랑에 빠진
principal [prínsəpəl] 주요한, 제1의, 중요한
delicate [délikət] 섬세한, 우아한, 고운

tern [təːrn] 제비갈매기
robber [rɑ́bər] 도둑, 강도, 약탈자

Vocabulary Of The Week

MON

beach [biːtʃ] 해변, 물가
bitch [bitʃ]
　암컷(개·이리·여우 따위의),
　심술궂은 여자
cape [keip] 곶(headland), 갑(岬)

mountaineer [màuntəníər]
　등산가, 산악인, 등산하다
nightmare [náitmὲər]
　악몽, 가위눌림

TUE

coast [koust] 연안, 해안
surf [səːrf] (해안에) 밀려드는 파도
roar [rɔːr]
　으르렁거리다, 포효하다, 울려 퍼지다

oakum [óukəm]
　뱃밥(낡은 밧줄을 푼 것,
　누수방지용으로 틈새를 메움)
breeze [briːz] 산들바람, 미풍

WED

storm [stɔːrm] 폭풍(우)
occurrence [əkə́ːrəns] 사건, 생긴 일
strength [streŋkθ] 세기, 힘
dusk [dʌsk]
　어둑어둑함, 땅거미, 황혼(twilight)

uspicious [ɔːspíʃəs]
　길조의, 경사스런, 상서로운

THU

nod [nɑd] 끄덕이다
trousers [tráuzərz] (남자의) 바지
pants [pænts] 바지
pant [pænt] 헐떡거리다, 숨차다
shoulder [ʃóuldər] 어깨

FRI

fond [fɑnd]
　좋아서(liking), 사랑에 빠진
principal [prínsəpəl]
　수요한, 제1의, 중요한
delicate [délikət]
　섬세한, 우아한, 고운

tern [təːrn] 제비갈매기
robber [rάbər] 도둑, 강도, 약탈자

MON

Why did they make birds so delicate and fine as those sea swallows

그들은 왜 제비갈매기처럼 연약하고 가냘픈 새를 만들어 냈을까?

Why did they make birds so delicate and fine as those sea swallows when the ocean can be so cruel? She is kind and very beautiful. But she can be so cruel and it comes so suddenly and such birds that fly, dipping and hunting, with their small sad voices are made too delicately for the sea.

바다가 이렇게 잔혹할 수도 있는데 왜 제비갈매기처럼 연약하고 가냘픈 새를 만들어 냈을까? 바다는 다정스럽고 아름답긴 해. 하지만 몹시 잔인해질 수도 있는 데다가 갑자기 그렇게 되기도 하지. 가냘프고 구슬픈 소리로 울며 날아가다가 수면에 주둥이를 처박고 먹이를 찾는 저 새들은 바다에서 살아가기에는 너무 연약하게 만들어졌단 말이야.

문장분석

Why did they make birds so delicate and fine/ as those sea swallows when the
처럼 ···인데
ocean can be so cruel? She is kind and very beautiful. But she can be so cruel
The ocean
and it comes so suddenly and such birds that fly, dipping and hunting, with their

small sad voices are made too delicately for the sea."

fine [fain] 미세한, 가는, 가냘픈, 예민한
swallow [swálou] 들이켜다, 삼키다, 제비
sea swallow 제비갈매기

cruel [krú:əl] 잔인한, 무자비한
dip [dip] 담그다, 적시다, 살짝 담그다

No one should be alone in their old age

늙어서는 어느 누구도 혼자 있어서는 안 돼

Then he said aloud, "I wish I had the boy. To help me and to see this." No one should be alone in their old age, he thought. But it is unavoidable. I must remember to eat the tuna before he spoils in order to keep strong. Remember, no matter how little you want to, that you must eat him in the morning. Remember, he said to himself.

노인은 큰 소리로 말했다. "그 애가 옆에 있다면 얼마나 좋을까. 나를 도와줄 수도 있고, 이걸 구경할 수도 있을 텐데." 늙어서는 어느 누구도 혼자 있어서는 안 돼, 하고 그는 생각했다. 하지만 어떨 도리가 없는걸. 잊지 말고 저 다랑어가 상하기 전에 먹고 기운을 차려야지. 아무리 먹기 싫더라도 아침에는 꼭 먹어야 해. 절대로 잊어서는 안 돼, 하고 그는 스스로를 타일렀다.

문장분석

Then he said aloud, "I wish I had the boy. To help me and to see this." No one should be alone in their old age, he thought. But it is unavoidable. I must remember to eat the tuna before he spoils (in order) to keep strong. Remember,
미래의 내용

no matter how little you want to, that you must eat him in the morning.
아무리~하더라도
Remember, he said to himself.

aloud [əláud] 소리를 내어, 큰 소리로
avoid [əvɔ́id] 피하다, 회피하다
unavoidable [ʌnəvɔ́idəbl]
   피할(어쩔) 수 없는, 무효로 할 수 없는

tuna [tjúːnə] 다랑어, 참치(의 살)
spoil [spɔil]
   망쳐놓다(destroy), 못쓰게 만들다, 손상하다

They play and make jokes and love one another

그들은 함께 놀고 장난도 치고 사랑도 하지

During the night two porpoise came around the boat and he could hear them rolling and blowing. He could tell the difference between the blowing noise the male made and the sighing blow of the female. "They are good," he said. "They play and make jokes and love one another. They are our brothers like the flying fish." Then he began to pity the great fish that he had hooked.

밤중에 돌고래 두 마리가 조각배 주위에 다가와 이리저리 뒹굴며 물을 내뿜는 소리가 들렸다. 노인은 수컷이 물을 내뿜는 소리와 암컷이 한숨을 쉬듯 물을 내뿜는 소리를 분간할 수 있었다. "착한 놈들이지. 놈들은 함께 놀고 장난도 치고 사랑도 하지. 저 돌고래들도 날치와 마찬가지로 우리의 형제들이지." 그가 말했다. 그리고 나서 노인은 자신의 낚시에 걸린 큰 고기가 불쌍하다는 생각이 들기 시작했다.

문장분석

During the night/ two porpoise came around the boat and he could hear them rolling and blowing. He could tell the difference between the blowing noise the
알아채다
male made and the sighing blow of the female. "They are good," he said. "They play and make jokes and love one another. They are our brothers like the flying
서로   처럼
fish." Then he began to pity the great fish that he had hooked.

porpoise [pɔ́ːrpəs] 돌고래
blow [blou] 불다, 숨을 내쉬다, 입김을 내뿜다
sigh [sai] 한숨 쉬다

pity [píti] 불쌍히 여김, 동정
hook [huk] 갈고리, 훅

Never have I had such a strong fish nor one who acted so strangely

이렇게 힘세고 별나게 구는 녀석은 처음이야

Never have I had such a strong fish nor one who acted so strangely. Perhaps he is too wise to jump. He could ruin me by jumping or by a wild rush. But perhaps he has been hooked many times before and he knows that this is how he should make his fight. He cannot know that it is only one man against him, nor that it is an old man.

이렇게 힘세고 별나게 구는 녀석은 처음이야. 날뛰는 것도 여간 똑똑하고, 작정하고 요동치면 내가 끝장날 것 같은데. 아마 전에도 여러 번 낚시에 걸린 경험이 있어 이럴 때는 지금처럼 싸워야 한다고 생각하고 있는 모양이야. 자신의 상대가 오직 한 사람뿐이며 게다가 나이 든 늙은이라는 사실은 전혀 모르고 있을 거야.

문장분석

Never have I had such a strong fish nor one who acted so strangely. Perhaps he
문두 부정어로 인한 도치   and also not
is too wise to jump. He could ruin me by jumping or by a wild rush. But perhaps

he has been hooked many times before and he knows that this is how he should

make his fight. He cannot know that it is only one man against him, nor that it is
~에 맞서

an old man.

act [ækt] 소행, 행위, 행하다
perhaps [pərhǽps]
  아마, 형편에 따라서는, 혹시, 어쩌면

wise [waiz] 슬기로운, 현명한
ruin [rúːin] 파멸, 파괴하다
rush [rʌʃ] 돌진하다, 쇄도

The male fish always let the female fish feed first

먹이를 발견하면 수놈은 언제나 암컷에게 먼저 먹게 한다

He remembered the time he had hooked one of a pair of marlin. The male fish always let the female fish feed first and the hooked fish, the female, made a wild, panic-stricken, despairing fight that soon exhausted her, and all the time the male had stayed with her, crossing the line and circling with her on the surface.

노인은 언젠가 청새치 한 쌍 중에서 한 마리를 낚았던 일이 기억났다. 먹이를 발견하면 수놈은 언제나 암컷에게 먼저 먹게 한다. 그때 낚시에 걸려든 놈은 암놈이었는데 겁에 질려 사방으로 마구 날뛰면서 필사적으로 투쟁하다가 곧 기진맥진해버렸고, 그러는 동안 수놈은 계속 암컷 옆에 붙어서 낚싯줄을 넘어 다니기도 하고 암컷과 함께 동그랗게 원을 그리며 수면을 맴돌기도 했다.

문장분석

He remembered (the time) he had hooked one of a pair of marlin. The male fish always let the female fish feed first and the hooked fish, the female, made a wild, panic-stricken, (despairing fight) that soon exhausted her, and all the time the
내내
male had stayed with her, crossing the line and circling with her on the surface.

marlin [máːrlin] 청새치류(類)
panic-stricken 공황에 휩쓸린, 당황한
despair [dispéər] 절망, 자포자기, 단념하다

exhaust [igzɔ́ːst]
다 써버리다(use up), 고갈시키다
surface [sə́ːrfis] 표면, 외면, 외부

Vocabulary Of The Week

MON

fine [faɪn]
미세한, 가는, 가냘픈, 예민한
swallow [swɑ́lou]
들이켜다, 삼키다, 제비
sea swallow 제비갈매기
cruel [krúːəl] 잔인한, 무자비한

dip [dip] 담그다, 적시다, 살짝 담그다

TUE

aloud [əláud] 소리를 내어, 큰 소리로
avoid [əvɔ́id] 피하다, 회피하다
unavoidable [ʌnəvɔ́idəbl]
피할(어쩔) 수 없는, 무효로 할 수 없는
tuna [tjúːnə] 다랑어, 참치(의 살)

spoil [spɔil]
망쳐놓다(destroy), 못쓰게 만들다,
손상하다

WED

porpoise [pɔ́ːrpəs] 돌고래
blow [blou]
불다, 숨을 내쉬다, 입김을 내뿜다
sigh [sai] 한숨 쉬다
pity [píti] 불쌍히 여김, 동정
hook [huk] 갈고리, 훅

THU

act [ækt] 소행, 행위, 행하다
perhaps [pərhǽps]
아마, 형편에 따라서는, 혹시, 어쩌면
wise [waiz] 슬기로운, 현명한
ruin [rúːin] 파멸, 파괴하다
rush [rʌʃ] 돌진하다, 쇄도

FRI

marlin [máːrlin] 청새치류(類)
panic-stricken
공황에 휩쓸린, 당황한
despair [dispέər]
절망, 자포자기, 단념하다

exhaust [igzɔ́ːst]
다 써버리다(use up), 고갈시키다
surface [sə́ːrfis] 표면, 외면, 외부

MON

That was the saddest thing I ever saw with them

그들과 함께하면서 목격한 일 중에서 가장 슬픈 사건이었다

He was beautiful, the old man remembered, and he had stayed. That was the saddest thing I ever saw with them, the old man thought. The boy was sad too and we begged her pardon and butchered her promptly.

참으로 아름다운 놈이었지, 하고 노인은 그때의 추억을 되새겼다. 그 녀석은 마지막까지 머물다 갔었지. 청새치를 잡으면서 목격한 일 중에서 가장 슬픈 사건이었어, 하고 노인은 생각했다. 그 애도 슬퍼했고, 우리는 암놈에게 용서를 빌고는 즉시 칼질을 해 버렸지.

문장분석

He was beautiful, (the old man remembered), and he had stayed. That was the saddest thing I ever saw with them, the old man thought. The boy was sad too and we begged her pardon and butchered her promptly.

beg [beg]
(먹고 입을 것·돈·허가·은혜 따위를) 빌다, 구하다
pardon [pά:rdn] 용서, 허용, 관대, 사면

amnesty [ǽmnəsti] 은사, 대사(大赦), 특사
butcher [bútʃər] 푸주한, 고깃간 주인
promptly [prάmptli] 신속히, 재빠르게, 즉시

Now we are joined together and have been since noon

그래서 우리는 지금 함께 있는 것이고, 정오부터 줄곧 이렇게 함께 있었던 거지

His choice had been to stay in the deep dark water far out beyond all snares and traps and treacheries. My choice was to go there to find him beyond all people. Beyond all people in the world. Now we are joined together and have been since noon. And no one to help either one of us.

그런데 이놈이 선택한 방법이란 온갖 올가미나 덫이나 계책이 미치지 못하는 먼바다의 깊고 어두운 물속에 잠겨 있자는 것이지. 내가 선택한 방법이란 모든 사람이 다다르지 못하는 그곳까지 쫓아가서 그놈을 찾아내는 것이고, 이 세상의 모든 사람이 가지 못하는 그곳까지 말이야. 그래서 우리는 지금 함께 있는 것이고, 정오부터 줄곧 이렇게 함께 있었던 거야. 더구나 우리를 도와주는 사람 하나 없이.

문장분석

His choice had been to stay in the deep dark water/ far out beyond all snares and traps and treacheries. My choice was to go there to find him/ beyond all people. Beyond all people in the world. Now we are joined together and have been since noon. And no one to help either one of us.

둘 중 어느 한쪽

snare [snɛər] 덫, 올가미
trap [træp] 올가미, 함정, 덫
treachery [trétʃəri] 배반, 반역, 변절

treacherous [trétʃərəs]
불충(不忠)한, (언동이) 불성실한, 배반하는
treach [tretʃ] 멋있는, 아주 근사한

Anyway I feel better with the sun

어쨌든 해가 떠오르니 한결 기분이 좋다

I must not jerk it ever, he thought. Each jerk widens the cut the hook makes and then when he does jump he might throw it. Anyway I feel better with the sun and for once I do not have to look into it.

절대로 잡아당겨서는 안 되겠는걸, 하고 그는 생각했다. 세게 잡아당길 때마다 낚시가 걸린 상처가 넓어질 것이고 그렇게 되면 고기가 뛰어오를 때 낚시가 벗겨져 버릴지도 몰라. 어쨌든 해가 떠오르니 한결 기분이 좋구나. 이번만은 해를 정면으로 바라보지 않아도 되고.

I must not jerk it ever, he thought. Each jerk widens (the cut) the hook makes and

then/ when he does jump/ he might throw it. Anyway I feel better with the sun
　　　　　　　　　　　　　　　　　　　　　　　　　　　　　좌우지간

and for once/ I do not have to look into it.
　　　　　　　～할 필요가 없다

jerk [dʒəːrk] 급격한 움직임, 갑자기 당기다
widen [wáidn] 넓히다, 넓게 되다
hook [huk] 갈고리, 훅

hooker [húkər] 매춘부, 사기꾼
throw [θrou] (내)던지다

Stay at my house if you like, bird

새야, 네가 좋다면 우리 집에 머물러도 좋아

"Take a good rest, small bird," he said. "Then go in and take your chance like any man or bird or fish." It encouraged him to talk because his back had stiffened in the night and it hurt truly now. "Stay at my house if you like, bird," he said. "I am sorry I cannot hoist the sail and take you in with the small breeze that is rising. But I am with a friend."

"실컷 푹 쉬어라, 작은 새야. 그러곤 뭍으로 날아가 인간이나 다른 새나 고기처럼 네 행운을 잡으려무나." 밤 동안에 등이 뻣뻣했고 지금은 심한 통증까지 있었는데, 새에게 말을 걸고 나니 노인은 힘이 솟았다. "새야, 네가 좋다면 우리 집에 머물러도 좋아. 지금 미풍이 불고 있는데 돛을 올리고 너를 뭍까지 데려다 주지 못해 미안해. 하지만 나는 지금 친구와 함께 있단다."

문장분석

"Take a good rest, small bird," he said. "Then go in and take your chance/ like any man or bird or fish." It encouraged him to talk/ because his back had stiffened in the night and it hurt truly now. "Stay at my house if you like, bird," he said. "I am sorry (that) I cannot hoist the sail and take you in with the small breeze that is rising. But I am with a friend."

encourage [enkə́ːridʒ]
용기를 돋우다, 격려하다, 고무하다
endanger [endéindʒər]
위태롭게 하다, 위험에 빠뜨리다

stiffen [stífən] 뻣뻣하게 하다, 딱딱하게 하다
hoist [hɔist] (기 따위를) 내걸다, 올리다
breeze [briːz] 산들바람, 미풍

I do this for you

널 위해 이렇게 하는 거야

"Be patient, hand," he said. "I do this for you." I wish I could feed the fish, he thought. He is my brother. But I must kill him and keep strong to do it. Slowly and conscientiously he ate all of the wedge-shaped strips of fish.

"조금만 참아, 이 손 친구야. 너를 위해 먹는 거니까." 그가 말했다. 물속의 고기 녀석한테도 먹을 것을 좀 줬으면 좋겠는데, 하고 그는 생각했다. 저놈하고 난 형제 사이니까. 하지만 나는 저놈을 꼭 죽여야 하고, 그러기 위해서는 힘이 빠져선 안 돼. 천천히 그리고 열심히 그는 쐐기 모양의 생선 조각을 모두 먹어 치웠다.

문장분석

"Be patient, hand," he said. "I do this for you." I (wish) I (could) feed the fish, he thought. He is my brother. But I must kill him and keep strong to do it. Slowly and conscientiously/ he ate all of the wedge-shaped strips of fish.

patient [péiʃənt] 인내심이 강한, 끈기 좋은
feed [fiːd] 음식을(먹이를) 주다
conscientious [kànʃiénʃəs] 양심적인, 성실한

wedge-shaped 쐐기 모양의, V 자 꼴의
strip [strip] 조각, 벗기다

MON

beg [beg]
(먹고 입을 것·돈·허가·은혜 따위를)
빌다, 구하다
pardon [páːrdn]
용서, 허용, 관대, 사면

amnesty [ǽmnəsti]
은사, 대사(大赦), 특사
butcher [bútʃər] 푸주한, 고깃간 주인
promptly [prάmptli]
신속히, 재빠르게, 즉시

TUE

snare [snɛər] 덫, 올가미
trap [træp] 올가미, 함정, 덫
treachery [trétʃəri] 배반, 반역, 변절
treacherous [trétʃərəs]
불충(不忠)한, (언동이) 불성실한,
배반하는

treach [tretʃ] 멋있는, 아주 근사한

WED

jerk [dʒəːrk]
급격한 움직임, 갑자기 당기다
widen [wáidn] 넓히다, 넓게 되다
hook [huk] 갈고리, 훅
hooker [húkər] 매춘부, 사기꾼
throw [θrou] (내)던지다

THU

encourage [enkə́ːridʒ]
용기를 돋우다, 격려하다, 고무하다
endanger [endéindʒər]
위태롭게 하다, 위험에 빠뜨리다
stiffen [stífən]
뻣뻣하게 하다, 딱딱하게 하다

hoist [hɔist]
(기 따위를) 내걸다, 올리다
breeze [briːz] 산들바람, 미풍

FRI

patient [péiʃənt]
인내심이 강한, 끈기 좋은
feed [fiːd] 음식을(먹이를) 주다
conscientious [kὰnʃiénʃəs]
양심적인, 성실한

wedge-shaped
쐐기 모양의, V 자 꼴의
strip [strip] 소삭, 벗기다

November
11

*You are so brave and quiet
I forget you are suffering.*

네가 너무 용감하고 조용히 있어서 고통 받고 있다는 걸 깜빡했어.

MON

He knew no man was ever alone on the sea

그는 어느 누구도 바다에서는 결코 외롭지 않다는 사실을 깨달았다

He looked across the sea and knew how alone he was now. But he could see the prisms in the deep dark water and the line stretching ahead and the strange undulation of the calm. The clouds were building up now for the trade wind and he looked ahead and saw a flight of wild ducks etching themselves against the sky over the water, then blurring, then etching again and he knew no man was ever alone on the sea.

노인은 바다 저편을 바라보며 자신이 얼마나 홀로 고독하게 있는지 새삼스럽게 깨달았다. 그러나 깊고 어두컴컴한 물속에서 프리즘이 보였고, 앞쪽으로 곧바로 뻗어 나간 낚싯줄이며 잔잔한 바다의 이상야릇한 파동이 보였다. 이제 무역풍이 불어오려는 듯 구름이 뭉게뭉게 피어오르기 시작했다. 문득 앞쪽을 바라보니 물오리 떼가 바다 위 하늘에 새겨 놓은 듯 뚜렷하게 모습을 드러냈다가 흩어지고 다시 나타나면서 바다 위를 날아가고 있었다. 그래서 그는 어느 누구도 바다에서는 결코 외롭지 않다는 사실을 깨달았다.

문장분석

He looked across the sea and knew how alone/ he was now. But he could see the prisms in the deep dark water and the line stretching ahead and the strange undulation of the calm. The clouds were building up now for the trade wind and he looked ahead and saw a flight of wild ducks etching themselves against the sky over the water, then blurring, then etching again and he knew (that) no man was ever alone on the sea.

undulate [ʌ́ndʒəlèit]
  (수면 등에) 물결이 일다, 굽이치다
calm [kɑːm] 고요한, 조용한(quiet), 온화한
flight [flait] 날기, 비상(飛翔), 비행

etch [etʃ]
  에칭으로 (그림·무늬를) 새기다, 선명하게 그리다
blur [bləːr] 더러움, 얼룩, 희미해지다, 흐려지다

A cramp humiliates oneself especially when one is alone

쥐가 난다는 건 특히 혼자 있을 때 그야말로 창피한 노릇이지

His left hand was still cramped, but he was unknotting it slowly. I hate a cramp, he thought. It is a treachery of one's own body. It is humiliating before others to have a diarrhoea from ptomaine poisoning or to vomit from it. But a cramp humiliates oneself especially when one is alone.

왼손은 여전히 쥐가 난 상태였지만 그는 천천히 쥐를 풀려고 하고 있었다. 쥐가 나는 건 딱 질색이야, 하고 노인은 생각했다. 그건 자신의 몸한테 배신을 당하는 꼴이거든. 사람들 앞에서 프토마인 중독을 일으켜 설사를 한다든지, 그 때문에 구토를 한다든지 하는 것도 창피한 일이지. 하지만 쥐가 난다는 건 특히 혼자 있을 때 그야말로 창피한 노릇이야.

문장분석

His left hand was still cramped, but he was unknotting it slowly. I hate a cramp, he thought. It is a treachery of one's own body. It is humiliating (before others) to have a diarrhoea from ptomaine poisoning or to vomit from it. But a cramp humiliates oneself especially when one is alone.

일반인

cramp [kræmp] 쥐, 경련, 꺾쇠, 침쇠
treachery [trétʃəri] 배반, 반역
humiliate [hjuːmílièit]
 욕보이다, 창피를 주다, 굴욕을 주다

diarrhoea [dàiəríːə] 설사
vomit [vámit] 토하다, 게우다

They are not as intelligent as we who kill them

저놈들은 저희들을 죽이는 우리 인간들보다는 똑똑하지가 않지

I must never let him learn his strength nor what he could do if he made his run. If I were him I would put in everything now and go until something broke. But, thank God, they are not as intelligent as we who kill them; although they are more noble and more able.

저놈이 힘이 세다는 것도, 저놈이 도망치기만 하면 무슨 짓이든 할 수 있다는 것도 알게 해서는 안 돼. 만약 내가 저놈이라면 있는 힘을 다해 뭔가 끊어질 때까지 계속 내달릴 텐데. 하지만 다행스럽게도 저놈들은 저희들을 죽이는 우리 인간들보다는 똑똑하지가 않단 말이야. 비록 저놈들이 우리 인간들보다 더 기품이 있고 힘이 세지만 말이지.

문장분석

I must never let him learn his strength nor what he could do if he made his run.

If I were him/ I would put in everything now and go until something broke. But,
쏟다, 들이다
thank God, they are not as intelligent as we who kill them; although they are
비록~이지만
more noble and more able.

strength [streŋkθ] 세기, 힘
intelligent [intélədʒənt]
　지적인, 지성을 갖춘, 지능이 있는
intelligible [intélədʒəbəl]
　이해할 수 있는, 알기 쉬운, 명료한

noble [nóubəl] 귀족의, 고귀한
able [éibəl] 능력 있는, 재능 있는, 유능한

Each time was a new time and he never thought about the past

매 순간이 새로운 순간이었고, 그는 과거에 대해서는 조금도 생각하지 않았다

"I told the boy I was a strange old man," he said. "Now is when I must prove it." The thousand times that he had proved it meant nothing. Now he was proving it again. Each time was a new time and he never thought about the past when he was doing it.

"나는 그 아이한테 내가 별난 늙은이라고 말했지. 지금 그 말을 입증해 보일 때지." 그가 말했다. 지금까지 그는 그런 입증을 수천 번이나 해 보였지만 결국 아무런 의미도 없었다. 지금 또다시 그것을 입증해 보이려고 하고 있었다. 매 순간이 새로운 순간이었고, 그것을 입증할 때 그는 과거에 대해서는 조금도 생각하지 않았다.

문장분석

"I told the boy I was a strange old man," he said. "Now is (the time) when I must prove it." (The thousand times) that he had proved it meant nothing. Now/ he was proving it again. Each time was a new time and he never thought about the past /when he was doing it.
~할 때

prove [pru:v] 증명하다, 입증(立證)하다
proof [pru:f]
　증명, 증거, 통과 안 시키는, (…에) 견디어내는

bulletproof [búlitpru:f] 방탄의
approve [əprú:v] 시인하다, 찬성하다
eccentric [ikséntrik] 보통과 다른, 괴상한, 괴짜인

Man is not much beside the great birds and beasts

이런 대단한 새나 짐승과 비교해 보면 인간이란 그리 대단한 게 못 돼

I do not think I could endure that or the loss of the eye and of both eyes and continue to fight as the fighting cocks do. Man is not much beside the great birds and beasts. Still I would rather be that beast down there in the darkness of the sea. "Unless sharks come," he said aloud. "If sharks come, God pity him and me."

싸움닭처럼 한쪽 눈이나 심지어 양쪽 눈이 다 빠지면서까지 계속 싸우지는 못할 거야. 이런 대단한 새나 짐승과 비교해 보면 인간이란 그리 대단한 게 못 돼. 난 차라리 저 캄캄한 바닷속에 사는 저런 놈이 되고 싶구나. "상어만 오지 않는다면 말이지만. 만약 상어가 나타난다면 저놈이나 나나 가엾은 꼴이 되고 말 거야." 그가 큰 소리로 말했다.

문장분석

I do not think I could endure that or the loss of the eye and of both eyes and

continue to fight/ as the fighting cocks do. Man is not much/ beside the great
　　　　　　　　　~처럼　　　　　　　fight　　　　　　　···와 비교하여
birds and beasts. Still I would rather be that beast down there in the darkness of
　　　　　　　　　　　　오히려
the sea. "Unless sharks come," he said aloud. "If sharks come, God pity him and
　　　　　If~not
me."

endure [endjúər] 견디다, 인내하다　　　　beast [bi:st] 짐승
continue [kəntínju:] 계속하다　　　　　　shark [ʃɑ:rk] 상어
cock [kɑk/kɔk] 수탉

Vocabulary Of The Week

MON

undulate [ʌ́ndʒəlèit]
(수면 등에) 물결이 일다, 굽이치다
calm [kɑːm]
고요한, 조용한(quiet), 온화한
flight [flait] 날기, 비상(飛翔), 비행

etch [etʃ]
에칭으로 (그림·무늬를) 새기다,
선명하게 그리다
blur [blə:r]
더러움, 얼룩, 희미해지다, 흐려지다

TUE

cramp [kræmp] 쥐, 경련, 꺾쇠, 죔쇠
treachery [trétʃəri] 배반, 반역
humiliate [hjuːmílièit]
욕보이다, 창피를 주다, 굴욕을 주다
diarrhoea [dàiərí:ə] 설사
vomit [vámit] 토하다, 게우다

WED

strength [streŋkθ] 세기, 힘
intelligent [intélədʒənt]
지적인, 지성을 갖춘, 지능이 있는
intelligible [intélədʒəbəl]
이해할 수 있는, 알기 쉬운, 명료한
noble [nóubəl] 귀족의, 고귀한

able [éibəl] 능력 있는, 재능 있는,
유능한

THU

prove [pru:v]
증명하다, 입증(立證)하다
proof [pru:f]
증명, 증거, 통과 안 시키는,
(…에) 견디어내는
bulletproof [búlitpru:f] 방탄의

approve [əprúːv] 시인하다, 찬성하다
eccentric [ikséntrik]
보통과 다른, 괴상한, 괴짜인

FRI

endure [endjúər] 견디다, 인내하다
continue [kəntínju:] 계속하다
cock [kɑk/kɔk] 수탉
beast [bi:st] 짐승
shark [ʃɑ:rk] 상어

MON

Also now I have gained on him in the question of sustenance

더구나 식량 문제라면 저놈보다는 내가 훨씬 유리한 입장이지

He did not truly feel good because the pain from the cord across his back had almost passed pain and gone into a dullness that he mistrusted. But I have had worse things than that, he thought. My hand is only cut a little and the cramp is gone from the other. My legs are all right. Also now I have gained on him in the question of sustenance.

실제로 노인은 정말로 기분이 좋은 상태가 아니었다. 낚싯줄을 멘 등이 통증의 수준을 넘어 거의 무감각 상태가 아닌가 의구심이 들 정도였기 때문이다. 하지만 나는 이보다 더 심한 일도 겪었는걸, 하고 그는 생각했다. 내 오른손은 조금 긁힌 정도에 지나지 않고, 이제 왼손의 쥐도 풀렸어. 두 다리도 끄떡없고. 더구나 식량 문제라면 저놈보다는 내가 훨씬 유리한 입장이지.

문장분석

He did not truly feel good because the pain from the cord across his back had almost passed pain and gone into a dullness that he mistrusted. But I have had worse things than that, he thought. My hand is only cut a little and the cramp is gone from the other. My legs are all right. Also now I have gained on him in the question of sustenance.

떼어놓다, 벌려놓다

dull [dʌl] 무딘, 둔한
mistrust [mistrʌ́st] 불신
cramp [kræmp] 경련, 쥐

gain [gein] 얻다, 획득하다
sustenance [sʌ́stənəns]
생명을 유지하는 물건, 지속

I am glad we do not have to try to kill the stars

별들은 죽이지 않아도 되니 다행이다

The first stars were out. He did not know the name of Rigel but he saw it and knew soon they would all be out and he would have all his distant friends. "The fish is my friend too," he said aloud. "I have never seen or heard of such a fish. But I must kill him. I am glad we do not have to try to kill the stars."

첫 별들이 나타났다. 그는 '리겔'성이라는 이름은 알지 못했지만 그 별을 보고 곧 뭇 별들이 떠오르리란 것을 알고 있었다. 그렇게 되면 먼 곳의 친구들을 모두 만나게 되리라. "하기야 저 고기도 내 친구이긴 하지." 그가 큰 소리로 말했다. "저런 고기는 여태껏 본 적도, 들은 적도 없어. 하지만 나는 저놈을 죽여야만 해. 별들은 죽이지 않아도 되니 다행이지 뭐야."

문장분석

The first stars were out. He did not know the name of Rigel but he saw it and knew soon they would all be out and he would have all <u>his distant friends</u>. "The fish is my friend too," he said aloud. "I have never seen or heard of such a fish. But I must kill him. I am glad (that) we <u>do not have to</u> try to kill the stars."

stars

~할 필요가 없다

distant [distənt] 먼, 떨어진
distance [dístəns] 거리, 간격
immense [iméns]
　막대한(enormous, vast), 광대한, 끝없는

aloud [əláud] 소리를 내어, 큰 소리로
lousy [láuzi] 천한, 치사한

It is good that we do not have to try to kill the sun or the moon or the stars

해나 달이나 별을 죽이려고 할 필요가 없다는 건 정말로 다행스러운 일이야

How many people will he feed, he thought. But are they worthy to eat him? No, of course not. There is no one worthy of eating him from the manner of his behaviour and his great dignity. I do not understand these things, he thought. But it is good that we do not have to try to kill the sun or the moon or the stars. It is enough to live on the sea and kill our true brothers.

저놈을 잡으면 얼마나 많은 사람의 배를 채울 수 있겠는가, 하고 그는 생각했다. 하지만 그들에게 저 고기를 먹을 만한 자격이 있을까? 아냐, 그럴 자격이 없어. 저렇게도 당당한 거동, 저런 위엄을 보면 저놈을 먹을 자격이 있는 인간이란 단 한 사람도 없어. 하지만 해나 달이나 별을 죽이려고 할 필요가 없다는 건 정말로 다행스러운 일이야. 바닷가에서 살아가면서 우리의 진정한 형제들을 죽이는 것만으로도 충분해.

문장분석

How many people/ will he feed, he thought. But are they worthy to eat him? No, of course not. There is no one (who is) worthy of eating him from the manner of his behaviour and his great dignity. I do not understand these things, he thought. But it is good that we do not have to try to kill the sun or the moon or the stars. It is enough to live on the sea and kill our true brothers.

~할 필요가 없다

feed [fi:d] 음식을 주다
worthy [wə́:rði] 훌륭한, 존경할 만한, 가치 있는
worth [wəːrθ] 가치, …할 만한 가치가 있는

behavior [bihéivjər] 행동, 행실, 동작, 태도
dignity [dígnəti] 존엄, 위엄

I am as clear as the stars that are my brothers

나는 나와 형제 사이인 별처럼 맑아

"It is half a day and a night and now another day and you have not slept. If you do not sleep you might become unclear in the head." I'm clear enough in the head, he thought. Too clear. I am as clear as the stars that are my brothers. Still I must sleep. They sleep and the moon and the sun sleep and even the ocean sleeps sometimes on certain days when there is no current and a flat calm.

"반나절과 하룻밤, 또 하루가 지났는데도 잠 한숨 못 잤잖아. 잠을 자지 않으면 머리가 흐리멍덩해질지 몰라." 머릿속은 충분히 맑아, 하고 노인은 생각했다. 너무나 맑아서 탈이지. 나와 형제 사이인 별처럼 맑아. 하지만 잠은 역시 자야 해. 별도 잠을 자고 달과 해도 잠을 자지 않는가. 심지어는 조류가 없는 아주 조용한 날이면 드넓은 바다도 가끔 잠들 때가 있지.

문장분석

"It is half a day and a night and now another day and you have not slept. If you do not sleep/ you might become unclear in the head." I'm clear enough in the head, he thought. Too clear. I am as clear as the stars that are my brothers. Still I must sleep. They sleep and the moon and the sun sleep and even the ocean sleeps sometimes on certain days when there is no current and a flat calm.

ocean [óuʃən] 대양, 해양
certain [sə́:rtən] 어떤, 확신하는
current [kə́:rənt] 흐름, 조류

flat [flæt] 편평한, 납작한, 평탄한
calm [ka:m] 고요한, 조용한

He waited to see if there would be more lions and he was happy

더 많은 사자가 나타나지는 않는지 보려고 기다리는 동안 그는 행복했다

After that he began to dream of the long yellow beach and he saw the first of the lions come down onto it in the early dark and then the other lions came and he rested his chin on the wood of the bows where the ship lay anchored with the evening off-shore breeze and he waited to see if there would be more lions and he was happy.

그런 다음 노인은 길게 뻗은 노란 해변이 나오는 꿈을 꾸기 시작했는데 처음에 사자 한 마리가 이른 새벽 어두컴컴한 바닷가로 내려오더니, 이어 다른 사자들 도 뒤따라 나타나기 시작했다. 그가 탄 배가 뭍에서 불어오는 저녁 미풍을 받으 며 닻을 내리고 있었고, 그는 이물의 널빤지에 턱을 괴고 있었다. 더 많은 사자 가 나타나지는 않는지 보려고 기다리는 동안 그는 행복했다.

문장분석

After that/ he began to dream of the long yellow beach and he saw the first of

the lions come down onto it/ in the early dark and then/ the other lions came

and he rested his chin on the wood of the bows where the ship lay anchored

with the evening off-shore breeze and he waited to see if there would be more
　　　　　　　　　　　앞바다로 향하는　　　　　　　　　　　　　　~인지 보다

lions and he was happy.

rest [rest] 놓다, 얹다, 휴식하다　　　　anchor [æŋkər] 닻, 닻을 내리다
chin [tʃin] 턱, 턱끝　　　　　　　　　breeze [bri:z] 산들바람, 미풍
bow [bau] 이물, 뱃머리

Vocabulary Of The Week

MON

dull [dʌl] 무딘, 둔한
mistrust [mistrʌst] 불신
cramp [kræmp] 경련, 쥐
gain [gein] 얻다, 획득하다
sustenance [sʌstənəns]
　생명을 유지하는 물건, 지속

TUE

distant [dístənt] 먼, 떨어진
distance [dístəns] 거리, 간격
immense [iméns]
　막대한(enormous, vast), 광대한,
　끝없는
aloud [əláud] 소리를 내어, 큰 소리로

lousy [láuzi] 천한, 치사한

WED

feed [fiːd] 음식을 주다
worthy [wə́ːrði]
　훌륭한, 존경할 만한, 가치 있는
worth [wəːrθ]
　가치, …할 만한 가치가 있는

behavior [bihéivjər]
　행동, 행실, 동작, 태도
dignity [dígnəti] 존엄, 위엄

THU

ocean [óuʃən] 대양, 해양
certain [sə́ːrtən] 어떤, 확신하는
current [kə́ːrənt] 흐름, 조류
flat [flæt] 편평한, 납작한, 평탄한
calm [kɑːm] 고요한, 조용한

FRI

rest [rest] 놓다, 얹다, 휴식하다
chin [tʃin] 턱, 턱끝
bow [bau] 이물, 뱃머리
anchor [æŋkər] 닻, 닻을 내리다
breeze [briːz] 산들바람, 미풍

MON

You are killing me, fish, but you have a right to

고기야 네놈이 지금 나를 죽이고 있구나, 하지만 네게도 그럴 권리는 있지

But again the fish righted himself and swam slowly away. You are killing me, fish, the old man thought. But you have a right to. Never have I seen a greater, or more beautiful, or a calmer or more noble thing than you, brother. Come on and kill me. I do not care who kills who.

그러나 고기는 또다시 몸을 곧추세우고 천천히 헤엄쳐 달아나 버렸다. 고기야 네놈이 지금 나를 죽이고 있구나, 하고 노인은 생각했다. 하지만 네게도 그럴 권리는 있지. 한데 이 형제야, 난 지금껏 너보다 크고, 너보다 아름답고, 또 너보다 침착하고 고결한 놈은 보지 못했구나. 자, 그럼 이리 와서 나를 죽여 보려무나. 누가 누구를 죽이든 그게 무슨 상관이란 말이냐.

문장분석

But again/ the fish righted himself and swam slowly away. You are killing me, fish, the old man thought. But you have a right to (swim away). Never have I
부정어로 인한 도치
seen a greater, or more beautiful, or a calmer or more noble thing than you, brother. Come on and kill me. I do not care who kills who.

right [rait] 일으키다, 다시 세우다, 권리
calm [kɑːm] 고요한, 조용한
calmness [kάːmnis] 평온, 냉정, 침착

noble [nóubəl] 귀족의, 고귀한
care [kɛər] 걱정하다, 마음을 쓰다

He took all his pain and what was left of his strength

노인은 모든 고통과 마지막 남아 있는 힘을 총동원했다

He took all his pain and what was left of his strength and his long gone pride and he put it against the fish's agony and the fish came over onto his side and swam gently on his side, his bill almost touching the planking of the skiff and started to pass the boat, long, deep, wide, silver and barred with purple and interminable in the water.

노인은 모든 고통과 마지막 남아 있는 힘, 그리고 오래전에 사라진 자부심을 총동원해 고기의 마지막 고통과 맞섰다. 고기는 그의 곁으로 다가와서 주둥이가 뱃전에 닿다시피 한 상태로 부드럽게 헤엄치면서 배 옆을 지나가기 시작했다. 은빛 살갖에 있는 자줏빛 줄무늬는 길고도 깊숙하고 넓게 물속까지 끝없이 이어져 있는 듯했다.

문장분석

He took all his pain and(what)was left of his strength and his long gone pride and he put it against the fish's agony and the fish came over onto his side and swam gently on his side, his bill almost touching the planking of the skiff and started to
선체 겉판자
pass the boat, long, deep, wide, silver and barred with purple and interminable in the water.

agony [ǽgəni] 고민, 고통
plank [plæŋk] 널, 두꺼운 판자, 판자로 깔다
barred [bɑːrd]
　가로대가 있는, 빗장을 건, 줄무늬가 있는

purple [pə́ːrpəl] 자줏빛의
interminable [intə́ːrmənəbəl]
　끝없는, 지루하게 긴

Is he bringing me in or am I bringing him in?

고기가 나를 데려가고 있는 건가, 아니면 내가 고기를 데려가고 있는 건가?

All I must do is keep the head clear. The hands have done their work and we sail well. With his mouth shut and his tail straight up and down we sail like brothers. Then his head started to become a little unclear and he thought, is he bringing me in or am I bringing him in?

이제 나는 정신을 똑바로 차리고 있기만 하면 되는 거야. 두 손은 할 일을 모두 잘 끝냈고, 우리는 지금 무사히 항구로 돌아가는 중이야. 고기는 아가리를 굳게 다물고 꼬리를 꼿꼿이 아래위로 흔들면서 우리는 지금 마치 형제처럼 항해하고 있지 않은가. 그런데 그때 노인의 머리가 다시 약간 흐려지기 시작했다. 고기가 나를 데려가고 있는 건가, 아니면 내가 고기를 데려가고 있는 건가, 하고 그는 생각했다.

문장분석

All I must do is keep the head clear. The hands have done their work and we sail well. With his mouth shut and his tail straight up and down we sail like brothers. Then his head started to become a little unclear and he thought, is he bringing
약간, 조금
me in or am I bringing him in?

sail [seil] 돛
tail [teil] 꼬리
confuse [kənfjúːz] 혼동하다

defuse [di(ː)fjúːz]
(폭탄·지뢰의) 신관을 제거하다, …의 긴장을 완화하다
refuse [rifjúːz] 거절하다, 거부하다

THU

I am only better than him through trickery and he meant me no harm

나는 꾀가 있어 저놈보다 나은 것일 뿐 저놈은 내게 아무런 적의도 품고 있지 않지

If I were towing him behind there would be no question. Nor if the fish were in the skiff, with all dignity gone, there would be no question either. But they were sailing together lashed side by side and the old man thought, let him bring me in if it pleases him. I am only better than him through trickery and he meant me no harm.

만약 내가 고기를 뒤에 두고 끌고 가는 것이라면 아무런 문제가 없어. 고기 놈이 모든 위엄을 잃어버린 채 지금 배 안에 있다고 해도 역시 아무런 문제가 없지. 하지만 고기와 배는 지금 서로 묶인 채 나란히 항해하는 중이야. 만약 고기 놈이 나를 데리고 가는 거라면 그렇게 하라지, 하고 그는 생각했다. 나는 꾀가 있어 저놈보다 나은 것일 뿐 저놈은 내게 아무런 적의도 품고 있지 않았거든.

문장분석

If I were towing him behind/ there would be no question. Nor if the fish were in

And also not

the skiff, with all dignity gone, there would be no question either. But they were

또한

sailing together/ lashed side by side and the old man thought, let him bring me

in if it pleases him. I am only better than him through trickery and he meant me

no harm.

tow [tou] 끌다, 견인하다
lash [læʃ] 묶다, 매다
please [pliːz] 기쁘게 하다, 만족시키다

trickery [tríkəri] 속임수, 사기, 책략
harm [haːrm] 손해, 손상, 위해

It was too good to last

좋은 일이란 오래가는 법이지

He did not like to look at the fish anymore since he had been mutilated. When the fish had been hit it was as though he himself were hit. It was too good to last, he thought. I wish it had been a dream now and that I had never hooked the fish and was alone in bed on the newspapers.

노인은 몸뚱이가 뜯겨 성하지 않게 되어 버린 고기를 이제 더 이상 바라보고 싶지가 않았다. 고기가 습격을 받을 때 마치 자신이 습격을 받는 듯한 느낌이 들었다. 좋은 일이란 오래가는 법이 없구나, 하고 그는 생각했다. 차라리 이게 한낱 꿈이었더라면 얼마나 좋을까. 이 고기는 잡은 적도 없고, 지금 이 순간 침대에 신문지를 깔고 혼자 누워 있다면 얼마나 좋을까.

He did not like to look at the fish anymore since he had been mutilated. When
the fish had been hit/ it was as though he himself were hit. It was too good to
　　　　　　　　　　　　　　　~이후로　　　　　　　　　　마치~인 것처럼　　　　　　　　　　　　　
last, he thought. I wish it had been a dream now and that I had never hooked
the fish and was alone in bed on the newspapers.

mutilate [mjúːtəlèit] 절단하다, 훼손하다 　　　raid [reid] 급습, 습격
last [læst, lɑːst] 지속되다, 계속하다 　　　　　skiff [skif] 소형 보트, 소형 범선
hook [huk] 갈고리, 낚시로 낚다

Vocabulary Of The Week

MON

right [rait]
일으키다, 다시 세우다, 권리
calm [kɑːm] 고요한, 조용한
calmness [kɑːmnis]
평온, 냉정, 침착
noble [nóubəl] 귀족의, 고귀한

care [kɛər] 걱정하다, 마음을 쓰다

TUE

agony [ǽgəni] 고민, 고통
plank [plæŋk]
널, 두꺼운 판자, 판자로 깔다
barred [bɑːrd]
가로대가 있는, 빗장을 건,
줄무늬가 있는

purple [pə́ːrpəl] 자줏빛의
interminable [intə́ːrmənəbəl]
끝없는, 지루하게 긴

WED

sail [seil] 돛
tail [teil] 꼬리
confuse [kənfjúːz] 혼동하다
defuse [di(ː)fjúːz]
(폭탄·지뢰의) 신관을 제거하다,
…의 긴장을 완화하다

refuse [rifjúːz] 거절하다, 거부하다

THU

tow [tou] 끌다, 견인하다
lash [læʃ] 묶다, 매다
please [pliːz]
기쁘게 하다, 만족시키다
trickery [tríkəri] 속임수, 사기, 책략
harm [hɑːrm] 손해, 손상, 위해

FRI

mutilate [mjúːtəlèit]
절단하다, 훼손하다
last [læst, lɑːst] 지속되다, 계속하다
hook [huk] 갈고리, 낚시로 낚다
raid [reid] 급습, 습격
skiff [skif] 소형 보트, 소형 범선

MON

A man can be destroyed but not defeated

인간은 파멸당할 수 있을지 몰라도 패배할 수는 없어

"But man is not made for defeat," he said. "A man can be destroyed but not defeated." I am sorry that I killed the fish though, he thought. Now the bad time is coming and I do not even have the harpoon. The dentuso is cruel and able and strong and intelligent. But I was more intelligent that he was. Perhaps not, he thought. Perhaps I was only better armed.

"하지만 인간은 패배하도록 창조된 게 아니야." 그기 말했다. "인간은 파멸당할 수 있을지 몰라도 패배할 수는 없어." 하지만 고기를 죽여서 정말 안 됐지 뭐야, 하고 그는 생각했다. 이제부터 정말 어려운 일이 닥쳐올 텐데 난 작살조차 갖고 있지 않으니, 덴투소란 놈은 무척이나 잔인하고 힘이 센 데다가 머리도 좋지. 하지만 그놈보다야 내가 더 똑똑하지. 아냐, 어쩌면 그렇지 않을는지도 몰라, 하고 그는 생각했다. 고놈보다 어쩌면 내가 좀 더 좋은 무기를 갖추고 있을 뿐인지 몰라.

문장분석

"But man is not made for defeat," he said. "A man can be destroyed but not

defeated." I am sorry that I killed the fish though, he thought. Now/ the bad time
<u>하지만</u>

is coming and I do not even have the harpoon. The dentuso is cruel and able
심지어   (Sp.) 뾰족한 이빨을 가진

and strong and intelligent. But I was more intelligent that he was (intelligent).

Perhaps not, he thought. Perhaps I was only better armed.

---

defeat [difí:t] 쳐부수다, 꺾다, 패배   cruel [krú:əl] 잔인한, 무자비한
destroy [distrói] 파괴하다, 부수다   armed [á:rmd] 무장한
harpoon [hɑ:rpún] (고래잡이용) 작살

It is silly not to hope

희망을 버린다는 건 어리석은 일이야

The breeze was fresh now and he sailed on well. He watched only the forward part of the fish and some of his hope returned. It is silly not to hope, he thought. Besides I believe it is a sin. Do not think about sin, he thought. There are enough problems now without sin. Also I have no understanding of it.

미풍이 다시 불어오기 시작했고, 배는 미끄러지듯 달렸다. 고기의 앞쪽 부분만을 보고 있으려니 희망이 조금 되살아났다. 희망을 버린다는 건 어리석은 일이야, 하고 그는 생각했다. 더구나 그건 죄악이거든. 죄에 대해서는 생각하지 말자, 하고 그는 생각했다. 지금은 죄가 아니라도 생각할 문제들이 얼마든지 있으니까. 게다가 나는 죄가 뭔지 아무것도 모르고 있지 않은가.

문장분석

The breeze was fresh now and he sailed on well. He watched only the forward part of the fish and some of his hope returned. It is silly not to hope, he thought.

Besides I believe it is a sin. Do not think about sin, he thought. There are enough
게다가
problems now/ without sin. Also I have no understanding of it.

breeze [briːz] 산들바람, 미풍
silly [síli] 어리석은(stupid)
sin [sin] (종교·도덕상의) 죄, 죄악

crime [kraim] (법률상의) 죄, 범죄 (행위)
criminal [krímənl] 범죄의, 범죄자

But then everything is a sin

하지만 그렇게 되면 모든 게 죄겠지

I have no understanding of it and I am not sure that I believe in it. Perhaps it was a sin to kill the fish. I suppose it was even though I did it to keep me alive and feed many people. But then everything is a sin.

난 죄가 뭔지 아무것도 모르고 있는 데다 죄를 믿고 있는지도 확실하지 않아. 고기를 죽이는 건 어쩌면 죄가 될지도 몰라. 설령 내가 먹고살아 가기 위해, 또 많은 사람들을 먹여 살리기 위해서 한 짓이라도 죄가 될 거야. 하지만 그렇게 되면 모든 게 죄겠지.

문장분석

I have no understanding of it and I am not sure that I believe in it. Perhaps it was a sin to kill the fish. I suppose it was (a sin) even though I did it to keep me alive
비록 ~할지라도
and feed many people. But then/ everything is a sin.

perhaps [pərhǽps]
　아마, 형편에 따라서는, 혹시, 어쩌면
sin tax '죄악'세(술·담배·도박 따위의 세금)

suppose [səpóuz] 가정하다(assume), 상상하다
alive [əláiv] 살아 있는, 생존해 있는
lively [láivli] 생기에 넘친, 기운찬, 팔팔한

You were born to be a fisherman as the fish was born to be a fish

고기가 고기로 태어난 것처럼 넌 어부로 태어났지

Do not think about sin. It is much too late for that and there are people who are paid to do it. Let them think about it. You were born to be a fisherman as the fish was born to be a fish.

죄에 대해서는 생각하지 말기로 하자. 그럴 것을 생각하기에는 이미 때가 너무 늦었고, 또 죄에 대해 생각하는 일로 벌어 먹고사는 사람도 있으니까 말이야. 죄에 대해선 그런 사람들에게 맡기면 돼. 고기가 고기로 태어난 것처럼 넌 어부로 태어났으니까.

문장분석

Do not think about sin. It is much too late for that and there are people who are paid to do it. Let them think about it. You were born to be a fisherman/ as the
처럼
fish was born to be a fish.

late [leit] 늦은, 지각한, 돌아가신
lately [léitli] 요즈음, 최근(of late)
confess [kənfés]
　(과실·죄를) 고백(자백)하다, 실토하다, 털어놓다

confide [kənfáid] (비밀 따위를) 털어놓다, 신용하다, 신뢰하다
confidential [kànfidénʃəl]
　은밀한, 내밀한(secret), 기밀의

You loved him when he was alive and you loved him after

너는 녀석이 아직 살아 있을 때도 사랑했고, 또 녀석이 죽은 뒤에도 사랑했지

You did not kill the fish only to keep alive and to sell for food, he thought. You killed him for pride and because you are a fisherman. You loved him when he was alive and you loved him after. If you love him, it is not a sin to kill him. Or is it more? "You think too much, old man," he said aloud.

네가 그 고기를 죽인 것은 다만 먹고 살기 위해서, 또는 식량으로 팔기 위해서만은 아니었어, 하고 그는 생각했다. 자존심 때문에, 그리고 어부이기 때문에 그 녀석을 죽인 거야. 너는 녀석이 아직 살아 있을 때도 사랑했고, 또 녀석이 죽은 뒤에도 사랑했지. 만약 네가 그놈을 사랑하고 있다면 죽여도 죄가 되지 않는 거야. 아니, 오히려 더 무거운 죄가 되는 걸까? "이 늙은이야, 생각을 너무 많이 하는 군." 그가 큰 소리로 말했다.

문장분석

You did not kill the fish only to keep alive and to sell for food, he thought. You killed him for pride and because you are a fisherman. You loved him when he was alive and you loved him after. If you love him, it is not a sin to kill him. Or is it more (than a sin)? "You think too much, old man," he said aloud.

aloud [əláud] 소리를 내어, 큰 소리로
loudly [láudli] 소리 높게, 떠들썩하게
lousy [láuzi] 천한, 치사한

mortal [mɔ́:rtl] 죽을 수밖에 없는 운명의
immortal [imɔ́:rtl] 죽지 않는(undying), 불멸의

Vocabulary Of The Week

MON

defeat [difíːt] 쳐부수다, 꺾다, 패배
destroy [distrɔ́i] 파괴하다, 부수다
harpoon [hɑːrpúːn]
 (고래잡이용) 작살
cruel [krúːəl] 잔인한, 무자비한
armed [áːrmd] 무장한

TUE

breeze [briːz] 산들바람, 미풍
silly [síli] 어리석은(stupid)
sin [sin] (종교·도덕상의) 죄, 죄악
crime [kraim]
 (법률상의) 죄, 범죄 (행위)
criminal [krímənl] 범죄의, 범죄자

WED

perhaps [pərhǽps]
 아마, 형편에 따라서는, 혹시, 어쩌면
sin tax
 '죄악'세(술·담배·도박 따위의 세금)
suppose [səpóuz]
 가정하다(assume), 상상하다

alive [əláiv] 살아 있는, 생존해 있는
lively [láivli]
 생기에 넘친, 기운찬, 팔팔한

THU

late [leit] 늦은, 지각한, 돌아가신
lately [léitli] 요즘은, 최근(of late)
confess [kənfés]
 (과실·죄를) 고백(자백)하다, 실토하다,
 털어놓다

confide [kənfáid]
 (비밀 따위를) 털어놓다, 신용하다,
 신뢰하다
confidential [kὰnfidénʃəl]
 은밀한, 내밀한(secret), 기밀의

FRI

aloud [əláud] 소리를 내어, 큰 소리로
loudly [láudli] 소리 높게, 떠들썩하게
lousy [láuzi] 천한, 치사한
mortal [mɔ́ːrtl]
 죽을 수밖에 없는 운명의

immortal [imɔ́ːrtl]
 죽지 않는(undying), 불멸의

December

12

*Writing, at its best, is a lonely life.
For he does his work alone and if he is a good
enough writer he must face eternity,
or the lack of it, each day.*

글을 쓴다는 것, 그것은 최상의 상태에서조차 고독한 삶입니다.
그의 작업은 오로지 혼자서 할 수밖에 없기 때문에 만약 그가 훌륭한 작가라면
그는 영원한 진리 혹은 그 진리의 결핍과 마주해야 합니다, 그것도 매일.

MON

Everything kills everything else in some way

이 세상의 모든 것은 어떤 형태로든 다른 것들을 죽이고 있어

"I killed him in self-defense," the old man said aloud. "And I killed him well." Besides, he thought, everything kills everything else in some way. Fishing kills me exactly as it keeps me alive. The boy keeps me alive, he thought. I must not deceive myself too much.

"내가 그 녀석을 죽인 건 정당방위였어. 그리고 정당한 방식으로 죽였다고." 노인은 큰 소리로 말했다. 더구나 이 세상의 모든 것은 어떤 형태로든 다른 것들을 죽이고 있어, 하고 그는 생각했다. 고기를 잡는 일은 나를 살려 주지만, 동시에 나를 죽이기도 하지. 그 소년은 나를 살려 주고 있어, 하고 노인은 생각했다. 나 자신을 너무 속여서는 안 되지.

문장분석

"I killed him in self-defense," the old man said aloud. "And I killed him well."

Besides, he thought, everything kills everything else in some way. Fishing kills
그 외에, 다른
me exactly as it keeps me alive. The boy keeps me alive, he thought. I must not
마찬가지로
deceive myself too much.

self-defense [sélfdiféns] 자기 방어, 정당방위　　exact [igzǽkt] 정확한, …을 요구하다, 강요하다
exactly [igzǽktli] 정확하게, 엄밀히, 정밀하게　　deceive [disíːv] 속이다, 기만하다
exactitude [igzǽktətjùːd] 정확, 엄밀, 정밀

I wish it were a dream and that I had never hooked him

이 일이 꿈이었더라면, 또 이 고기를 잡지 않았더라면 좋았을 걸

"They must have taken a quarter of him and of the best meat," he said aloud.
"I wish it were a dream and that I had never hooked him. I'm sorry about it, fish. It makes everything wrong."

"놈들이 고기 사 분의 일은 뜯어 간 것 같군. 그것도 가장 좋은 부위를 말이야." 노인은 큰 소리로 말했다.
"차라리 이 일이 꿈이었더라면 좋았을걸. 또 이 고기를 잡지 않았더라면 좋았을 걸. 고기야, 너한테는 정말 미안하게 되었구나. 그래서 모든 게 엉망이 되어 버렸던 거야."

I shouldn't have gone out so far, neither for you nor for me

이렇게 멀리 나오지 말았어야 했는데, 너를 위해서도 나를 위해서도

He stopped and he did not want to look at the fish now. Drained of blood and awash he looked the colour of the silver backing of a mirror and his stripes still showed. "I shouldn't have gone out so far, fish," he said. "Neither for you nor for me. I'm sorry, fish."

그는 말을 멈추었고 이제 더 이상 고기를 바라보고 싶지 않았다. 피가 빠져나가고 바닷물에 깨끗이 씻긴 고기는 거울의 뒷면처럼 은색을 띠고 있었으나 줄무늬만은 아직도 선명했다. "고기야, 난 이렇게 멀리 나오지 말았어야 했는데. 너를 위해서나 나를 위해서나 말이다. 고기야, 미안하구나." 그가 말했다.

문장분석

He stopped and he did not want to look at (the fish) now. Drained of blood and

awash/(he) looked the colour of the silver backing of a mirror and his stripes still
　　　~처럼 보이다

showed. "I shouldn't have gone out so far, fish," he said. "Neither for you nor for
　　　　　~하지 말았어야 했는데(했다)

me. I'm sorry, fish."

drain [drein]
　…의 물을 빼내다, …을 배출하다, 뚝뚝 떨어지다
awash [əwɔ́ːʃ] 물을 뒤집어쓰고
blood [blʌd] 피

stripe [straip] 줄무늬, 줄
strip [strip]
　(겉껍질 따위를) 벗기다, 까다, 떼어내다, 조각

Now is no time to think of what you do not have

지금은 갖고 오지 않은 물건을 생각할 때가 아니야

"I wish I had a stone for the knife," the old man said after he had checked the lashing on the oar butt. "I should have brought a stone." You should have brought many things, he thought. But you did not bring them, old man. Now is no time to think of what you do not have. Think of what you can do with what there is.

"칼을 갈 숫돌이 있으면 좋으련만." 노인은 노 끝부분에 묶은 끈을 살펴보고 나서 말했다. "숫돌을 가지고 올 걸 그랬어." 갖고 왔어야 할 것이 많군, 하고 그는 생각했다. 하지만 이 늙은이야, 넌 그것들을 가지고 오지 않았잖아. 지금은 갖고 오지 않은 물건을 생각할 때가 아니야. 지금 갖고 있는 물건으로 뭘 할 수 있는지 생각해 보란 말이야.

문장분석

"I wish I had a stone for the knife," the old man said/ after he had checked the lashing on the oar butt. "I should have brought a stone." You should have
~했어야 했는데(하지 않았다)
brought many things, he thought. But you did not bring them, old man. Now is no time to think of what you do not have. Think of what you can do with what there is.

lash [læʃ]
묶다, 매다, (파도·바람이) 세차게 부닥치다, 내리치다
slash [slæʃ]
휙(썩) 베다, (칼 따위로) 난도질하다, 깊숙이 베다
flash [flæʃ]
번쩍이다, 빛나다, 번개처럼 스치다, 갑자기 움직이다

oar [ɔːr] 노, 젓는 배
butt [bʌt]
(무기·도구 등) 굵은 쪽의 끝, 궁둥이(buttocks)

God knows how much that last one took

마지막 놈이 얼마나 많이 뜯어 먹었는지 모르겠군

"God knows how much that last one took," he said. "But she's much lighter now." He did not want to think of the mutilated under-side of the fish. He knew that each of the jerking bumps of the shark had been meat torn away and that the fish now made a trail for all sharks as wide as a highway through the sea.

"마지막 놈이 얼마나 많이 뜯어 먹었는지 모르겠군." 그가 말했다. "하지만 덕분에 배는 훨씬 가벼워졌어." 그는 물어뜯긴 고기의 아랫배 부분에 대해선 생각하고 싶지 않았다. 상어가 쿵 하고 덮칠 때마다 살점이 떨어져 나갔을 테니 지금쯤 고기는 온갖 상어가 뒤쫓아 **오도록** 바다에 고속도로처럼 널찍한 수로를 만들어 놓고 있다는 것을 잘 알고 **있었다.**

문장분석

"God knows (that) how much/ that last one took," he said. "But she is much
<u>Nobody knows</u>   <u>boat</u>
lighter now." He did not want to think of the mutilated under-side of the fish.

He knew that each of the jerking bumps of the shark had been meat torn away

and (knew) that the fish now made a trail (for all sharks) as wide as a highway

through the sea.

mutilate [mjúːtəlèit] 절단하다
jerk [dʒəːrk]
　갑자기 당김, 홱 움직이게 하다, 급히 당기다

bump [bʌmp] 부딪치다, 충돌, 혹
meat [miːt] (식용 짐승의) 고기
trail [treil] 자국, 흔적

Vocabulary Of The Week

MON

self-defense [sélfdifèns]
자기 방어, 정당방위
exactly [igzǽktli]
정확하게, 엄밀히, 정밀하게
exactitude [igzǽktətjù:d]
정확, 엄밀, 정밀

exact [igzǽkt]
정확한, …을 요구하다, 강요하다
deceive [disí:v] 속이다, 기만하다

TUE

meat [mi:t] (식용 짐승의) 고기
flesh [fleʃ] 살(뼈·가죽에 대하여)
quarter [kwɔ́:rtər]
4분의 1, 15분, 25센트
hook [huk] 갈고리, 훅, 걸쇠
hooker 매춘부, 사기꾼

WED

drain [drein]
…의 물을 빼내다, …을 배출하다,
뚝뚝 떨어지다
awash [əwɔ́:ʃ] 물을 뒤집어쓰고
blood [blʌd] 피
stripe [straip] 줄무늬, 줄

strip [strip]
(겉껍질 따위를) 벗기다, 까다,
떼어내다, 조각

THU

lash [læʃ]
묶다, 매다, (파도·바람이) 세차게
부딪치다, 내리치다
slash [slæʃ]
휙(썩) 베다, (칼 따위로) 난도질하다,
깊숙이 베다

flash [flæʃ]
번쩍이다, 빛나다, 번개처럼 스치다,
갑자기 움직이다
oar [ɔ:r] 노, 젓는 배
butt [bʌt] (무기·도구 등) 굵은 쪽의 끝,
궁둥이(buttocks)

FRI

mutilate [mjú:təlèit] 절단하다
jerk [dʒə:rk]
갑자기 당김, 홱 움직이게 하다,
급히 당기다
bump [bʌmp] 부딪치다, 충돌, 혹
meat [mi:t] (식용 짐승의) 고기

trail [treil] 자국, 흔적

MON

Just rest and try to get your hands in shape to defend what is left of him

이젠 휴식을 취하면서 남은 고기를 지킬 수 있도록 손이나 제대로 풀어 둬

Just rest and try to get your hands in shape to defend what is left of him. The blood smell from my hands means nothing now with all that scent in the water. Besides they do not bleed much. There is nothing cut that means anything. The bleeding may keep the left from cramping.

이젠 그저 휴식을 취하면서 남은 고기를 지킬 수 있도록 손이나 제대로 풀어 두도록 해. 이제 바다에는 피 냄새가 진동할 테니 내 손에서 나는 피 냄새쯤이야 아무것도 아닐 테지. 더구나 지금은 내 손의 출혈도 대단치가 않아. 또 걱정될 만한 상처도 없고. 피를 흘린 덕분에 왼손에 쥐가 나지 않는 건지도 몰라.

Just rest and try to get your hands in shape to defend what is left of him. The
최상의 상태인
blood smell from my hands means nothing now with all that scent in the water.
~와 비교하면
Besides/ they do not bleed much. There is nothing cut that means anything. The
게다가
bleeding may keep the left (hand) from cramping.

shape [ʃeip] 모양, (건강한) 상태
defend [difénd] 막다, 지키다
scent [sent] 냄새, 향기

bleed [bliːd] 피를 흘리다
cramp [kræmp] 경련, 쥐가 나다

TUE

I must think of nothing and wait for the next ones

아무 생각도 하지 말고 다만 다음 수순을 기다리기로 하자

What can I think of now? he thought. Nothing. I must think of nothing and wait for the next ones. I wish it had really been a dream, he thought. But who knows? It might have turned out well.

이제 무슨 생각을 해야 하나? 하고 노인은 생각했다. 아무것도 없어. 아무 생각도 하지 말고 다만 다음 상어 놈들을 기다리기로 하자. 차라리 이게 꿈이라면 얼마나 좋을까, 하고 노인은 생각했다. 하지만 누가 알겠어? 일이 모두 잘 풀리게 될지도 모르잖아.

문장분석

What can I think of now? he thought. Nothing. I must think of nothing and wait

for the next ones. I wish it had really been a dream, he thought. But who knows?

It might have turned out well.
　　　　　　　　　나타나다, 드러나다

prove [pru:v] 증명하다, 입증(立證)하다
approve [əprú:v] (좋다고) 시인하다, 찬성하다
improve [imprú:v] 개량하다, 개선하다

proof [pru:f]
　증명, 증거, 통과 안 시키는, (…에) 견디어내는
waterproof [wɔ́:tərprù:f] 방수의, 물이 새지 않는

Now they have beaten me

이제 난 그들한테 완전히 지고 말았다

Now they have beaten me, he thought. I am too old to club sharks to death. But I will try it as long as I have the oars and the short club and the tiller. He put his hands in the water again to soak them. It was getting late in the afternoon and he saw nothing but the sea and the sky. There was more wind in the sky than there had been, and soon he hoped that he would see land.

이제 난 상어 놈들한테 완전히 지고 말았구나, 하고 노인은 생각했다. 이제 너무 늙어서 몽둥이로 상어를 때려죽일 만한 힘도 없어. 그렇지만 내게 노와 짤막한 몽둥이와 키 손잡이가 있는 한 끝까지 싸워 볼 테다. 노인은 다시 두 손을 바닷물 속에 담갔다. 벌써 오후가 저물어 가고 있었고, 바다와 하늘밖에는 아무것도 보이지 않았다. 바람은 전보다 훨씬 세차게 불고 있었고, 그래서 그는 어서 뭍이 보이기를 바랐다.

문장분석

Now they have beaten me, he thought. I am too old to club sharks to death. But

I will try it as long as I have the oars and the short club and the tiller. He put his
　　　　　~하는 한

hands in the water again to soak them. It was getting late in the afternoon and

he saw nothing but the sea and the sky. There was more wind in the sky than
　　　　　　　　only

there had been, and soon he hoped that he would see land.

beat [biːt] 치다, 두드리다, ~에 이기다, …보다 낫다　　oar [ɔːr] 노, 젓는 배
till [til] 갈다, 경작하다, 조종하다　　　　　　　　　　soak [souk] 홈뻑 젖다, 적시다
tiller 키의 손잡이, 조종 장치, 경작자

I hope no one has been too worried

아무도 나 때문에 걱정을 하지 않았으면 좋겠는데

"It will be dark soon," he said. "Then I should see the glow of Havana." I cannot be too far out now, he thought. I hope no one has been too worried. There is only the boy to worry, of course. But I am sure he would have confidence. Many of the older fishermen will worry. Many others too, he thought. I live in a good town.

"이제 곧 어두워지겠는걸. 그럼 이제 아바나의 불빛이 보이겠지." 그가 말했다. 이제 그다지 멀리 떨어져 있지는 않을 텐데, 하고 노인은 생각했다. 아무도 나 때문에 걱정을 하지 않았으면 좋겠는데. 물론 그 아이는 내 걱정을 하고 있을 거야. 하지만 그 아이는 확신하고 있을 거야. 늙은 어부들도 내 걱정을 할 테지. 그 밖에 다른 많은 사람도 역시 걱정하고 있겠지, 하고 노인은 생각했다. 난 정말 좋은 마을에 살고 있구나.

문장분석

"It will be dark soon," he said. "Then I should see the glow of Havana." I cannot
be too far out now, he thought. I hope no one has been too worried. There is
only the boy to worry, of course. But I am sure (that) he would have confidence.
Many of the older fishermen will worry. Many others too, he thought. I live in a
good town.

glow [glou] 붉은 빛, 빛을 내다, 빛나다
confidence [kánfidəns/kɔ́n-] 신용, 신뢰
confide [kənfáid]
(비밀 따위를) 털어놓다, 위탁하다, 맡기다

confident [kánfidənt] 확신하는, 자신만만한
confidential [kànfidénʃəl]
은밀한, 내밀한(secret), 기밀의

I ruined us both

내가 우리 둘을 모두 망쳐 버렸어

He could not talk to the fish anymore because the fish had been ruined too badly. Then something came into his head. "Half fish," he said. "Fish that you were. I am sorry that I went too far out. I ruined us both. But we have killed many sharks, you and I, and ruined many others. How many did you ever kill, old fish? You do not have that spear on your head for nothing."

고기는 너무 심하게 뜯겨 있었기 때문에 노인은 이제 더 이상 고기에게 말을 걸 수가 없었다. 문득 이떤 생각이 그의 머리를 스쳐 갔다. "고기는 이제 반동강이 가 되었구나. 한때는 온전한 한 마리였는데. 내가 너무 멀리까지 나왔어. 내가 우리 둘을 모두 망쳐 버렸어." 노인이 말했다. "하지만 너랑 나 둘이서 많은 상 어를 죽이고 다른 고기들도 죽이지 않았느냐. 고기야, 지금까지 넌 얼마나 많이 죽였니? 대가리에 뾰족한 창날 같은 주둥이를 공연히 달고 있는 건 아니잖아."

문장분석

He could not talk to the fish anymore because the fish had been ruined too badly. Then something came into his head. "Half fish," he said. "Fish that you were. I am sorry that I went too far out. I ruined us both. But we have killed many sharks, you and I, and ruined many others. How many did you ever kill, old fish?
지금까지
You do not have that spear on your head for nothing."
거저, 까닭 없이

ruin [rúːin] 파멸, 파산, 파멸시키다
wreck [rek] (배의) 난파
shark [ʃɑːrk] 상어

homicide [háməsàid]
　살인(정당 방위나 범죄를 구성하는 경우)
murder [məːrdər]
　살인(살의(殺意)를 지닌 범죄), 죽이다

MON

shape [ʃeip] 모양, (건강한) 상태
defend [difénd] 막다, 지키다
scent [sent] 냄새, 향기
bleed [bli:d] 피를 흘리다
cramp [kræmp] 경련, 쥐가 나다

TUE

prove [pru:v]
　증명하다, 입증(立證)하다
approve [əprú:v]
　(좋다고) 시인하다, 찬성하다
improve [imprú:v]
　개량하다, 개선하다

proof [pru:f]
　증명, 증거, 통과 안 시키는,
　(…에) 견디어내는
waterproof [wɔ́:tərprù:f]
　방수의, 물이 새지 않는

WED

beat [bi:t]
　치다, 두드리다, ~에 이기다,
　…보다 낫다
till [til] 갈다, 경작하다, 조종하다
tiller 키의 손잡이, 조종 장치, 경작자
oar [ɔ:r] 노, 젓는 배

soak [souk] 흠뻑 젖다, 적시다

THU

glow [glou]
　붉은 빛, 빛을 내다, 빛나다
confidence [kánfidəns/kón-]
　신용, 신뢰
confide [kənfáid]
　(비밀 따위를) 털어놓다, 위탁하다,

맡기다
confident [kánfidənt]
　확신하는, 자신만만한
confidential [kànfidénʃəl]
　은밀한, 내밀한(secret), 기밀의

FRI

ruin [rú:in] 파멸, 파산, 파멸시키다
wreck [rek] (배의) 난파
shark [ʃɑ:rk] 상어
homicide [háməsàid]
　살인(정당 방위나 범죄를 구성하는
　경우)

murder [mə́:rdər]
　살인(살의(殺意)를 지닌 범죄), 죽이다

MON

He felt that perhaps he was already dead

그는 어쩌면 자신이 죽은 몸은 아닐까 하는 느낌이 들었다

He felt that perhaps he was already dead. He put his two hands together and felt the palms. They were not dead and he could bring the pain of life by simply opening and closing them. He leaned his back against the stern and knew he was not dead. His shoulders told him. I have all those prayers I promised if I caught the fish, he thought. But I am too tired to say them now.

노인은 어쩌면 자신이 죽은 몸은 아닐까 하는 느낌이 늘났다. 그래서 두 손을 마주 잡고 손바닥을 만져 보았다. 손은 죽어 있지 않았고, 그래서 두 손을 폈다 오므렸다 함으로써 살아 있다는 고통을 느낄 수 있었다. 고물에 몸을 기대어 보고 자신이 죽지 않았다는 것을 알았다. 어깨가 그렇게 말해 주었던 것이다. 만약 이 고기를 잡으면 기도를 하겠다고 약속했었지, 하고 그는 생각했다. 하지만 지금은 너무 지쳐서 기도를 드릴 수 없어.

문장분석

He felt that perhaps he was already dead. He put his two hands together and
　　　　　혹시, 어쩌면
felt the palms. They were not dead and he could bring the pain of life/ by simply

opening and closing them. He leaned his back against the stern and knew he

was not dead. His shoulders told him. I have all those prayers I promised if I

caught the fish, he thought. But I am too tired to say them now.

palm [pɑːm] 손바닥　　　　　　　　　shoulder [ʃóuldər] 어깨
lean [liːn] 기대다, 의지하다　　　　　　prayer [prɛər] 빌기, 기도
stern [stəːrn] 선미(船尾), 고물, 엄격한, 단호한

I'd like to buy some if there's any place they sell luck

행운을 파는 곳이 있다면 조금 사고 싶군

"I'd like to buy some if there's any place they sell it[luck]," he said. What could I buy it with? he asked himself. Could I buy it with a lost harpoon and a broken knife and two bad hands? "You might," he said. "You tried to buy it with eighty-four days at sea. They nearly sold it to you too."

"행운을 파는 곳이 있다면 조금 사고 싶군." 그가 말했다. 하지만 뭣으로 사지? 그는 자신에게 물어보았다. 잃어버린 작살과 부러진 칼과 부상당한 이 손으로 그걸 살 수 있을까? "어쩌면 살 수 있을지도 몰라. 넌 바다에서 보낸 여든 날하고도 나홀로 그것을 사려고 했어. 그들도 네게 그걸 거의 팔아 줄 듯했잖아." 그가 말했다.

문장분석

"I'd like to buy some if there's any place they sell it[luck]," he said. What could I buy it with? he asked himself. Could I buy it with a lost harpoon and a broken knife and two bad hands? "You might (buy it with them)," he said. "You tried to buy it with eighty-four days at sea. They nearly sold it to you too."
_____
almost

harpoon [hɑːrpún] (고래잡이용) 작살
fortune [fɔ́ːrtʃən] 운, 행운
fluke [fluːk] 뜻밖의 행운, (당구 등) 요행히 맞음

bonanza [bənǽnzə] 풍부한 광맥, 뜻밖의 행운, 횡재
serendipity [sèrəndípəti]
　재수 좋게 우연히 찾아낸 것, 뜻밖의 발견

Luck is a thing that comes in many forms and who can recognize her?

행운의 여신이란 여러 모습으로 나타나는 법인데 누가 그것을 알아본단 말인가?

I must not think nonsense, he thought. Luck is a thing that comes in many forms and who can recognize her? I would take some though in any form and pay what they asked. I wish I could see the glow from the lights, he thought. I wish too many things. But that is the thing I wish for now.

쓸데없는 생각은 하지 말자, 하고 노인은 생각했다. 행운의 여신이란 여러 모습으로 나타나는 법인데 누가 그것을 알아본단 말인가? 어쨌든 어떤 모습의 행운이라도 얼마쯤 손에 넣고 그것이 요구하는 대로 값을 치를 테야. 하늘에 흰한 불빛이 나타나면 좋을 텐데, 하고 그는 생각했다. 나는 바라는 게 너무 많구나. 하지만 지금 당장 절실히 바라는 건 그 흰한 불빛을 바라보는 거야.

문장분석

I must not think nonsense, he thought. Luck is a thing that comes in many forms
and who can recognize her? I would take some though in any form and pay
······한다 하더라도
what they asked. I wish I could see the glow from the lights, he thought. I wish
too many things. But that is the thing I wish for now.

recognize [rékəgnàiz] 알아보다, 인식하다
recognition [rèkəgníʃən] 인지, 인식, 승인, 허가
glow [glou] 빛을 내다, 빛나다, 붉은 빛

expect [ikspékt] 예상하다, 기대하다
desire [dizáiər] 욕망, 원하다

It was then he knew the depth of his tiredness

그제야 비로소 그는 자신이 얼마나 녹초가 되었는지 깨달을 수 있었다

He unstepped the mast and furled the sail and tied it. Then he shouldered the mast and started to climb. It was then he knew the depth of his tiredness. He stopped for a moment and looked back and saw in the reflection from the street light the great tail of the fish standing up well behind the skiff's stern. He saw the white naked line of his backbone and the dark mass of the head with the projecting bill and all the nakedness between.

노인은 돛대를 빼내어 돛을 감아서 묶었다. 그리고 돛대를 어깨 위에 걸머메고 언덕길을 오르기 시작했다. 그제야 비로소 그는 자신이 얼마나 녹초가 되었는지 깨달을 수 있었다. 잠깐 발걸음을 멈추고 뒤를 돌아보니 가로등 불빛에 고기의 커다란 꼬리가 조각배의 고물 뒤쪽에 꼿꼿이 서 있는 것이 보였다. 그리고 허옇게 드러난 등뼈의 선과 뾰족한 주둥이가 달린 시커먼 머리통, 그리고 그 사이가 모조리 앙상하게 텅 비어 있는 것이 보였다.

문장분석

He unstepped the mast and furled the sail and tied it. Then he shouldered the
　　　돛대를 떼내다
mast and started to climb. It was then he knew the depth of his tiredness. He

stopped for a moment and looked back and saw (in the reflection from the

street light) the great tail of the fish standing up well behind the skiff's stern. He

saw the white naked line of his backbone and the dark mass of the head with the
　　　　　　　　　　　　　　　　　　　　　　　　　　　　　덩어리
projecting bill and all the nakedness between.
　　　　　　　　　벌거숭이, 적나라

furl [fəːrl]
　(돛·기 따위를) 말아 걷다, 개키다, (우산 따위를) 접다
reflection [riflékʃən] 반사, 반영

stern [stəːrn] 고물, 선미, 엄격한
project [prədʒékt] 삐죽 나오다, 입안하다, 계획하다
bill [bil] 부리

A cat passed on the far side going about its business

마침 길 저쪽으로 고양이 한 마리가 오줌을 누려고 지나가고 있었다

He started to climb again and at the top he fell and lay for some time with the mast across his shoulder. He tried to get up. But it was too difficult and he sat there with the mast on his shoulder and looked at the road. A cat passed on the far side going about its business and the old man watched it. Then he just watched the road.

노인은 다시 언덕길을 오르기 시작했고, 언덕 꼭대기에 이르렀을 때 그만 넘어져 돛대를 어깨에 걸머멘 채 한참 동안 누워 있었다. 일어나려고 애썼지만 너무 힘이 들었다. 그래서 가까스로 돛대를 어깨에 멘 채 앉아 길 쪽을 바라보았다. 마침 길 저쪽으로 고양이 한 마리가 오줌을 누려고 지나가고 있었고, 노인은 고양이를 물끄러미 바라보았다. 그러고는 다시 길 쪽을 물끄러미 바라다보았다.

문장분석

He started to climb again and at the top/ he fell and lay/ for some time/ with the

mast across his shoulder. He tried to get up. But it was too difficult and he sat
　　　　가로 질러서

there/ with the mast on his shoulder and looked at the road. A cat passed on

the far side/ going about its business and the old man watched it. Then he just

watched the road.

lie [lai]　　　　　　　　　　　　　　mast [mæst, mɑːst] 돛대, 기둥, 장대
　(lay [lei]- lain [lein]) 눕다, (물건이) 놓여 있다　　shoulder [ʃóuldər] 어깨, 짊어지다, 메다
climb [klaim] (산 따위에) 오르다　　　　do one's business 배변(排便)하다

Vocabulary Of The Week

MON

palm [pɑːm] 손바닥
lean [liːn] 기대다, 의지하다
stern [stəːrn]
　선미(船尾), 고물, 엄격한, 단호한
shoulder [ʃóuldər] 어깨
prayer [prɛər] 빌기, 기도

TUE

harpoon [hɑːrpún]
　(고래잡이용) 작살
fortune [fɔ́ːrtʃən] 운, 행운
fluke [fluːk]
　뜻밖의 행운, (당구 등) 요행히 맞음

bonanza [bənǽnzə]
　풍부한 광맥, 뜻밖의 행운, 횡재
serendipity [sèrəndípəti]
　재수 좋게 우연히 찾아낸 것,
　뜻밖의 발견

WED

recognize [rékəgnàiz]
　알아보다, 인식하다
recognition [rèkəgníʃən]
　인지, 인식, 승인, 허가
glow [glou]
　빛을 내다, 빛나다, 붉은 빛

expect [ikspékt] 예상하다, 기대하다
desire [dizáiər] 욕망, 원하다

THU

furl [fəːrl]
　(돛·기 따위를) 말아 걷다, 개키다,
　(우산 따위를) 접다
reflection [riflékʃən] 반사, 반영
stern [stəːrn] 고물, 선미, 엄격한

project [prədʒékt]
　삐죽 나오다, 입안하다, 계획하다,
bill [bil] 부리

FRI

lie [lai]
　(lay [lei]- lain [lein]) 눕다,
　(물건이) 놓여 있다
climb [klaim] (산 따위에) 오르다
mast [mæst, mɑːst] 돛대, 기둥, 장대

shoulder [ʃóuldər]
　어깨, 짊어지다, 메다
do one's business 배변(排便)하다

MON

He saw the old man's hands and he started to cry

소년은 노인의 두 손을 보더니 울기 시작했다

He was asleep when the boy looked in the door in the morning. It was blowing so hard that the drifting-boats would not be going out and the boy had slept late and then come to the old man's shack as he had come each morning. The boy saw that the old man was breathing and then he saw the old man's hands and he started to cry. He went out very quietly to go to bring some coffee and all the way down the road he was crying.

이튿날 아침에 소년이 판잣집 문 안을 들여다보았을 때 노인은 잠을 자고 있었다. 그날은 바람이 몹시 사납게 불어서 유망어선이 바다에 나갈 수 없었기 때문에 소년은 늦잠을 자고 일어나 아침마다 그랬듯이 노인의 판잣집에 와 본 것이었다. 소년은 노인이 숨을 쉬고 있는지 확인하고 나서 노인의 두 손을 보더니 울기 시작했다. 그리고 커피를 가져오려고 조용히 판잣집을 빠져나와 길을 따라 내려가면서도 줄곧 엉엉 울었다.

문장분석

He was asleep when the boy looked in the door in the morning. It was blowing

so hard that the drifting-boats would not be going out and the boy had slept late

and then come to the old man's shack/ as he had come each morning. The boy
~하듯

saw that the old man was breathing and then he saw the old man's hands and

he started to cry. He went out very quietly/ to go to bring some coffee and all the
처음부터 끝까지

way down the road/ he was crying.

blow [blou] (바람이) 불다
drift [drift] 표류(drifting), 떠내려가다
shack [ʃæk] (초라한) 오두막

breathe [briːð] 호흡하다, 숨을 쉬다, 살아 있다
breath [breθ] 숨, 호흡

Sleeping, let no one disturb him

주무시고 계세요, 그분을 깨우지 않는 게 좋겠어요

Many fishermen were around the skiff looking at what was lashed beside it and one was in the water, his trousers rolled up, measuring the skeleton with a length of line. The boy did not go down. He had been there before and one of the fishermen was looking after the skiff for him. "How is he?" one of the fishermen shouted. "Sleeping," the boy called. He did not care that they saw him crying. "Let no one disturb him."

많은 어부들이 조각배 주위에 모여 서서 뱃전에 매달려 있는 것을 구경하고 있었다. 한 어부는 바지를 걷어 올리고 물속으로 들어가 낚싯줄로 고기 잔해의 길이를 재고 있었다. 소년은 내려가지 않았다. 벌써 가 보았던 것이다. 한 어부가 소년을 대신해 배를 살펴보고 있었다. "노인은 좀 어떠시냐?" 어느 어부가 큰소리로 물었다. "주무시고 계세요." 소년이 큰 소리로 대답했다. 자기가 울고 있는 것을 어부들이 바라보고 있었지만 소년은 개의치 않았다. "그분을 깨우지 않는 게 좋겠어요."

문장분석

Many fishermen were around the skiff/ looking at ⟨what⟩was lashed beside it and

one (fisherman) was in the water, his trousers rolled up, measuring the skeleton

with a length of line. The boy did not go down. He had been there before and

one of the fishermen was looking after the skiff for him. "How is he?" one of the
                                                                    그를 대신해
fishermen shouted. "Sleeping," the boy called. He did not care that they saw him

crying. "Let no one disturb him."

measure [méʒər] 재다, 측정하다
lash [læʃ] 묶다, 매다
skeleton [skélətn] 골격, 해골

length [leŋkθ] 길이
disturb [distə́ːrb]
(휴식·일·생각 중인 사람을) 방해하다

I'll bring the luck with me

운은 제가 갖고 가면 돼요

"Now we fish together again."
"No. I am not lucky. I am not lucky anymore."
"The hell with luck," the boy said. "I'll bring the luck with me."
"What will your family say?"
"I do not care. I caught two yesterday. But we will fish together now for I still have much to learn."

"이젠 할아버지하고 같이 나가서 잡기로 해요."
"그건 안 돼. 내겐 운이 없어. 운이 다했거든."
"그런 소리 하지 마세요. 운은 제가 갖고 가면 되잖아요." 소년이 대꾸했다.
"네 가족들이 뭐라고 하지 않을까?"
"상관없어요. 어제도 두 마리나 잡았는걸요. 하지만 전 아직도 배울 게 많으니까, 이제부턴 할아버지와 함께 나갈래요."

문장분석

"Now/ we fish together again."

"No. I am not lucky. I am not lucky anymore."

"The hell with luck," the boy said. "I'll bring the luck with me."

"What will your family say?"

"I do not care. I caught two (fish) yesterday. But we will fish together now/ for I
because
still have much to learn."

sail [seil] 항해하다, 출범하다, 돛
navigate [nǽvəgèit] 항해하다, 조종하다
voyage [vɔ́iidʒ] 항해, 탐험, 여행하다

cruise [kruːz] 유람선, 순항하다, 돌아다니다
explore [iksplɔ́ːr]
　(미지의 땅·바다 등을) 탐험하다, (우주를) 탐사하다

You must get well fast for there is much that I can learn

얼른 나으셔야 해요, 전 아직 할아버지한테 배울 게 많으니까요

"Bring any of the papers of the time that I was gone," the old man said.
"You must get well fast for there is much that I can learn and you can teach me everything. How much did you suffer?"
"Plenty," the old man said.
"I'll bring the food and the papers," the boy said.
"Rest well, old man. I will bring stuff from the drug-store for your hands."

"내가 없던 동안에 온 신문이 있거든 좀 가져다주렴." 노인이 말했다.
"얼른 나으셔야 해요. 전 아직 할아버지한테 배울 게 많으니까요. 또 할아버지는 제게 모든 걸 가르쳐 주셔야 해요. 대체 얼마나 고생하신 거예요?"
"많이 했지." 노인이 대답했다.
"그럼 드실 것이랑 신문을 가져올게요." 소년이 말했다.
"푹 쉬세요, 할아버지. 약국에서 손에 바를 약도 사 올게요."

문장분석

"Bring any of the papers of (the time) that I was gone," the old man said.

"You must get well fast/ for there is (much) that I can learn and you can teach me
회복하다   because
everything. How much did you suffer?"

"Plenty," the old man said.

"I'll bring the food and the papers," the boy said.

"Rest well, old man. I will bring stuff from the drug-store for your hands."

suffer [sʌ́fər] (고통·변화 따위를) 경험하다, 겪다
suffering [sʌ́fəriŋ] 괴로움, 고통, 고생
plenty [plénti] 많음, 가득, 풍부, 다량, 충분

rest [rest] 휴식, 쉬다
stuff [stʌf] (막연히) 물건, 재료, 물자, ~에 채워 넣다

The old man was dreaming about the lions

노인은 사자 꿈을 꾸고 있었다

Up the road, in his shack, the old man was sleeping again. He was still sleeping on his face and the boy was sitting by him watching him. The old man was dreaming about the lions.

길 위쪽의 판잣집에서 노인은 다시금 잠이 들어 있었다. 얼굴을 파묻고 엎드려 여전히 잠을 자고 있었고, 소년이 곁에 앉아서 그를 지켜보고 있었다. 노인은 사자 꿈을 꾸고 있었다.

문장분석

Up the road, in his shack, the old man was sleeping again. He was still sleeping on his face and the boy was sitting by him/ watching him. The old man was dreaming about the lions.

shack [ʃæk] (초라한) 오두막(hut)
see
　시력을 작동시키지 않고 시야에 들어오는 것을 보다
look 얼굴·눈을 상대방 쪽으로 향하고 보다

watch
　감시자가 정지해 상대의 움직임 등을 지켜보다
stare
　놀람·호기심 등으로 눈을 크게 뜨고 눈여겨보다

Vocabulary Of The Week

MON

blow [blou] (바람이) 불다
drift [drift] 표류(drifting), 떠내려가다
shack [ʃæk] (초라한) 오두막
breathe [bri:ð]
  호흡하다, 숨을 쉬다, 살아 있다
breath [breθ] 숨, 호흡

TUE

measure [méʒər] 재다, 측정하다
lash [læʃ] 묶다, 매다
skeleton [skélətn] 골격, 해골
length [leŋkθ] 길이
disturb [distə́:rb]
  (휴식·일·생각 중인 사람을) 방해히다

WED

sail [seil] 항해하다, 출범하다, 돛
navigate [nǽvəgèit]
  항해하다, 조종하다
voyage [vɔ́iidʒ] 항해, 탐험, 여행하다
cruise [kru:z]
  유람선, 순항하다, 돌아다니다

explore [iksplɔ́:r]
  (미지의 땅·바다 등을) 탐험하다,
  (우주를) 탐사하다

THU

suffer [sʌ́fər]
  (고통·변화 따위를) 경험하다, 겪다
suffering [sʌ́fəriŋ]
  괴로움, 고통, 고생
plenty [plénti]
  많음, 가득, 풍부, 다량, 충분

rest [rest] 휴식, 쉬다
stuff [stʌf]
  (막연히) 물건, 재료, 물자,
  ~에 채워 넣다

FRI

shack [ʃæk] (초라한) 오두막(hut)
see
  시력을 작동시키지 않고 시야에
  들어오는 것을 보다
look
  얼굴·눈을 상대방 쪽으로 향하고 보다

watch
  감시자가 정지해 상대의 움직임 등을
  지켜보다
stare
  놀람·호기심 등으로 눈을 크게 뜨고
  눈여겨보다

지금,
멋진 영어 한 줄의
타이밍

3. Ernest Hemingway

초판 1쇄 펴낸 날 | 2020년 6월 19일

지은이 | 이충호
펴낸이 | 홍정우
펴낸곳 | 브레인스토어

책임편집 | 이슬기
편집진행 | 양은지
디자인 | 이유정
마케팅 | 김에너벨리

주소 | (04035) 서울특별시 마포구 양화로7안길 31(서교동, 1층)
전화 | (02)3275-2915~7
팩스 | (02)3275-2918
이메일 | brainstore@chol.com
블로그 | https://blog.naver.com/brain_store
페이스북 | http://www.facebook.com/brainstorebooks

등록 | 2007년 11월 30일(제313-2007-000238호)

© 브레인스토어, 이충호, 2020
ISBN 979-11-88073-52-8 (03740)

이 도서의 국립중앙도서관 출판예정도서목록(CIP)은 서지정보유통지원시스템 홈페이지
(http://seoji.nl.go.kr)와 국가자료종합목록시스템(http://www.nl.go.kr/kolisnet)에서 이용
하실 수 있습니다. (CIP제어번호 : CIP2020022574)